POEMS AND PROSE OF

JOHN DRYDEN

A SELECTION BY

DOUGLAS GRANT

PENGUIN BOOKS

Penguin Books Ltd, Harmondsworth, Middlesex
U.S.A.: Penguin Books Inc., 3300 Clipper Mill Road, Baltimore, 11, Md
CANADA: Penguin Books (Canada) Ltd, 47 Green Street,
Saint Lambert, Montreal, P.Q.
AUSTRALIA: Penguin Books Pty Ltd, 762 Whitehorse Road,
Mitcham, Victoria
SOUTH AFRICA: Penguin Books (S.A.) Pty Ltd, Gilbraltar House,
Regent Road, Sea Point, Cape Town
—
This selection first published 1955

Made and printed in Great Britain
by Unwin Brothers Ltd
Woking and London

CONTENTS

CONTENTS

INTRODUCTION

WHEN Elizabeth of Bohemia – the 'Queen of Hearts' – died in 1661, Lord Leicester, her contemporary, wrote: 'It is a pity that she lived not a few hours more, to die upon her wedding-day, and that there is not as good a poet to make her epitaph as Doctor Donne, who wrote her Epithalamium upon that day, unto St Valentine.' Though Leicester's complaint at the lack of poets must be attributed in part to the regret of an ageing man at the loss of the brightness which seemed in memory to have surrounded his youth, it was not an unreasonable judgement on the apparent condition of the poetry at the time. But had he read appreciatively the poem which a young poet, John Dryden, had published in 1660 to commemorate the restoration of Charles II, he might have recognized in it the marks of a poet who was to exceed Donne in reputation and to dominate over the literature of the second half of the century, relaying and reforming the traditions of English poetry.

John Dryden was born in 1631, and his poetic career began effectively with the Restoration; at the time when, in his own words, 'revived poesy' was 'lifting up its head' after being buried under 'the ruins of monarchy'. Of his early life, the little that is known can be quickly summarized: he was educated at Westminster School and Trinity College, Cambridge, and may have acted as clerk to his cousin Sir Gilbert Pickering, Lord Chamberlain to Oliver Cromwell. He published a panegyrical poem on the death of Cromwell in 1659 but his political sympathies lay entirely with the restored monarchy, and were rewarded with the offices of Poet Laureate in 1668 and of Historiographer Royal in 1670.

Dryden's early poems are marked by uncertainty. Reacting against the metaphysical school in response to the spirit of the new age, he was at first unable to settle his style. The most important of the early poems, *Annus Mirabilis*, 1667, was written not in the heroic couplet, which he was later to perfect, but in the heroic stanza – used earlier by Sir William Davenant in *Gondibert* – which he claimed to be 'more noble and of greater dignity, both for the sound and number, than any other verse in use amongst us.' He gave the reason for his rejection of the metaphysicals in a succinct comparison of contemporary poets with Donne: 'if we are not so great wits as Donne,' he wrote, 'yet certainly we are better poets.' In other words, while respecting Donne's genius, he condemned his style – a condemnation which we to-day are unable to accept. He found the example he needed in the poetry of Edmund Waller and Sir John Denham; poets far below Donne and other metaphysicals in stature but showing in their use of the heroic couplet an important concern with form; making in this way the kind of fertile contribution to the development of poetry which is the privilege of the minor poet.

Dryden established his style by writing for the theatre, revived at the Restoration. The new drama in fashion, and fashion was dictated by a Court largely under French influence in literature, was the heroic play, and convention required that it should be written in heroic verse; a convention which received Dryden's unqualified support, brilliantly expressed in *An Essay of Dramatic Poesy*. Dryden derived the heroic play from the epic poem and saw it as 'an imitation in little' of the epic, concerned with the same themes, love and valour.

We are generally unsympathetic to the heroic play; the conflict and, in consequence, the sentiments and characters are too far 'beyond the common words and actions of human life' to move us deeply; but we can at least admire the construction, the force with which the characters are blocked out, and, particularly, the verse. Experience of the theatre taught Dryden to write verse which could be spoken effectively, and the rhythm of his couplets is wonderfully managed to avoid monotony, the danger to which the couplet is peculiarly susceptible. And as much as Wordsworth, he based his diction upon the spoken language; in his case, upon the language of the Court, whose example, he claimed, had 'improved and refined the language, wit, and conversation of our age above the last.'

The themes of the heroic play are love and valour but the rank of the protagonists – kings and queens, and heirs and pretenders to the thrones – required the plot to be largely concerned with a struggle for political power; and considered under this aspect, the play becomes a commentary, direct and indirect, upon the politics of the age. The dissensions of the Civil War were continued after the Restoration, and as the reign of Charles II advanced, the interests and ambitions of the different parties and classes came more openly into conflict, threatening a renewal of the earlier violence. Dryden was deeply engaged in the struggle in favour of tradition and authority and used the heroic play to state his opinions and to prove, in action and argument, their superiority over those of his opponents. By the time the crisis came to a head in 1680 over the Exclusion Bill, he had learnt how political ideas could be most effectively debated in verse.

The success of *Absalom and Achitophel*, the first result of Dryden's direct involvement in political controversy, depended largely upon the lessons learnt in writing heroic plays. The characterization, argument, and verse of the poem had been anticipated in the plays; but appeared to greater advantage in the poem, which raised English satire to an art. Dryden's concern with tradition has already been seen in the connexion which he made between the heroic play and epic poetry; similarly, he related English satire to classical satire, endowing it from that source with a form and a seriousness which it had never before achieved.

Dryden's religious development ran parallel to his political. The belief in the need for authority led him to accept at first the Church of England and later to transfer his allegiance to the Church of Rome. The stages in his progress were marked by two poems, *Religio Laici* and *The Hind and the Panther*; and if the first is the better poem, the second is irrefutable proof of the sincerity of his conversion to Roman Catholicism. But his progress ran counter to the course of politics and after the Revolution of 1688 he lost his places and pension, being forced to write again for a living. He was writing with undiminished energy up to his death in 1700.

A sketch of Dryden's career cannot do justice to one of his greatest characteristics – his variety. Comedies and translations, familiar verses, songs and odes – he may not have always excelled in everything he tried but he was always excellent. And the reason for his success can be seen in his criticism, which accompanied and related his other work. Prompted by his own experience, he brought to bear on literature an open and powerful mind, constantly refreshed by his devotion to letters. His prose certainly equals his poetry in its achievement; never at a loss, it rapidly and unerringly follows up the argument, and is as alive as the finest conversation.

DOUGLAS GRANT

NOTE

The dates of publication of the works chosen for this selection are given after each in the table of contents. The spelling and punctuation have been modernized.

Dryden's most popular play, *All for Love*, has already been included in another Penguin (*Four English Tragedies*, ed. J. M. Morrell), and since it is thus readily available, I have been free to choose *Aureng-Zebe*, the last of the heroic plays.

I am indebted to Mr D. F. S. Thomson for the translations of the classical quotations.

1955   D.G.

ANNUS MIRABILIS

THE YEAR OF

WONDERS

1666

THE cheerful soldiers, with new stores supplied,
  Now long to execute their spleenful will;
And in revenge for those three days they tried,
  Wish one, like Joshua's, when the sun stood still.

Thus re-inforced, against the adverse fleet
  Still doubling ours, brave Rupert leads the way.[1]
With the first blushes of the morn they meet,
  And bring night back upon the new-born day.

His presence soon blows up the kindling fight,
  And his loud guns speak thick like angry men;
It seemed as slaughter had been breathed all night,
  And death new pointed his dull dart agen.

The Dutch, too well his mighty conduct knew,
  And matchless courage since the former fight;
Whose navy like a stiff stretched cord did show
  Till he bore in and bent them into flight.

1. Prince Rupert (1619–82), joint-commander of the English fleet.

The wind he shares while half their fleet offends
    His open side, and high above him shows;
Upon the rest at pleasure he descends,
    And, doubly harmed, he double harms bestows.

Behind, the Gen'ral mends his weary pace,[1]
    And sullenly to his revenge he sails;
So glides some trodden serpent on the grass,
    And long behind his wounded volume trails.

Th' increasing sound is borne to either shore,
    And for their stakes the throwing nations fear.
Their passions double with the cannons' roar,
    And with warm wishes each man combats there.

Plied thick and close as when the fight begun,
    Their huge unwieldy navy wastes away;
So sicken waning moons too near the sun,
    And blunt their crescents on the edge of day.

And now reduced on equal terms to fight,
    Their ships like wasted patrimonies show:
Where the thin scatt'ring trees admit the light,
    And shun each other's shadows as they grow.

The warlike Prince had severed from the rest
    Two giant ships, the pride of all the main;
Which, with his one, so vigorously he pressed
    And flew so home they could not rise again.

Already battered, by his lee they lay,
    In vain upon the passing winds they call;
The passing winds through their torn canvas play,
    And flagging sails on heartless sailors fall.

1. George Monk, Duke of Albemarle (1608–70), joint-commander
  of the English fleet.

Their opened sides receive a gloomy light,
    Dreadful as day let in to shades below;
Without, grim death rides bare-faced in their sight,
    And urges ent'ring billows as they flow.

When one dire shot, the last they could supply,
    Close by the board the Prince's main-mast bore.
All three now, helpless, by each other lie,
    And this offends not, and those fear no more.

So have I seen some fearful hare maintain
    A course till tired before the dog she lay;
Who, stretched behind her, pants upon the plain,
    Past pow'r to kill as she to get away.

With his lolled tongue he faintly licks his prey,
    His warm breath blows her flix up as she lies;
She, trembling, creeps upon the ground away,
    And looks back to him with beseeching eyes.

The Prince unjustly does his stars accuse,
    Which hindered him to push his fortune on;
For what they to his courage did refuse,
    By mortal valour never must be done.

This lucky hour the wise Batavian takes,
    And warns his tattered fleet to follow home;
Proud to have so got off with equal stakes,
    Where 'twas a triumph not to be o'ercome.

ABSALOM AND ACHITOPHEL

A POEM

———————— Si propiùs stes
Te capiet magis————————[1]

NOTE

Absalom and Achitophel was published in November 1681 when the
Earl of Shaftesbury, the leader of the Whigs, was imprisoned in the
Tower, awaiting trial on a charge of high treason. Using the intense
popular feeling against Roman Catholics aroused by the Popish Plot
of 1678 – a plot which existed largely in the deposition of Titus
Oates, the perjurer – to further his own purposes, Shaftesbury had
attempted to force through Parliament a Bill excluding James, Duke
of York, an avowed Catholic, from the succession and substituting
for him James, Duke of Monmouth, Charles II's illegitimate son and
a Protestant. Charles waited until Shaftesbury had proceeded to
extremes and then, having freed himself from financial dependence
on Parliament by accepting a subsidy from Louis XIV, had him
arrested. Dryden timed the publication of his poem to prejudice the
people against Shaftesbury, but it had no effect upon the issue of his
trial; the bill of indictment against him was thrown out by a London
jury on 24 November 1681.

A KEY TO ABSALOM AND ACHITOPHEL

Aaron's Race, The Clergy.
Abbethdin, Lord Chancellor.
Absalom, James Scott, Duke of Monmouth and Buccleuch (1649–85),
    the natural son of Charles II and Lucy Walters, who took the
    name of Scott upon his marriage with *Annabel*.
Achitophel, Anthony Ashley Cooper, Earl of Shaftesbury (1621–83).
Adriel, John Sheffield, Earl of Mulgrave (1648–1721).
Agag, Sir Edmund Berry Godfrey (1621–78).

1. One kind will attract you more, if you stand nearer to it.
   (Horace, *Ars Poetica* 361–2.)

Amiel, Edward Seymour (1633–1708).

Annabel, Anne Scott, Countess of Bucchleuch in her own right, and wife of *Absalom*.

Balaam, Theophilus Hastings, Earl of Huntingdon (1650–1701).

Barzillai, James Butler, Duke of Ormonde (1610–88).

Bathsheba, Louise Renée de Kéroualle, Duchess of Portsmouth and Aubigny (1649–1734), Charles II's mistress.

Caleb, Forde, Lord Grey of Werke (*d*. 1701).

Corah, Titus Oates (1648–1705).

David, Charles II.

Egypt, France.

Ethnic Plot, Popish Plot.

Gath, Brussels.

Hebrew Priests, Church of England clergy.

Hebron, Scotland.

Hushai, Laurence Hyde, Earl of Rochester (1641–1711).

Ishbosheth, Richard Cromwell (1626–1712).

Israel, England.

Issachar, Thomas Thynne of Longleat (1648–82), known on account of his wealth as 'Tom of Ten Thousand'.

Jebusites, Roman Catholics.

Jerusalem, London.

Jewish Rabbins, Doctors of the Church of England.

Jonas, Sir William Jones (1631–82).

Jordan, The English seas or, as '*Jordan's Flood*', the Irish Channel.

Jotham, George Savile, Marquis of Halifax (1633–95).

Levites, The Presbyterian ministers displaced by the Act of Uniformity.

Michal, Catherine of Braganza (1638–1705), the childless Queen of Charles II.

Nadab, William, Lord Howard of Escrick (1626?–94).

Pharaoh, Louis XIV of France.

Sagan of Jerusalem, Bishop of London.

Sanhedrin, Parliament.

Saul, Oliver Cromwell.

Shimei, Slingsby Bethel (1617–97).

Sion, London.

Solymean rout, London mob.

Tyre, Holland.

Zadoc, William Sancroft (1617–93), Archbishop of Canterbury.

Zimri, George Villiers, Duke of Buckingham (1628–87).

ABSALOM AND ACHITOPHEL

A POEM

In pious times ere priest-craft did begin,
Before polygamy was made a sin;
When man on many multiplied his kind,
Ere one to one was, cursedly, confined;
When nature prompted and no law denied
Promiscuous use of concubine and bride;
Then Israel's monarch, after Heaven's own heart,
His vigorous warmth did, variously, impart
To wives and slaves; and, wide as his command,
Scattered his Maker's image through the land.
Michal, of royal blood, the crown did wear;
A soil ungrateful to the tiller's care.
Not so the rest; for several mothers bore
To God-like David several sons before.
But since like slaves his bed they did ascend,
No true succession could their seed attend.
Of all this numerous progeny was none
So beautiful, so brave as Absalon.
Whether, inspired by some diviner lust,
His father got him with a greater gust;
Or that his conscious destiny made way
By manly beauty to imperial sway.
Early in foreign fields he won renown,
With kings and states allied to Israel's crown.[1]
In peace the thoughts of war he could remove,
And seemed as he were only born for love.

---

1. Monmouth had commanded the British troops serving under the French against the Dutch in 1672-73, and under the Dutch against the French in 1678. He gained distinction in both campaigns.

Whate'er he did was done with so much ease,
In him alone 'twas natural to please:
His motions all accompanied with grace,
And Paradise was opened in his face.
With secret joy indulgent David viewed
His youthful image in his son renewed;
To all his wishes nothing he denied,
And made the charming Annabel his bride.
What faults he had (for who from faults is free?),
His father could not or he would not see.
Some warm excesses, which the law forbore,
Were construed youth that purged by boiling o'er;
And Amnon's murder, by a specious name,
Was called a just revenge for injured fame.[1]
Thus praised and loved the noble youth remained,
While David undisturbed in Sion reigned.
But life can never be sincerely blest;
Heav'n punishes the bad, and proves the best.
The Jews, a headstrong, moody, murm'ring race,
As ever tried th' extent and stretch of grace;
God's pampered people whom, debauched with
        ease,
No king could govern, nor no god could please
(Gods they had tried of every shape and size,
That god-smiths could produce, or priests devise):
These Adam-wits, too fortunately free,
Began to dream they wanted liberty;
And when no rule, no precedent, was found
Of men, by laws less circumscribed and bound

---

1. This is a reference to the attack made on Sir John Coventry (d, 1682) in 1670 at the instigation of Monmouth. Coventry reflected on the King's affairs with actresses in a debate in the Commons, and was later waylaid and had his nose slit to the bone with a penknife.

They led their wild desires to woods and caves,
And thought that all but savages were slaves.
They who, when Saul was dead, without a blow
Made foolish Ishbosheth the crown forgo;
Who banished David did from Hebron bring[1]
And, with a general shout, proclaimed him king:
Those very Jews, who at their very best
Their humour more than loyalty expressed,
Now wondered why so long they had obeyed
An idol-monarch which their hands had made;
Thought they might ruin him they could create,
Or melt him to that Golden Calf, a state.
But these were random bolts; no formed design
Nor interest made the factious crowd to join.
The sober part of Israel, free from stain,
Well knew the value of a peaceful reign,
And, looking backward with a wise affright,
Saw seams of wounds, dishonest to the sight;
In contemplation of whose ugly scars
They cursed the memory of civil wars.
The moderate sort of men, thus qualified,
Inclined the balance to the better side;
And David's mildness managed it so well
The bad found no occasion to rebel.
But when to sin our biassed nature leans
The careful devil is still at hand with means,
And providently pimps for ill desires:
The good Old Cause revived a Plot requires.
Plots, true or false, are necessary things
To raise up commonwealths and ruin kings.

1. Charles II was crowned King in Scotland in 1651 but not in England until 1661; therefore, although he entered England in 1660 from the Continent, Dryden can say that his people brought him from Scotland.

Th' inhabitants of old Jerusalem
Were Jebusites; the town so called from them,
And theirs the native right —
But when the chosen people grew more strong
The rightful cause at length became the wrong;
And every loss the men of Jebus bore,
They still were thought God's enemies the more.
Thus worn and weakened, well or ill content,
Submit they must to David's government.
Impoverished and deprived of all command,
Their taxes doubled as they lost their land;
And, what was harder yet to flesh and blood,
Their gods disgraced and burnt like common wood.
This set the heathen priesthood in a flame;
For priests of all religions are the same:
Of whatsoe'er descent their godhead be,
Stock, stone, or other homely pedigree,
In his defence his servants are as bold
As if he had been born of beaten gold.
The Jewish Rabbins, though their enemies,
In this conclude them honest men and wise;
For 'twas their duty, all the learned think,
T' espouse his cause by whom they eat and drink.
From hence began that Plot, the nation's curse,
Bad in itself, but represented worse;
Raised in extremes, and in extremes decried;
With oaths affirmed, with dying vows denied;
Not weighed or winnowed by the multitude,
But swallowed in the mass, unchewed and crude.
Some truth there was, but dashed and brewed with
    lies
To please the fools and puzzle all the wise.
Succeeding times did equal folly call,
Believing nothing, or believing all.

Th' Egyptian rites the Jebusites embraced,
Where gods were recommended by their taste;
Such sav'ry deities must needs be good
As served at once for worship and for food.[1]
By force they could not introduce these gods,
For ten to one in former days was odds;
So fraud was used (the sacrificer's trade):
Fools are more hard to conquer than persuade.
Their busy teachers mingled with the Jews,
And raked for converts even the Court and stews;
Which Hebrew priests the more unkindly took
Because the fleece accompanies the flock.
Some thought they God's anointed meant to slay
By guns, invented since full many a day.
Our author swears it not; but who can know
How far the devil and Jebusites may go?
This Plot, which failed for want of common sense,
Had yet a deep and dangerous consequence;
For as when raging fevers boil the blood,
The standing lake soon floats into a flood,
And ev'ry hostile humour, which before
Slept quiet in its channels, bubbles o'er;
So several factions from this first ferment
Work up to foam, and threat the government.
Some by their friends, more by themselves thought wise,
Opposed the Pow'r to which they could not rise;
Some had in courts been great, and thrown from thence,
Like fiends, were hardened in impenitence;
Some, by their monarch's fatal mercy grown,
From pardon'd rebels, kinsmen to the throne,
Were raised in pow'r and public office high:
Strong bands, if bands ungrateful men could tie.
Of these the false Achitophel was first:

1. A gibing reference to the Catholic doctrine of Transubstantiation.

A name to all succeeding Ages cursed.
For close designs, and crooked counsels fit;
Sagacious, bold, and turbulent of wit;
Restless, unfixed in principles and place;
In pow'r unpleased, impatient of disgrace;
A fiery soul, which working out its way,
Fretted the pigmy-body to decay,
And o'er-informed the tenement of clay.[1]
A daring pilot in extremity;
Pleased with the danger, when the waves went high
He sought the storms; but for a calm unfit,
Would steer too nigh the sands to boast his wit.
Great wits are sure to madness near allied,
And thin partitions do their bounds divide;
Else why should he, with wealth and honour blest,
Refuse his age the needful hours of rest?
Punish a body which he could not please;
Bankrupt of life, yet prodigal of ease?
And all to leave, what with his toil he won,
To that unfeathered, two-legged thing, a son;
Got while his soul did huddled notions try,
And born a shapeless lump, like anarchy.[2]
In friendship false, implacable in hate;
Resolved to ruin or to rule the state:
To compass this the triple bond he broke,
The pillars of the public safety shook,
And fitted Israel for a foreign yoke.[3]

1. Shaftesbury was a man of poor physique and sickly constitution.
2. Shaftesbury's son, the second Earl, was entirely without character or ability.
3. Shaftesbury was a signatory to the second Treaty with France in 1670 which ended the Triple Alliance of 1667 between England, Sweden, and Holland, directed against France. He was ignorant of the first Treaty with France of 1670 by which Charles II pledged himself to re-establish Roman Catholicism in England.

Then, seized with fear, yet still affecting fame,
Usurped a patriot's all-atoning name;
So easy still it proves in factious times,
With public zeal to cancel private crimes.
How safe is treason, and how sacred ill,
Where none can sin against the people's will;
Where crowds can wink and no offence be known,
Since in another's guilt they find their own.
Yet, fame deserved no enemy can grudge:
The statesman we abhor but praise the judge.[1]
In Israel's courts ne'er sat an Abbethdin
With more discerning eyes or hands more clean;
Unbribed, unsought, the wretched to redress;
Swift of dispatch, and easy of access.
Oh, had he been content to serve the crown
With virtues only proper to the gown;
Or had the rankness of the soil been freed
From cockle that oppressed the noble seed;
David for him his tuneful harp had strung,
And heav'n had wanted one immortal song.
But wild ambition loves to slide, not stand;
And fortune's ice prefers to virtue's land.
Achitophel, grown weary to possess
A lawful fame and lazy happiness,
Disdained the golden fruit to gather free,
And lent the crowd his arm to shake the tree.
Now, manifest of crimes, contrived long since,
He stood at bold defiance with his prince;
Held up the buckler of the people's cause
Against the Crown, and skulked behind the laws.
The wished occasion of the Plot he takes;
Some circumstances finds, but more he makes.

1. Shaftesbury was Lord Chancellor in 1672–73 but was dismissed
from office.

By buzzing emissaries fills the ears
Of list'ning crowds with jealousies and fears
Of arbitrary counsels brought to light,
And proves the King himself a Jebusite.
Weak arguments! which yet he knew full well
Were strong with people easy to rebel;
For, governed by the moon, the giddy Jews
Tread the same track when she the prime renews;
And once in twenty years, their scribes record,
By natural instinct they change their lord.
Achitophel still wants a chief, and none
Was found so fit as warlike Absalon.
Not that he wished his greatness to create
(For politicians neither love nor hate),
But for he knew his title not allowed
Would keep him still depending on the crowd;
That kingly power, thus ebbing out, might be
Drawn to the dregs of a democracy.
Him he attempts with studied arts to please,
And sheds his venom, in such words as these:
   'Auspicious Prince! at whose nativity
Some royal planet ruled the southern sky;
Thy longing country's darling and desire;
Their cloudy pillar and their guardian fire;
Their second Moses, whose extended wand
Divides the seas and shows the promised land;
Whose dawning day, in every distant age,
Has exercised the sacred prophets' rage;
The people's pray'r, the glad diviners' theme,
The young men's vision, and the old men's dream!
Thee, Saviour, thee, the nation's vows confess,
And, never satisfied with seeing, bless.
Swift unbespoken pomps thy steps proclaim,
And stammering babes are taught to lisp thy name.

How long wilt thou the general joy detain,
Starve and defraud the people of thy reign?
Content ingloriously to pass thy days,
Like one of virtue's fools that feeds on praise,
Till thy fresh glories, which now shine so bright,
Grow stale and tarnish with our daily sight.
Believe me, royal youth, thy fruit must be
Or gathered ripe or rot upon the tree.
Heav'n has to all allotted, soon or late,
Some lucky revolution of their fate,
Whose motions, if we watch and guide with skill
(For human good depends on human will),
Our fortune rolls as from a smooth descent
And from the first impression takes the bent;
But if unseized, she glides away like wind
And leaves repenting folly far behind.
Now, now she meets you with a glorious prize,
And spreads her locks before her as she flies.
Had thus old David, from whose loins you
        spring,
Not dared, when fortune called him, to be King,
At Gath an exile he might still remain;
And heav'n's anointing oil had been in vain.
Let his successful youth your hopes engage;
But shun th' example of declining age:
Behold him setting in his western skies,
The shadows length'ning as the vapours rise.
He is not now as when on Jordan's sand
The joyful people thronged to see him land,
Cov'ring the beach and black'ning all the strand;
But, like the Prince of Angels from his height,
Comes tumbling downward with diminished light.
Betrayed by one poor Plot to public scorn
(Our only blessing since his cursed return);

Those heaps of people, which one sheaf did bind,
Blown off and scattered by a puff of wind.
What strength can he to your designs oppose,
Naked of friends, and round beset with foes?
If Pharaoh's doubtful succour he should use,
A foreign aid would more incense the Jews;
Proud Egypt would dissembled friendship bring,
Foment the war but not support the King.
Nor would the royal party e'er unite
With Pharaoh's arms t' assist the Jebusite;
Or if they should, their interest soon would break,
And, with such odious aid, make David weak.
All sorts of men, by my successful arts
Abhorring kings, estrange their altered hearts
From David's rule; and 'tis the general cry,
Religion, commonwealth, and liberty.
If you, as champion of the public good,
Add to their arms a chief of royal blood,
What may not Israel hope? and what applause
Might such a general gain by such a cause?
Not barren praise alone, that gaudy flow'r,
Fair only to the sight, but solid pow'r;
And nobler is a limited command,
Giv'n by the love of all your native land,
Than a successive title, long and dark,
Drawn from the mouldy rolls of Noah's Ark.'
    What cannot praise effect in mighty minds
When flattery soothes and when ambition blinds!
Desire of pow'r, on earth a vicious weed,
Yet, sprung from high, is of celestial seed;
In God 'tis glory; and when men aspire,
'Tis but a spark too much of heav'nly fire.
Th' ambitious youth, too covetous of fame,
Too full of angel's metal in his frame,

Unwarily was led from virtue's ways;
Made drunk with honour, and debauched with praise.
Half loath and half consenting to the ill
(For loyal blood within him struggled still),
He thus replied: — 'And what pretence have I
To take up arms for public liberty?
My father governs with unquestioned right,
The Faith's defender and mankind's delight;
Good, gracious, just, observant of the laws;
And heav'n by wonders has espoused his cause.
Whom has he wronged in all his peaceful reign?
Who sues for justice to his throne in vain?
What millions has he pardoned of his foes,
Whom just revenge did to his wrath expose?
Mild, easy, humble, studious of our good;
Inclin'd to mercy, and averse from blood.
If mildness ill with stubborn Israel suit,
His crime is God's beloved attribute.
What could he gain his people to betray,
Or change his right for arbitrary sway?
Let haughty Pharaoh curse with such a reign
His fruitful Nile, and yoke a servile train!
If David's rule Jerusalem displease,
The dog-star heats their brains to this disease.
Why then should I, encouraging the bad,
Turn rebel and run popularly mad?
Were he a tyrant, who by lawless might
Oppressed the Jews and raised the Jebusite,
Well might I mourn; but nature's holy bands
Would curb my spirits and restrain my hands.
The people might assert their liberty,
But what was right in them were crime in me.
His favour leaves me nothing to require;
Prevents my wishes and out-runs desire.

What more can I expect while David lives?
All but his kingly diadem he gives:
And that — ' but there he paused; then sighing said —
' Is justly destined for a worthier head.
For when my father from his toils shall rest
And late augment the number of the blest,
His lawful issue shall the throne ascend;
Or the collat'ral line where that shall end.
His brother, though oppressed with vulgar spite,
Yet dauntless and secure of native right,
Of every royal virtue stands possessed;
Still dear to all the bravest, and the best.
His courage foes, his friends his truth proclaim;
His loyalty the King, the world his fame.
His mercy ev'n th' offending crowd will find,
For sure he comes of a forgiving kind.
Why should I then repine at heaven's decree,
Which gives me no pretence to royalty?
Yet oh! that fate, propitiously inclined,
Had raised my birth, or had debased my mind;
To my large soul not all her treasure lent,
And then betrayed it to a mean descent.
I find, I find my mounting spirits bold,
And David's part disdains my mother's mould.
Why am I scanted by a niggard-birth?
My soul disclaims the kindred of her earth,
And, made for empire, whispers me within:
"Desire of greatness is a god-like sin." '
Him staggering so when hell's dire agent found,
While fainting virtue scarce maintained her ground,
He pours fresh forces in, and thus replies:
'Th' eternal God, supremely good and wise,
Imparts not these prodigious gifts in vain;
What wonders are reserved to bless your reign?

Against your will your arguments have shown,
Such virtue's only giv'n to guide a throne.
Not that your father's mildness I contemn;
But manly force becomes the diadem.
'Tis true, he grants the people all they crave,
And more perhaps than subjects ought to have:
For lavish grants suppose a monarch tame,
And more his goodness than his wit proclaim.
But when should people strive their bonds to break,
If not when kings are negligent or weak?
Let him give on till he can give no more,
The thrifty Sanhedrin shall keep him poor;
And every shekel which he can receive
Shall cost a limb of his prerogative.
To ply him with new plots shall be my care;
Or plunge him deep in some expensive war,
Which, when his treasure can no more supply,
He must, with the remains of kingship, buy.
His faithful friends our jealousies and fears
Call Jebusites and Pharaoh's pensioners;
Whom, when our fury from his aid has torn,
He shall be naked left to public scorn.
The next successor, whom I fear and hate,
My arts have made obnoxious to the state;
Turned all his virtues to his overthrow,
And gained our elders to pronounce a foe.
His right, for sums of necessary gold,
Shall first be pawned, and afterwards be sold;
Till time shall ever-wanting David draw
To pass your doubtful title into law.
If not, the people have a right supreme
To make their kings; for kings are made for them.
All empire is no more than pow'r in trust,
Which when resumed can be no longer just.

Succession, for the general good designed,
In its own wrong a nation cannot bind;
If altering that the people can relieve,
Better one suffer than a nation grieve.
The Jews well know their pow'r: ere Saul they chose,
God was their king, and God they durst depose.
Urge now your piety, your filial name,
A father's right, and fear of future fame;
The public good, that universal call,
To which even heav'n submitted, answers all.
Nor let his love enchant your generous mind;
'Tis nature's trick to propagate her kind.
Our fond begetters, who would never die,
Love but themselves in their posterity.
Or let his kindness by th' effects be tried,
Or let him lay his vain pretence aside.
God said he loved your father; could he bring
A better proof than to anoint him King?
It surely show'd he loved the shepherd well
Who gave so fair a flock as Israel.
Would David have you thought his darling son?
What means he then to alienate the crown?
The name of godly he may blush to bear;
'Tis after God's own heart to cheat his heir.
He to his brother gives supreme command,
To you a legacy of barren land;
Perhaps th' old harp on which he thrums his lays,
Or some dull Hebrew ballad in your praise.
Then the next heir, a prince severe and wise,
Already looks on you with jealous eyes;
Sees through the thin disguises of your arts,
And marks your progress in the people's hearts.
Though now his mighty soul its grief contains,
He meditates revenge who least complains;

Cow'ring and quaking at a conqu'ror's sword,
But lofty to a lawful prince restored;
Saw with disdain an Ethnick Plot begun,
And scorned by Jebusites to be outdone.
Hot Levites headed these; who pulled before
From th' Ark, which in the Judge's days they bore,
Resumed their cant and with a zealous cry
Pursued their old beloved theocracy;
Where Sanhedrin and priest enslaved the nation,
And justified their spoils by inspiration:
For who so fit for reign as Aaron's race,
If once dominion they could found in grace?
These led the pack; though not of surest scent
Yet deepest mouthed against the government.
A numerous host of dreaming saints succeed,
Of the true old enthusiastic breed.
'Gainst form and order they their pow'r employ;
Nothing to build and all things to destroy.
But far more numerous was the herd of such
Who think too little and who talk too much.
These, out of mere instinct, they knew not why,
Adored their father's god, and property;
And by the same blind benefit of fate
The devil and the Jebusite did hate.
Born to be saved, even in their own despite,
Because they could not help believing right.
Such were the tools; but a whole hydra more
Remains of sprouting heads too long to score.
Some of their chiefs were princes of the land.
In the first rank of these did Zimri[1] stand:

1. The Duke of Buckingham, poet, wit, and politician, was a man of
brilliant gifts but of unstable and profligate character. He was at
this time a supporter of Shaftesbury. He had ridiculed Dryden
and his plays in *The Rehearsal*, 1671.

A man so various that he seemed to be
Not one, but all mankind's epitome.
Stiff in opinions, always in the wrong,
Was everything by starts and nothing long;
But in the course of one revolving moon
Was chemist, fiddler, statesman, and buffoon.
Then all for women, painting, rhyming, drinking;
Besides ten thousand freaks that died in thinking.
Blest madman, who could every hour employ
With something new to wish or to enjoy!
Railing and praising were his usual themes;
And both (to show his judgement) in extremes;
So over violent, or over civil,
That every man with him was god or devil.
In squandering wealth was his peculiar art:
Nothing went unrewarded, but desert.
Beggared by fools, whom still he found too late;
He had his jest, and they had his estate.
He laughed himself from court; then sought relief
By forming parties, but could ne'er be chief;
For, spite of him, the weight of business fell
On Absalom and wise Achitophel.
Thus, wicked but in will, of means bereft,
He left not faction but of that was left.

   Titles and names 'twere tedious to rehearse
Of lords below the dignity of verse.
Wits, warriors, commonwealthsmen, were the best;
Kind husbands and mere nobles all the rest.
And, therefore, in the name of dullness be
The well-hung Balaam and cold Caleb free.
And canting Nadab let oblivion damn,
Who made new porridge for the Paschal Lamb.[1]

1. Lord Howard was said to have taken the Sacrament in 'lamb's
wool', a concoction of ale, sauce, and roasted apples, instead of
in wine.

Let friendship's holy band some names assure;
Some their own worth, and some let scorn secure.
Nor shall the rascal rabble here have place,
Whom kings no titles gave, and God no grace.
Not bull-faced Jonas,[1] who could statutes draw
To mean rebellion, and make treason law.
But he, though bad, is followed by a worse;
The wretch who heav'n's anointed dared to curse:
Shimei,[2] whose youth did early promise bring
Of zeal to God and hatred to his King,
Did wisely from expensive sins refrain,
And never broke the sabbath, but for gain;
Nor ever was he known an oath to vent,
Or curse, unless against the government.
Thus, heaping wealth by the most ready way
Among the Jews, which was to cheat and pray,
The City, to reward his pious hate
Against his master, chose him magistrate.
His hand a vare[3] of justice did uphold;
His neck was loaded with a chain of gold.
During his office treason was no crime:
The sons of Belial had a glorious time;
For Shimei, though not prodigal of pelf,
Yet loved his wicked neighbour as himself.
When two or three were gathered to declaim
Against the monarch of Jerusalem,
Shimei was always in the midst of them.

1. Sir William Jones, as attorney-general, conducted the prosecu-
   tions of the Popish Plot but resigned office in order to support
   Shaftesbury. He secured the passage through the Commons in
   1680 of the Bill – which he may have drawn up – to exclude the
   Duke of York from the succession.

2. Slingsby Bethel, a wealthy merchant and conspicuous republican,
   was elected sheriff of London in 1680 but his mean state during
   his term of office offended many citizens.

3. Vare, from the Spanish *vara*, means a wand.

And if they cursed the King when he was by
Would rather curse than break good company.
If any durst his factious friends accuse,
He packed a jury of dissenting Jews;
Whose fellow-feeling in the godly cause
Would free the suffering saint from human laws.
For laws are only made to punish those
Who serve the King, and to protect his foes.
If any leisure time he had from pow'r
(Because 'tis sin to misemploy an hour),
His bus'ness was, by writing, to persuade
That kings were useless and a clog to trade;
And, that his noble style he might refine,
No Rechabite more shunned the fumes of wine.
Chaste were his cellars, and his shrieval board
The grossness of a City feast abhorred;
His cooks with long disuse their trade forgot:
Cool was his kitchen though his brains were hot.
Such frugal virtue malice may accuse,
But sure 'twas necessary to the Jews;
For towns once burnt such magistrates require
As dare not tempt God's providence by fire.
With spiritual food he fed his servants well,
But free from flesh that made the Jews rebel;
And Moses' laws he held in more account
For forty days of fasting in the Mount.
To speak the rest, who better are forgot,
Would tire a well-breathed witness of the Plot;
Yet, Corah, thou shalt from oblivion pass:
Erect thyself, thou Monumental Brass,
High as the Serpent of thy metal made,
While nations stand secure beneath thy shade.
What though his birth were base, yet comets rise
From earthy vapours ere they shine in skies.

Prodigious actions may as well be done
By weaver's issue as by prince's son.
This arch-attestor for the public good
By that one deed ennobles all his blood.
Who ever asked the witnesses' high race
Whose oath with martyrdom did Stephen grace?
Ours was a Levite[1] and, as times went then,
His tribe were God-Almighty's gentlemen.
Sunk were his eyes, his voice was harsh and loud,
Sure signs he neither choleric was nor proud;
His long chin proved his wit; his saint-like grace
A church vermilion and a Moses' face.[2]
His memory, miraculously great,
Could plots exceeding man's belief repeat;
Which, therefore, cannot be accounted lies,
For human wit could never such devise.
Some future truths are mingled in his book,
But where the witness failed the prophet spoke.
Some things like visionary flights appear;
The spirit caught him up, the Lord knows where,
And gave him his Rabbinical degree,
Unknown to foreign university.[3]
His judgement yet his mem'ry did excel,
Which pieced his wondrous evidence so well;
And suited to the temper of the times,
Then groaning under Jebusitic crimes.
Let Israel's foes suspect his heav'nly call,
And rashly judge his writ apocryphal;

1. Titus Oates had taken orders in the Church of England following his father's lead who, after being a ribbon-weaver and an Anabaptist minister, was also a Church of England clergyman.
2. The ruddy complexion of a clergyman and a shining expression like Moses' when he came down from Mount Sinai.
3. Oates claimed to have received the degree of Doctor of Divinity from Salamanca, a place which he is known never to have visited.

Our laws for such affronts have forfeits made:
He takes his life who takes away his trade.
Were I myself in witness Corah's place,
The wretch who did me such a dire disgrace
Should whet my memory, though once forgot,
To make him an appendix of my Plot.
His zeal to heav'n made him his prince despise
And load his person with indignities;
But zeal peculiar privilege affords,
Indulging latitude to deeds and words.
And Corah might for Agag's[1] murder call
In terms as coarse as Samuel used to Saul.
What others in his evidence did join
(The best that could be had for love or coin),
In Corah's own predicament will fall;
For witness is a common name to all.
    Surrounded thus with friends of every sort,
Deluded Absalom forsakes the Court;
Impatient of high hopes, urged with renown,
And fired with near possession of a crown.
Th' admiring crowd are dazzled with surprise,
And on his goodly person feed their eyes.
His joy concealed, he sets himself to show,
On each side bowing popularly low;
His looks, his gestures, and his words he frames,
And with familiar ease repeats their names.
Thus, formed by nature, furnished out with arts,
He glides unfelt into their secret hearts;

1. Sir Edmund Berry Godfrey, the London Magistrate before whom
Oates deposed on oath his story of the Popish Plot, was murdered
on Primrose Hill on 12 October 1678. The Protestants accused
the Catholics of his murder and the Catholics retaliated by
accusing the Whigs of murdering him in order to give substance
to the Plot.

Then with a kind compassionating look
And sighs bespeaking pity ere he spoke.
Few words he said, but easy those and fit;
More slow than Hybla drops and far more sweet:
   'I mourn, my countrymen, your lost estate,
Though far unable to prevent your fate.
Behold a banished man,[1] for your dear cause
Exposed a prey to arbitrary laws!
Yet oh! that I alone could be undone,
Cut off from empire, and no more a son!
Now all your liberties a spoil are made;
Egypt and Tyrus intercept your trade,
And Jebusites your sacred rites invade.
My father, whom with reverence yet I name,
Charmed into ease is careless of his fame,
And, bribed with petty sums of foreign gold,
Is grown in Bathsheba's embraces old.
Exalts his enemies, his friends destroys,
And all his pow'r against himself employs.
He gives and let him give my right away,
But why should he his own and yours betray?
He, only he, can make the nation bleed,
And he alone from my revenge is freed.
Take then my tears' (with that he wiped his eyes)
' 'Tis all the aid my present pow'r supplies.
No court-informer can these arms accuse;
These arms may sons against their fathers use;
And, 'tis my wish, the next successor's reign
May make no other Israelite complain.'

1. Monmouth had been sent out of the country by the King in September 1679, but returned without permission in November. He was ordered to leave the country again and, when he disobeyed, was deprived of all his offices and banished from the Court.

40

Youth, beauty, graceful action, seldom fail,
But common interest always will prevail;
And pity never ceases to be shown
To him who makes the people's wrongs his own.
The crowd (that still believe their kings oppress),
With lifted hands their young Messiah bless;
Who now begins his progress to ordain,
With chariots, horsemen, and a num'rous train.[1]
From east to west his glories he displays,
And, like the sun, the Promised Land surveys.
Fame runs before him as the Morning Star,
And shouts of joy salute him from afar.
Each house receives him as a guardian god,
And consecrates the place of his abode.
But hospitable treats did most commend
Wise Issachar, his wealthy western friend.
This moving court, that caught the people's eyes
And seemed but pomp, did other ends disguise.
Achitophel had formed it with intent
To sound the depths, and fathom where it went,
The people's hearts; distinguish friends from foes;
And try their strength before they come to blows.
Yet all was coloured with a smooth pretence
Of specious love and duty to their prince.
Religion and redress of grievances,
Two names that always cheat and always please,
Are often urged; and good King David's life
Endangered by a brother and a wife.
Thus in a pageant show a plot is made,
And peace itself is war in masquerade.
Oh foolish Israel! never warned by ill;

1. Monmouth made a royal progress through western England
after his banishment from Court and his attractive personality
gained him and the Whigs many supporters.

Still the same bait, and circumvented still!
Did ever men forsake their present ease,
In midst of health imagine a disease;
Take pains contingent mischiefs to foresee,
Make heirs for monarchs and for God decree?
What shall we think! Can people give away
Both for themselves and sons their native sway?
Then they are left defenceless to the sword
Of each unbounded arbitrary lord;
And laws are vain, by which we right enjoy,
If kings unquestioned can those laws destroy.
Yet, if the crowd be judge of fit and just,
And kings are only officers in trust,
Then this resuming cov'nant was declared
When kings were made, or is for ever barred:
If those who gave the sceptre could not tie
By their own deed their own posterity,
How then could Adam bind his future race?
How could his forfeit on mankind take place?
Or how could heavenly justice damn us all,
Who ne'er consented to our father's fall?
Then kings are slaves to those whom they command,
And tenants to their people's pleasure stand.
Add, that the pow'r for property allowed
Is mischievously seated in the crowd;
For who can be secure of private right
If sovereign sway may be dissolved by might?
Nor is the people's judgement always true,
The most may err as grossly as the few;
And faultless kings run down by common cry
For vice, oppression and for tyranny.
What standard is there in a fickle rout
Which, flowing to the mark, runs faster out?
Nor only crowds but Sanhedrins may be

Infected with this public lunacy;
And share the madness of rebellious times
To murder monarchs for imagined crimes.
If they may give and take whene'er they please
Not kings alone (the Godhead's images)
But government itself at length must fall
To nature's state, where all have right to all.
Yet grant our lords the people kings can make,
What prudent men a settled throne would shake ?
For whatsoe'er their sufferings were before,
That change they covet makes them suffer more.
All other errors but disturb a state;
But innovation is the blow of fate.
If ancient fabrics nod and threat to fall,
To patch the flaws and buttress up the wall
Thus far 'tis duty; but here fix the mark,
For all beyond it is to touch our Ark.
To change foundations, cast the frame anew,
Is work for rebels who base ends pursue;
At once divine and human laws control,
And mend the parts by ruin of the whole.
The tamp'ring world is subject to this curse,
To physic their disease into a worse.
    Now what relief can righteous David bring ?
How fatal 'tis to be too good a king!
Friends he has few, so high the madness grows;
Who dare be such must be the people's foes.
Yet some there were, ev'n in the worst of days;
Some let me name, and naming is to praise.
    In this short file Barzillai[1] first appears;
Barzillai crowned with honour and with years.
Long since the rising rebels he withstood

---

1. The Duke of Ormonde, Lord-Lieutenant of Ireland, was an ardent
royalist, and a man of remarkable purity and integrity of character,

In regions waste beyond the Jordan's flood.
Unfortunately brave to buoy the state,
But sinking underneath his master's fate
In exile with his god-like prince he mourned;
For him he suffered and with him returned.
The Court he practised, not the courtier's art.
Large was his wealth but larger was his heart,
Which well the noblest objects knew to choose,
The fighting warrior and recording muse.
His bed could once a fruitful issue boast;
Now more than half a father's name is lost.
His eldest hope,[1] with every grace adorned,
By me (so heav'n will have it) always mourned
And always honoured, snatched in manhood's prime
B' unequal fates and providence's crime.
Yet not before the goal of honour won,
All parts fulfilled of subject and of son;
Swift was the race but short the time to run.
Oh, narrow circle but of pow'r divine,
Scanted in space, but perfect in thy line!
By sea, by land, thy matchless worth was known;
Arms thy delight, and war was all thy own.
Thy force, infused, the fainting Tyrians propped,
And haughty Pharaoh found his fortune stopped.
Oh, ancient honour, oh, unconquered hand,
Whom foes unpunished never could withstand!
But Israel was unworthy of thy name:

who, after being defeated in Ireland during the Civil War, was in
exile until the Restoration when he was restored to the offices he
had held under Charles I.

1. Ormonde's eldest son was Thomas, Earl of Ossory (1634–80),
   who, in John Evelyn's words, 'deserved all that a sincere friend,
   a brave soldier, a virtuous courtier, a loyal subject, an honest
   man, a bountiful master, and good christian, could deserve of his
   prince and country'.

Short is the date of all immoderate fame.
It looks as heav'n our ruin had designed,
And durst not trust thy fortune and thy mind.
Now, free from earth, thy disencumbered soul
Mounts up and leaves behind the clouds and starry pole;
From thence thy kindred legions may'st thou bring
To aid the guardian angel of thy King.
Here stop my muse, here cease thy painful flight;
No pinions can pursue immortal height.
Tell good Barzillai thou canst sing no more,
And tell thy soul she should have fled before;
Or fled she with his life, and left this verse
To hang on her departed patron's hearse?
Now take thy steepy flight from heav'n, and see
If thou canst find on earth another he;
Another he would be too hard to find,
See then whom thou canst see not far behind.
Zadoc the priest, whom, shunning pow'r and place,
His lowly mind advanced to David's grace.
With him the Sagan of Jerusalem,[1]
Of hospitable soul and noble stem;
Him of the western dome,[2] whose weighty sense
Flows in fit words and heavenly eloquence.
The prophet's sons, by such example led,
To learning and to loyalty were bred;
For colleges on bounteous kings depend,
And never rebel was to arts a friend.
To these succeed the pillars of the laws,

1. The Bishop of London was Henry Compton (1632–1713), who
   had superintended the education of the Duke of York's daughters,
   Mary and Anne.
2. A reference to John Dolben (1625–86), Bishop of Rochester and
   Dean of Westminster. The 'Western dome' is Westminster
   Abbey, and the 'Prophet's Sons' the boys of Westminster School.

Who best could plead and best can judge a cause.
Next them a train of loyal peers ascend.
Sharp judging Adriel,[1] the muses' friend,
Himself a muse — in Sanhedrin's debate
True to his prince, but not a slave of state;
Whom David's love with honours did adorn
That from his disobedient son were torn.[2]
Jotham[3] of piercing wit and pregnant thought,
Endued by nature, and by learning taught
To move assemblies, who but only tried
The worse awhile then chose the better side,
Nor chose alone but turned the balance too;
So much the weight of one brave man can do.
Hushai,[4] the friend of David in distress,
In public storms of manly steadfastness;
By foreign treaties he informed his youth,
And joined experience to his native truth.
His frugal care supplied the wanting throne;
Frugal for that but bounteous of his own.
'Tis easy conduct when exchequers flow,
But hard the task to manage well the low;
For sovereign power is too depressed or high
When kings are forced to sell or crowds to buy.
Indulge one labour more, my weary muse,

1. The Earl of Mulgrave was both a poet and a particular friend and patron of Dryden.
2. Mulgrave was invested with some of the offices taken from Monmouth in 1679.
3. The Marquis of Halifax had once supported Shaftesbury but, alarmed at his excess, had become a supporter of the Court. It was by his eloquence that the Exclusion Bill was defeated in the Lords in 1680.
4. Laurence Hyde was an ardent royalist, a confidant of the Duke of York, and a patron of Dryden. He was First Commissioner of the Treasury and an important power in the administration.

For Amiel,[1] who can Amiel's praise refuse?
Of ancient race by birth but nobler yet
In his own worth, and without title great.
The Sanhedrin long time as chief he ruled,
Their reason guided and their passion cooled;
So dext'rous was he in the crown's defence,
So formed to speak a loyal nation's sense,
That as their band was Israel's Tribes in small,
So fit was he to represent them all.
Now rasher charioteers the seat ascend,
Whose loose careers his steady skill commend.
They, like th' unequal ruler of the day,
Misguide the seasons and mistake the way;
While he withdrawn at their mad labour smiles,
And safe enjoys the Sabbath of his toils.
    These were the chief; a small but faithful band
Of worthies, in the breach who dared to stand
And tempt th' united fury of the land.
With grief they viewed such powerful engines bent
To batter down the lawful government;
A numerous faction with pretended frights
In Sanhedrins to plume the regal rights;
The true successor from the Court removed;
The Plot by hireling witnesses improved.
These ills they saw and, as their duty bound,
They showed the King the danger of the wound;
That no concessions from the throne would please,
But lenitives fomented the disease;
That Absalom, ambitious of the crown,
Was made the lure to draw the people down;
That false Achitophel's pernicious hate

1. Edward Seymour, who had been Speaker of the House of Commons from 1673 to 1678, was re-elected as Speaker in 1679, but the King refused to accept him. A Tory and Churchman, he opposed the Exclusion Bill in 1680.

Had turned the Plot to ruin Church and State;
The council violent, the rabble worse;
That Shimei taught Jerusalem to curse.

  With all these loads of injuries oppressed,
And long revolving in his careful breast
Th' event of things, at last his patience tired,
Thus from his royal throne, by heav'n inspired,
The god-like David spoke; with awful fear
His train their Maker in their master hear.

  'Thus long have I, by native mercy swayed,
My wrongs dissembled, my revenge delayed;
So willing to forgive th' offending age,
So much the father did the King assuage.
But now so far my clemency they slight,
Th' offenders question my forgiving right.
That one was made for many, they contend;
But 'tis to rule, for that's a monarch's end.
They call my tenderness of blood my fear,
Though manly tempers can the longest bear.
Yet, since they will divert my native course,
'Tis time to show I am not good by force.
Those heaped affronts that haughty subjects bring,
Are burdens for a camel, not a king;
Kings are the public pillars of the state,
Born to sustain and prop the nation's weight.
If my young Samson will pretend a call
To shake the column, let him share the fall.
But oh, that yet he would repent and live!
How easy 'tis for parents to forgive!
With how few tears a pardon might be won
From nature, pleading for a darling son!
Poor pitied youth! by my paternal care
Raised up to all the height his frame could bear;
Had God ordained his fate for empire born,

He would have giv'n his soul another turn.
Gulled with a patriot's name, whose modern sense
Is one that would by law supplant his prince;
The people's brave, the politicians' tool;
Never was patriot yet but was a fool.
Whence comes it that religion and the laws
Should more be Absalom's than David's cause?
His old instructor, ere he lost his place,
Was never thought endued with so much grace.
Good heav'ns, how faction can a patriot paint!
My rebel ever proves my people's saint.
Would *they* impose an heir upon the throne?
Let Sanhedrins be taught to give their own.
A king's at least a part of government,
And mine as requisite as their consent;
Without my leave a future king to choose
Infers a right the present to depose.
True, they petition me t' approve their choice,
But Esau's hands suit ill with Jacob's voice.
My pious subjects for my safety pray,
Which to secure they take my pow'r away.
From plots and treasons heav'n preserve my years,
But save me most from my petitioners.
Unsatiate as the barren womb or grave,
God cannot grant so much as they can crave.
What then is left but with a jealous eye
To guard the small remains of royalty?
The law shall still direct my peaceful sway,
And the same law teach rebels to obey.
Votes shall no more established pow'r control,
Such votes as make a part exceed the whole;
No groundless clamours shall my friends remove,
Nor crowds have pow'r to punish ere they prove;
For gods and god-like kings their care express

Still to defend their servants in distress.
Oh, that my pow'r to saving were confined!
Why am I forced, like heav'n, against my mind
To make examples of another kind?
Must I at length the sword of justice draw?
Oh, cursed effects of necessary law!
How ill my fear they by my mercy scan;
Beware the fury of a patient man.
Law they require, let law then show her face;
They could not be content to look on grace,
Her hinder parts, but with a daring eye
To tempt the terror of her front and die.
By their own arts 'tis righteously decreed
Those dire artificers of death shall bleed.
Against themselves their witnesses will swear,
Till viper-like their mother-Plot they tear;
And suck for nutriment that bloody gore
Which was their principle of life before.
Their Belial with their Belzebub will fight;
Thus on my foes my foes shall do me right.
Nor doubt th' event: for factious crowds engage
In their first onset all their brutal rage;
Then let 'em take an unresisted course,
Retire and traverse and delude their force,
But when they stand all breathless urge the fight
And rise upon 'em with redoubled might.
For lawful pow'r is still superior found
When long driv'n back at length it stands the ground.'
    He said. Th' Almighty, nodding, gave consent,
And peals of thunder shook the firmament.
Henceforth a series of new time began,
The mighty years in long procession ran;
Once more the god-like David was restored,
And willing nations knew their lawful lord.

THE MEDAL

ALMIGHTY crowd, thou shorten'st all dispute;
Pow'r is thy essence, wit thy attribute!
Nor faith nor reason make thee at a stay,
Thou leap'st o'er all eternal truths in thy pindaric way!
Athens, no doubt, did righteously decide
When Phocion and when Socrates were tried,
As righteously they did those dooms repent;
Still they were wise whatever way they went.
Crowds err not though to both extremes they run,
To kill the father and recall the son.
Some think the fools were most, as times went then;
But now the world's o'erstock'd with prudent men.
The common cry is ev'n religion's test;
The Turk's is, at Constantinople, best,
Idols in India, popery at Rome,
And our own worship only true at home.
And true but for the time! 'tis hard to know
How long we please it shall continue so.
This side to-day, and that to-morrow burns;
So all are god-a'mightys in their turns.
A tempting doctrine, plausible and new:
What fools our fathers were, if this be true!

MAC FLECKNOE

OR A SATIRE UPON THE

TRUE-BLUE PROTESTANT POET

T. S.

ALL human things are subject to decay,
And when Fate summons monarchs must obey.
This Flecknoe found,[1] who, like Augustus, young
Was called to Empire and had governed long;
In prose and verse was owned, without dispute
Through all the realms of Nonsense, absolute.
This aged prince, now flourishing in peace
And blest with issue of a large increase,
Worn out with business, did at length debate
To settle the succession of the state;
And pond'ring which of all his sons was fit
To reign and wage immortal war with wit,
Cried: ' 'Tis resolved; for nature pleads that he
Should only rule who most resembles me.
Shadwell alone my perfect image bears,[2]
Mature in dullness from his tender years.
Shadwell alone, of all my sons, is he
Who stands confirmed in full stupidity.
The rest to some faint meaning make pretence,
But Shadwell never deviates into sense.
Some beams of wit on other souls may fall,
Strike through and make a lucid interval,

1. Richard Flecknoe (*d.* 1678), Irish priest and poet.
2. Thomas Shadwell (1642–92), the dramatist. Dryden attacked
   him largely on account of his support of Shaftesbury and the
   Whigs; but professional jealousy also played its part.

But Shadwell's genuine night admits no ray,
His rising fogs prevail upon the day.
Besides his goodly fabric fills the eye,
And seems designed for thoughtless majesty:
Thoughtless as monarch oaks that shade the plain
And, spread in solemn state, supinely reign.
Heywood and Shirley[1] were but types of thee,
Thou last great prophet of tautology.
Even I, a dunce of more renown than they,
Was sent before but to prepare thy way;
And coarsely clad in Norwich drugget came
To teach the nations in thy greater name.
My warbling lute, the lute I whilom strung
When to King John of Portugal I sung,[2]
Was but the prelude to that glorious day
When thou on silver Thames did'st cut thy
     way
With well-timed oars before the Royal Barge,
Swelled with the pride of thy celestial charge;
And big with hymn, commander of an host,
The like was ne'er in Epsom blankets tossed.[3]
Methinks I see the new Arion sail,
The lute still trembling underneath thy nail,
At thy well-sharpened thumb from shore to shore
The treble squeaks for fear, the basses roar;
Echoes from Pissing-Alley Shadwell call,
And Shadwell they resound from Aston Hall.

1. Thomas Heywood (*d.* 1650) and James Shirley (1596–1666), the dramatists.
2. Flecknoe had lived in Lisbon for some years and been patronized by King John.
3. Shadwell published his play of *Epsom Wells* in 1673 but the phrase to which Dryden refers, – 'Such a fellow as he deserves to be tossed in a blanket' – occurs in another of Shadwell's plays, *The Sullen Lovers.*

About thy boat the little fishes throng
As at the morning toast that floats along.
Sometimes as prince of thy harmonious band
Thou wield'st thy papers in thy threshing hand.
St Andre's[1] feet ne'er kept more equal time,
Not ev'n the feet of thy own Psyche's rhyme[2]
Though they in number as in sense excel;
So just, so like tautology they fell,
That, pale with envy, Singleton forswore
The lute and sword which he in triumph bore
And vowed he ne'er would act Villerius more.'[3]
Here stopped the good old sire, and wept for joy
In silent raptures of the hopeful boy.
All arguments, but most his plays, persuade
That for anointed dullness he was made.

    Close to the walls which fair Augusta bind
(The fair Augusta much to fears inclined),
An ancient fabric, raised t' inform the sight,
There stood of yore and Barbican[4] it hight.
A watchtower once; but now, so Fate ordains,
Of all the pile an empty name remains.
From its old ruins brothel-houses rise,
Scenes of lewd loves and of polluted joys.
Where their vast courts the mother-strumpets keep,
And, undisturbed by watch, in silence sleep.
Near these a Nursery[5] erects its head,
Where queens are formed and future heroes bred;

1. A dancing master.
2. Shadwell's verse opera of *Psyche* was produced in 1676.
3. Singleton, a singer, played the part of Villerius in Sir William
   D'Avenant's opera of *The Siege of Rhodes*.
4. The Barbican stood in Aldersgate Street.
5. The Nursery, a theatrical school for training boys and girls for
   the stage, was established in 1662.

Where unfledged actors learn to laugh and cry,
Where infant punks their tender voices try,
And little Maximins[1] the gods defy.
Great Fletcher never treads in buskins here,
Nor greater Jonson dares in socks appear;
But gentle Simkin[2] just reception finds
Amidst this monument of vanished minds;
Pure clinches the suburban muse affords,
And Panton[3] waging harmless war with words.
Here Flecknoe, as a place to fame well-known,
Ambitiously designed his Shadwell's throne.
For ancient Decker[4] prophesied long since
That in this pile should reign a mighty prince,
Born for a scourge of wit and flail of sense;
To whom true dullness should some Psyches owe,
But worlds of Misers from his pen should flow;
Humorists and hypocrites it should produce,
Whole Raymond families and tribes of Bruce.[5]

    Now Empress Fame had published the renown
Of Shadwell's coronation through the town.
Roused by report of fame the nations meet
From near Bunhill and distant Watling Street.
No Persian carpets spread th' imperial way,
But scattered limbs of mangled poets lay;
From dusty shops neglected authors come,
Martyrs of pies and relics of the bum.

---

1. The hero of Dryden's *Tyrannic Love.*
2. A character of a cobbler in an interlude.
3. A celebrated punster.
4. Thomas Dekker (1570?–1632), dramatist and miscellaneous writer.
5. *The Miser,* and *The Humorists,* are two of Shadwell's less successful plays. Raymond is a character in *The Humorists,* and Bruce a character in another of Shadwell's plays, *The Virtuoso.*

Much Heywood, Shirley, Ogleby[1] there lay,
But loads of Shadwell almost choked the way.
Bilked stationers for Yeomen stood prepared,
And Herringman[2] was captain of the guard.
The hoary Prince in majesty appeared,
High on a throne of his own labours reared.
At his right hand our young Ascanius sat,
Rome's other hope and pillar of the State.
His brows thick fogs, instead of glories, grace,
And lambent dullness played around his face.
As Hannibal did to the altars come,
Sworn by his sire a mortal foe to Rome;
So Shadwell swore, nor should his vow be vain,
That he till death true dullness would maintain,
And in his father's right and realm's defence
Ne'er to have peace with wit nor truce with sense.
The King himself the sacred unction made,
As King by office, and as priest by trade.
In his sinister hand instead of ball
He placed a mighty mug of potent ale;
Love's Kingdom[3] to his right he did convey,
At once his sceptre and his rule of sway,
Whose righteous lore the Prince had practised young
And from whose loins recorded Psyche sprung.
His temples last with poppies were o'erspread,
That nodding seemed to consecrate his head.
Just at that point of time, if fame not lie,
On his left hand twelve reverend owls did fly:
So Romulus, 'tis sung, by Tiber's brook
Presage of sway from twice six vultures took.

1. John Ogilby (1600–76), the translator of Vergil.
2. Henry Herringman had been Dryden's publisher.
3. Flecknoe's pastoral tragi-comedy of *Love's Kingdom* was published in 1664.

Th' admiring throng loud acclamations make,
And omens of his future empire take.
The sire then shook the honours of his head,
And from his brows damps of oblivion shed
Full on the filial dullness. Long he stood
Repelling from his breast the raging god;
At length burst out in this prophetic mood:
    'Heavens bless my son, from Ireland let him reign
To far Barbadoes on the western main;
Of his dominion may no end be known,
And greater than his father's be his throne.
Beyond Love's Kingdom let him stretch his pen.'
He paused and all the people cried 'Amen.'
'Then thus,' continued he, 'my son, advance
Still in new impudence, new ignorance.
Success let others teach, learn thou from me
Pangs without birth and fruitless industry.
Let Virtuoso's in five years be writ;
Yet not one thought accuse thy toil of wit.
Let gentle George[1] in triumph tread the stage,
Make Dorimant betray, and Loveit rage;
Let Cully, Cockwood, Fopling, charm the pit,
And in their folly show the writer's wit.
Yet still thy fools shall stand in thy defence,
And justify their author's want of sense.
Let 'em be all by thy own model made
Of dullness and desire no foreign aid,
That they to future ages may be known
Not copies drawn but issue of thy own.
Nay, let thy men of wit, too, be the same,
All full of thee and differing but in name;
But let no alien Sedley interpose

1. Sir George Etherege (1634?–91?), the dramatist. The names in
   the two following lines are characters in his comedies.

To lard with wit thy hungry Epsom prose.[1]
And when false flowers of rhetoric thou would'st cull,
Trust nature, do not labour to be dull
But write thy best and top; and in each line
Sir Formal's oratory will be thine.[2]
Sir Formal, though unsought, attends thy quill
And does thy northern dedications fill.[3]
Nor let false friends seduce thy mind to fame
By arrogating Jonson's hostile name.[4]
Let father Flecknoe fire thy mind with praise,
And uncle Ogleby thy envy raise.
Thou art my blood, where Jonson has no part;
What share have we in nature or in art?
Where did his wit on learning fix a brand
And rail at arts he did not understand?
Where made he love in Prince Nicander's[5] vein,
Or swept the dust in Psyche's humble strain?
Where sold he bargains, whip-stitch, kiss my arse,[6]
Promised a play and dwindled to a farce?
When did his muse from Fletcher scenes purloin,
As thou whole Eth'rege dost transfuse to thine?
But so transfused as oil on waters flow,
His always floats above, thine sinks below.
This is thy province, this thy wondrous way,
New humours to invent for each new play;

1. Sir Charles Sedley (1639?–1701), the dramatist, was supposed to have helped Shadwell in the composition of *Epsom Wells*.
2. Sir Formal Trifle, an oratorical character in Shadwell's comedy of *The Virtuoso*.
3. A reference to Shadwell's dedications addressed to the Duke of Newcastle (1592–1676), himself a dramatist.
4. Shadwell was an eulogist of Ben Jonson, whose theory of drama, particularly his conception of 'humours', he copied.
5. A character in Shadwell's *Psyche*.
6. The catch-phrase of a character in Shadwell's *The Virtuoso*.

This is that boasted bias of thy mind
By which one way, to dullness, 'tis inclined,
Which makes thy writings lean on one side still,
And in all changes that way bends thy will.
Nor let thy mountain belly make pretence
Of likeness; thine's a tympany of sense.
A tun of man in thy large bulk is writ,
But sure thou 'rt but a kilderkin of wit.
Like mine thy gentle numbers feebly creep,
Thy tragic muse gives smiles, thy comic sleep.
With whate'er gall thou sett'st thyself to write,
Thy inoffensive satires never bite.
In thy felonious heart though venom lies,
It does but touch thy Irish pen and dies.
Thy genius calls thee not to purchase fame
In keen iambics but mild anagram;
Leave writing plays and choose for thy command
Some peaceful province in acrostic land.
There thou may'st wings display and altars raise,[1]
And torture one poor word ten thousand ways.
Or, if thou would'st thy diff'rent talents suit,
Set thy own songs and sing them to thy lute.'
He said, but his last words were scarcely heard,
For Bruce and Longville had a trap prepared,
And down they sent the yet declaiming bard.[2]
Sinking, he left his drugget robe behind;
Born upwards by a subterranean wind
The mantle fell to the young prophet's part,
With double portion of his father's art.

1. It was a fashion during the earlier years of the seventeenth century
   to write verses in such a variety of metres that their shapes on
   the printed page resembled, among other objects, wings and altars.
2. Bruce and Longville, in Shadwell's *The Virtuoso*, dismiss Sir For-
   mal Trifle by opening a trap-door while he is delivering a speech.

THE SECOND PART OF

ABSALOM AND ACHITOPHEL

DOEG,[1] though without knowing how or why,
Made still a blundering kind of melody;
Spurred boldly on, and dashed through thick and thin,
Through sense and nonsense, never out nor in;
Free from all meaning, whether good or bad,
And in one word, heroically mad.
He was too warm on picking-work to dwell
But faggoted his notions as they fell,
And if they rhymed and rattled all was well.
Spiteful he is not, though he wrote a satire,
For still there goes some *thinking* to ill-nature;
He needs no more than birds and beasts to think,
All his occasions are to eat and drink.
If he call rogue and rascal from a garret
He means you no more mischief than a parrot;
The words for friend and foe alike were made,
To fetter 'em in verse is all his trade.
For almonds he'll cry whore to his own mother,
And call young Absalom King David's brother.
Let him be gallows-free by my consent,
And nothing suffer since he nothing meant;
Hanging supposes human soul and reason,
This animal's below committing treason.
Shall he be hanged who never could rebel?
That's a preferment for Achitophel.

1. Elkanah Settle (1648–1724) replied to *Absalom and Achitophel* in a satire defending the Whigs, clumsily entitled *Absalom Senior: or, Achitophel Transprosed*, 1682. Dryden makes fun of this title in the line 'For to write verse with him is to *transprose*.'

The woman that committed buggary
Was rightly sentenced by the law to die;
But 'twas hard fate that to the gallows led
The dog that never heard the statute read.
Railing in other men may be a crime,
But ought to pass for mere instinct in him;
Instinct he follows and no farther knows,
For to write verse with him is to *transprose*.
'Twere pity treason at his door to lay,
Who *makes heaven's gate a lock to its own key*.[1]
Let him rail on, let his invective muse
Have four and twenty letters to abuse,
Which if he jumbles to one line of sense,
Indict him of a capital offence.
In fireworks give him leave to vent his spite,
Those are the only serpents he can write.
The height of his ambition is we know
But to be master of a puppet-show;
On that one stage his works may yet appear,
And a month's harvest keeps him all the year.

  Now stop your noses, readers, all and some,
For here's a tun of midnight-work to come,
Og[2] from a treason tavern rolling home,
Round as a globe, and liquored ev'ry chink,
Goodly and great he sails behind his link;
With all this bulk there's nothing lost in Og,
For ev'ry inch that is not fool is rogue:
A monstrous mass of foul corrupted matter,
As all the devils had spewed to make the batter.
When wine has given him courage to blaspheme,
He curses God, but God before cursed him;

1. A line from Settle's *Absalom Senior: or, Achitophel Transprosed*.
2. Thomas Shadwell, the hero of *Mac Flecknoe*.

And if man could have reason, none has more
That made his paunch so rich and him so poor.
With wealth he was not trusted, for heav'n knew
What 'twas of old to pamper up a Jew;
To what would he on quail and pheasant swell,
That ev'n on tripe and carrion could rebel?
But though heav'n made him poor (with rev'rence
    speaking)
He never was a poet of God's making;
The midwife laid her hand on his thick skull
With this prophetic blessing – 'Be thou dull.'
Drink, swear and roar, forbear no lewd delight
Fit for thy bulk, do anything but write.
Thou art of lasting make like thoughtless men;
A strong nativity – but for the pen!
Eat opium, mingle arsenic in thy drink,
Still thou may'st live avoiding pen and ink.
I see, I see, 'tis counsel given in vain,
For treason botched in rhyme will be thy bane;
Rhyme is the rock on which thou art to wreck,
'Tis fatal to thy fame and to thy neck.
Why should thy metre good king David blast?
A psalm of his will surely be thy last!
Dar'st thou presume in verse to meet thy foes,
Thou whom the penny pamphlet foiled in prose?
Doeg, whom God for mankind's mirth has
    made,
O'er-tops thy talent in thy very trade;
Doeg to thee, thy paintings are so coarse,
A poet is, though he's the poet's horse.
A double noose thou on thy neck dost pull,
For writing treason and for writing dull;
To die for faction is a common evil,
But to be hanged for nonsense is the devil.

Had'st thou the glories of thy King expressed,
Thy praises had been satire at the best;
But thou in clumsy verse, unlicked, unpointed,
Hast shamefully defied the Lord's anointed.
I will not rake the dunghill of thy crimes,
For who would read thy life that reads thy rhymes?
But of King David's foes be this the doom,
May all be like the young man Absalom;
And for my foes may this their blessing be,
To talk like Doeg, and to write like thee.

RELIGIO LAICI

OR A LAYMAN'S FAITH

Ornari res ipsa negat; contenta doceri[1]

DIM, as the borrowed beams of moon and stars
To lonely, weary, wand'ring travellers,
Is reason to the soul; and as on high
Those rolling fires discover but the sky
Not light us here, so reason's glimmering ray
Was lent not to assure our doubtful way
But guide us upward to a better day.
And as those nightly tapers disappear
When day's bright lord ascends our hemisphere,
So pale grows reason at religion's sight,
So dies and so dissolves in supernatural light.
Some few, whose lamp shone brighter, have been led
From cause to cause to nature's secret head,
And found that one first principle must be.
But what, or who, that universal He;
Whether some soul encompassing this ball,
Unmade, unmoved, yet making, moving all;
Or various atoms' interfering dance
Leapt into form (the noble work of chance);
Or this great All was from eternity;
Not even the Stagirite himself could see,
And Epicurus guessed as well as he.
As blindly groped they for a future state;
As rashly judged of providence and fate.

1. My very subject, content to be taught, spurns adornment.
   (Manilius, *Astronomica* 3. 39.)

But least of all could their endeavours find
What most concerned the good of human kind;
For happiness was never to be found,
But vanished from 'em like enchanted ground.
One thought content the good to be enjoyed;
This, every little accident destroyed.
The wiser madmen did for virtue toil,
A thorny or at best a barren soil.
In pleasure some their glutton souls would steep,
But found their line too short, the well too deep,
And leaky vessels which no bliss could keep.
Thus anxious thoughts in endless circles roll,
Without a centre where to fix the soul.
In this wild maze their vain endeavours end:
How can the less the greater comprehend?
Or finite reason reach infinity?
For what could fathom God were more than He.

Opinions of the several sects of philosophers concerning the Summum Bonum.

    The Deist thinks he stands on firmer ground;
Cries εὑρηκα: the mighty secret's found:
God is that spring of good, supreme and best;
We, made to serve, and in that service blest.
If so, some rules of worship must be given,
Distributed alike to all by heaven;
Else God were partial, and to some denied
The means His justice should for all provide.
This general worship is to praise, and pray;
One part to borrow blessings, one to pay;
And when frail nature slides into offence,
The sacrifice for crimes is penitence.
Yet since th' effects of providence we find
Are variously dispensed to human kind;
That vice triumphs, and virtue suffers here
(A brand that sovereign justice cannot bear),

System of deism.

Our reason prompts us to a future state;
The last appeal from fortune and from fate,
Where God's all-righteous ways will be declared,
The bad meet punishment, the good, reward.

Of revealed religion.

    Thus man by his own strength to heaven would
        soar,
And would not be obliged to God for more.
Vain, wretched creature, how art thou misled
To think thy wit these God-like notions bred!
These truths are not the product of thy mind,
But dropped from heaven and of a nobler kind.
Revealed religion first informed thy sight,
And reason saw not, till faith sprung the light.
Hence all thy natural worship takes the source;
'Tis revelation what thou think'st discourse.
Else how com'st thou to see these truths so clear,
Which so obscure to heathens did appear?
Not Plato these, nor Aristotle found;

Socrates.

Nor he whose wisdom oracles renowned.
Hast thou a wit so deep, or so sublime,
Or can'st thou lower dive, or higher climb?
Can'st thou, by reason, more of God-head know
Than Plutarch, Seneca, or Cicero?
Those giant wits, in happier ages born
(When arms and arts did Greece and Rome adorn),
Knew no such system; no such piles could raise
Of natural worship, built on pray'r and praise,
To one sole God.
Nor did remorse, to expiate sin, prescribe,
But slew their fellow creatures for a bribe;
The guiltless victim groaned for their offence,
And cruelty and blood was penitence.
If sheep and oxen could atone for men,
Ah! at how cheap a rate the rich might sin!

And great oppressors might heaven's wrath beguile
By offering his own creatures for a spoil!
    Dar'st thou, poor worm, offend infinity?
And must the terms of peace be given by thee?
Then thou art justice in the last appeal;
Thy easy God instructs thee to rebel,
And, like a king remote and weak, must take
What satisfaction thou art pleased to make.
    But if there be a pow'r too just and strong
To wink at crimes and bear unpunished wrong;
Look humbly upward, see His will disclose
The forfeit first, and then the fine impose;
A mulct thy poverty could never pay,
Had not eternal wisdom found the way
And with celestial wealth supplied thy store.
His justice makes the fine, His mercy quits the
    score.
See God descending in thy human frame;
Th' offended suff'ring in th' offender's name;
All thy misdeeds to him imputed see,
And all his righteousness devolved on thee.
    For granting we have sinned, and that th' offence
Of man is made against omnipotence,
Some price that bears proportion must be paid,
And infinite with infinite be weighed.
See then the Deist lost, remorse for vice
Not paid, or paid, inadequate in price;
What farther means can reason now direct,
Or what relief from human wit expect?
That shows us sick; and sadly are we sure
Still to be sick till heav'n reveal the cure.
If then heaven's will must needs be understood
(Which must if we want cure and heaven be
    good),

Let all records of will revealed be shown;
With Scripture all in equal balance thrown,
And our one sacred Book will be that one.
    Proof needs not here, for whether we compare
That impious, idle, superstitious ware
Of rites, lustrations, offerings (which before
In various ages various countries bore),
With Christian faith and virtues, we shall find
None answ'ring the great ends of human kind
But this one rule of life; that shows us best
How God may be appeased, and mortals blest.
Whether from length of time its worth we draw,
The world is scarce more ancient than the law;
Heav'n's early care prescribed for every age,
First, in the soul, and after, in the page.
Or whether more abstractedly we look,
Or on the writers or the written Book,
Whence but for heav'n could men unskilled in arts,
In several ages born, in several parts,
Weave such agreeing truths? or how or why
Should all conspire to cheat us with a lie?
Unasked their pains, ungrateful their advice,
Starving their gain, and martyrdom their price.
    If on the Book itself we cast our view,
Concurrent heathens prove the story true,
The doctrine, miracles; which must convince,
For heav'n in them appeals to human sense.
And though they prove not, they confirm the
        cause,
When what is taught agrees with nature's laws.
    Then for the style, majestic and divine,
It speaks no less than God in every line;
Commanding words, whose force is still the same
As the first fiat that produced our frame.

All faiths beside or did by arms ascend,
Or sense indulged has made mankind their friend.
This only doctrine does our lusts oppose;
Unfed by nature's soil in which it grows;
Cross to our interests, curbing sense and sin;
Oppressed without and undermined within,
It thrives through pain, its own tormentors tires,
And with a stubborn patience still aspires.
To what can reason such effects assign,
Transcending nature, but to laws divine,
Which in that sacred volume are contained,
Sufficient, clear, and for that use ordained.

But stay! the Deist here will urge anew, *Objection of*
No supernatural worship can be true, *the Deist.*
Because a general law is that alone
Which must to all and everywhere be known.
A style so large as not this book can claim,
Nor aught that bears revealed religion's name.
'Tis said the sound of a Messiah's birth
Is gone through all the habitable earth;
But still that text must be confined alone
To what was then inhabited and known,
And what provision could from thence accrue
To Indian souls and worlds discovered new?
In other parts it helps, that ages past
The Scriptures there were known and were embraced
Till sin spread once again the shades of night.
What's that to these who never saw the light?

Of all objections this indeed is chief *The objec-*
To startle reason, stagger frail belief. *tion an-*
We grant, 'tis true, that heav'n from human sense *swered.*
Has hid the secret paths of providence;
But boundless wisdom, boundless mercy, may
Find ev'n for those bewildered souls a way.

If from His nature foes may pity claim,
Much more may strangers who ne'er heard His name;
And though no name be for salvation known
But that of His eternal Son's alone,
Who knows how far transcending goodness can
Extend the merits of that Son to man?
Who knows what reasons may His mercy lead,
Or ignorance invincible may plead?
Not only charity bids hope the best,
But more, the great Apostle has expressed
That if the Gentiles (whom no law inspired)
By nature did what was by law required,
They who the written rule had never known
Were to themselves both rule and law alone;
To nature's plain indictment they shall plead,
And by their conscience be condemned or freed.
Most righteous doom! because a rule revealed
Is none to those from whom it was concealed.
Then those who followed reason's dictates right,
Lived up and lifted high their natural light,
With Socrates may see their Maker's face,
While thousand rubric-martyrs want a place.
  Nor does it balk my charity to find
Th' Egyptian Bishop of another mind;
For, though his Creed eternal truth contains,
'Tis hard for man to doom to endless pains
All who believed not all his zeal required,
Unless he first could prove he was inspired.[1]
Then let us either think he meant to say
This faith, where published, was the only way;
Or else conclude that, Arius to confute,
The good old man, too eager in dispute,

---

1. A reference to St Athanasius and the Creed that bears his name.

Flew high and, as his Christian fury rose,
Damned all for heretics who durst oppose.
   Thus far my charity this path has tried
(A much unskilful but well meaning guide);
Yet what they are, ev'n these crude thoughts were
      bred
By reading that which better thou hast read,
Thy matchless author's work; which thou, my friend,
By well translating better dost commend.[1]
Those youthful hours which, of thy equals most
In toys have squandered or in vice have lost,
Those hours hast thou to nobler use employed,
And the severe delights of truth enjoyed.
Witness this weighty book, in which appears
The crabbed toil of many thoughtful years,
Spent by thy author in the sifting care
Of Rabbins' old sophisticated ware
From gold divine; which he who well can sort
May afterwards make algebra a sport.
A treasure, which if country curates buy
They Junius and Tremellius may defy;[2]
Save pains in various readings and translations,
And without Hebrew make most learned quotations.
A work so full with various learning fraught,
So nicely pondered yet so strongly wrought,
As nature's height and art's last hand required;
As much as man could compass uninspired.
Where we may see what errors have been made
Both in the copiers' and translators' trade;
How Jewish, Popish, interests have prevailed,
And where infallibility has failed.

Digression to the translator of Father Simon's Critical History of the Old Testament.

1. Henry Dickinson was the translator of Father Simon's work, and
   Dryden addressed this poem to him.
2. Calvinist translators of the Scriptures.

For some, who have his secret meaning guessed,
Have found our author not too much a priest.
For fashion-sake he seems to have recourse
To Pope and Councils and tradition's force;
But he that old traditions could subdue
Could not but find the weakness of the new.
If Scripture, though derived from heavenly birth,
Has been but carelessly preserved on earth;
If God's own People — who of God before
Knew what we know, and had been promised more,
In fuller terms, of heaven's assisting care,
And who did neither time nor study spare
To keep this Book untainted, unperplexed,
Let in gross errors to corrupt the text,
Omitted paragraphs, embroiled the sense,
With vain traditions stopped the gaping fence
Which every common hand pulled up with ease;
What safety from such brushwood-helps as these?
If written words from time are not secured,
How can we think have oral sounds endured?
Which thus transmitted, if one mouth has failed,
Immortal lies on ages are entailed;
And that some such have been is proved too plain,
If we consider interest, church, and gain.

Of the infal-
libility of
tradition, in
general.

    Oh! but, says one, tradition set aside,
Where can we hope for an unerring guide?
For since th' original Scripture has been lost,
All copies disagreeing, maimed the most,
Or Christian faith can have no certain ground,
Or truth in church tradition must be found.
    Such an omniscient Church we wish indeed;
'Twere worth both Testaments, and cast in the Creed.
But if this mother be a guide so sure
As can all doubts resolve, all truth secure,

Then her infallibility as well
Where copies are corrupt or lame can tell,
Restore lost Canon with as little pains,
As truly explicate what still remains;
Which yet not council dare pretend to do,
Unless, like Esdras,[1] they could write it new.
Strange confidence, still to interpret true,
Yet not be sure that all they have explained
Is in the blest original contained.
More safe and much more modest 'tis to say
God would not leave mankind without a way;
And that the Scriptures, though not every-
    where
Free from corruption or entire or clear,
Are uncorrupt, sufficient, clear, entire
In all things which our needful faith require.
If others in the same glass better see,
'Tis for themselves they look, but not for me;
For my salvation must its doom receive
Not from what others but what I believe.

   Must all tradition then be set aside?
This to affirm were ignorance or pride.
Are there not many points, some needful sure
To saving faith, that Scripture leaves obscure?
Which every sect will wrest a several way
(For what one sect interprets, all sects may).
We hold, and say we prove from Scripture plain,
That Christ is God; the bold Socinian
From the same Scripture urges he's but man.
Now what appeal can end th' important suit?
Both parts talk loudly but the rule is mute.

   Shall I speak plain, and in a nation free
Assume an honest layman's liberty?

Objection in behalf of tradition urged by Father Simon.

1. See 1 *Esdras*, viii, 7.

I think (according to my little skill,
To my own Mother-Church submitting still)
That many have been saved, and many may,
Who never heard this question brought in play.
Th' unlettered Christian, who believes in gross,
Plods on to heaven, and ne'er is at a loss;
For the strait gate would be made straiter yet
Were none admitted there but men of wit.
The few, by nature formed, with learning fraught,
Born to instruct, as others to be taught,
Must study well the sacred page and see
Which doctrine, this or that, does best agree
With the whole tenor of the work divine,
And plainliest points to heaven's revealed design;
Which exposition flows from genuine sense,
And which is forced by wit and eloquence.
Not that tradition's parts are useless here,
When general, old, disinteressed and clear.
That ancient Fathers thus expound the page,
Gives truth the reverend majesty of age,
Confirms its force by biding every test;
For best authority's next rules are best,
And still the nearer to the spring we go
More limpid, more unsoiled the waters flow.
Thus, first traditions were a proof alone
Could we be certain such they were, so known;
But since some flaws in long descent may be,
They make not truth but probability.
Even Arius and Pelagius durst provoke
To what the centuries preceding spoke.
Such difference is there in an oft-told tale;
But truth by its own sinews will prevail.
Tradition written therefore more commends
Authority than what from voice descends;

And this, as perfect as its kind can be,
Rolls down to us the sacred history,
Which, from the Universal Church received,
Is tried, and after for itself believed.
    The partial Papists would infer from hence, *The second*
Their Church, in last resort, should judge the sense. *objection.*
But first they would assume, with wondrous art, *Answer to*
Themselves to be the whole, who are but part *the objec-*
Of that vast frame, the Church. Yet grant they were *tion.*
The handers down, can they from thence infer
A right t' interpret? or would they alone
Who brought the present claim it for their own?
The Book's a common largess to mankind;
Not more for them than every man designed.
The welcome news is in the letter found;
The carrier's not commissioned to expound.
It speaks itself, and what it does contain,
In all things needful to be known, is plain.
    In times o'ergrown with rust and ignorance,
A gainful trade their clergy did advance.
When want of learning kept the laymen low,
And none but priests were authorized to know;
When what small knowledge was in them did dwell,
And he a god who could but read or spell;
Then Mother Church did mightily prevail:
She parcelled out the Bible by retail,
But still expounded what she sold or gave
To keep it in her power to damn and save.
Scripture was scarce, and as the market went,
Poor laymen took salvation on content,
As needy men take money, good or bad;
God's Word they had not, but the priests' they had.
Yet, whate'er false conveyances they made,
The lawyer still was certain to be paid.

In those dark times they learned their knack so well
That by long use they grew infallible.
At last a knowing age began t' enquire
If they the Book, or that did them inspire;
And making narrower search they found, tho' late,
That what they thought the priest's, was their
    estate;
Taught by the will produced (the written Word),
How long they had been cheated on record.
Then every man who saw the title fair
Claimed a child's part, and put in for a share;
Consulted soberly his private good,
And saved himself as cheap as e'er he could.
   'Tis true, my Friend, (and far be flattery hence)
This good had full as bad a consequence.
The Book thus put in every vulgar hand,
Which each presumed he best could understand,
The common rule was made the common prey
And at the mercy of the rabble lay.
The tender page with horny fists was gall'd,
And he was gifted most that loudest bawled.
The spirit gave the doctoral degree;
And every member of a company
Was of his trade and of the Bible free.
Plain truths enough for needful use they found,
But men would still be itching to expound;
Each was ambitious of th' obscurest place,
No measure ta'en from knowledge, all from grace.
Study and pains were now no more their care;
Texts were explained by fasting and by prayer.
This was the fruit the private spirit brought,
Occasioned by great zeal and little thought.
While crowds unlearned, with rude devotion warm,
About the sacred viands buzz and swarm,

The fly-blown text creates a crawling brood
And turns to maggots what was meant for food.
A thousand daily sects rise up and die;
A thousand more the perished race supply.
So all we make of heaven's discovered will
Is, not to have it or to use it ill.
The danger's much the same; on several shelves
If others wreck us, or we wreck ourselves.

　　What then remains but, waiving each extreme,
The tides of ignorance and pride to stem?
Neither so rich a treasure to forgo,
Nor proudly seek beyond our power to know.
Faith is not built on disquisitions vain;
The things we must believe are few and plain.
But since men will believe more than they need
And every man will make himself a creed,
In doubtful questions 'tis the safest way
To learn what unsuspected ancients say;
For 'tis not likely we should higher soar
In search of heav'n than all the Church before.
Nor can we be deceived, unless we see
The Scripture and the Fathers disagree.
If after all they stand suspected still
(For no man's faith depends upon his will),
'Tis some relief that points not clearly known
Without much hazard may be let alone.
And after hearing what our Church can say
If still our reason runs another way,
That private reason 'tis more just to curb
Than by disputes the public peace disturb;
For points obscure are of small use to learn,
But common quiet is mankind's concern.

　　Thus have I made my own opinions clear,
Yet neither praise expect nor censure fear;

And this unpolished, rugged verse I chose
As fittest for discourse and nearest prose;
For while from sacred truth I do not swerve,
Tom Sternhold's or Tom Shadwell's rhymes will serve.[1]

1. Thomas Sternhold (d. 1570) collaborated with John Hopkins (d.
1549) in a famous collection of versified psalms, 1549. Thomas
Shadwell, the hero of *Mac Flecknoe*.

THE HIND
AND THE PANTHER

The Swallow,[1] privileged above the rest
Of all the birds as man's familiar guest,
Pursues the sun in summer brisk and bold,
But wisely shuns the persecuting cold;
Is well to chancels and to chimneys known,
Though 'tis not thought she feeds on smoke alone.
From hence she has been held of heav'nly line,
Endued with particles of soul divine.
This merry chorister had long possessed
Her summer seat and feathered well her nest,
Till frowning skies began to change their cheer
And time turned up the wrong side of the year.
The shedding trees began the ground to strow
With yellow leaves, and bitter blasts to blow:
Sad auguries of winter thence she drew,
Which by instinct, or prophecy, she knew;
When prudence warned her to remove betimes
And seek a better heav'n and warmer climes.

Her sons were summoned on a steeple's height,[2]
And, called in common council, vote a flight;

1. The fable of the Swallow is told by the Panther (the Church of
England) to warn the Hind (the Roman Catholic Church) of the
dangers confronting the English Roman Catholics, in spite of
the favour extended to them by James II.
2. A reference to an assembly of Roman Catholics held in 1686, at
which it was proposed that they should petition the King for
permission to emigrate to France. Father Edward Petre (1631–
1699), the King's confessor, the *Martin* of this fable, counselled
them to remain in England and trust to the King's protection.

The day was named, the next that should be fair.
All to the gen'ral rendezvous repair;
They try their flutt'ring wings and trust themselves
    in air.
But whether upward to the moon they go,
Or dream the winter out in caves below,
Or hawk at flies elsewhere, concerns not us to know.
  Southwards, you may be sure, they bent their flight,
And harboured in a hollow rock at night.
Next morn they rose and set up ev'ry sail,
The wind was fair, but blew a mackrel gale.
The sickly young sat shiv'ring on the shore,
Abhorred salt-water never seen before,
And prayed their tender mothers to delay
The passage and expect a fairer day.
  With these the Martin readily concurred,
A church-begot and church-believing bird;
Of little body but of lofty mind,
Round bellied for a dignity designed,
And much a dunce, as martins are by kind.
Yet often quoted canon-laws and Code,
And Fathers which he never understood;
But little learning needs in noble blood.
For, sooth to say, the Swallow brought him in,
Her household chaplain and her next of kin.
In superstition silly to excess,
And casting schemes by planetary guess;
In fine, short-winged, unfit himself to fly,
His fear foretold foul weather in the sky.
  Besides, a raven from a withered oak,
Left of their lodging, was observed to croak.
That omen liked him not, so his advice
Was present safety, bought at any price
(A seeming pious care that covered cowardice).

To strengthen this, he told a boding dream
Of rising waters and a troubled stream,
Sure signs of anguish, dangers and distress,
With something more not lawful to express;
By which he slyly seemed to intimate
Some secret revelation of their fate.
For he concluded, once upon a time
He found a leaf inscribed with sacred rhyme,
Whose antique characters did well denote
The Sibyl's hand of the Cumaean grot.
The mad divineress had plainly writ,
A time should come (but many ages yet)
In which, sinister destinies ordain,
A dame should drown with all her feathered train,
And seas from thence be called the Chelidonian main.
At this some shook for fear; the more devout
Arose and blessed themselves from head to foot.
  'Tis true, some stagers of the wiser sort
Made all these idle wonderments their sport;
They said their only danger was delay,
And he who heard what ev'ry fool could say
Would never fix his thoughts but trim his time away.
The passage yet was good, the wind, 'tis true,
Was somewhat high, but that was nothing new,
Nor more than usual equinoxes blew.
The sun (already from the scales declined)
Gave little hopes of better days behind
But change from bad to worse of weather and of
    wind.
Nor need they fear the dampness of the sky
Should flag their wings and hinder them to fly,
'Twas only water thrown on sails too dry.
But least of all philosophy presumes
Of truth in dreams, from melancholy fumes.

Perhaps the Martin, housed in holy ground,
Might think of ghosts that walk their midnight round
Till grosser atoms, tumbling in the stream
Of fancy, madly met and clubbed into a dream.
As little weight his vain presages bear,
Of ill effect to such alone who fear.
Most prophecies are of a piece with these,
Each Nostradamus[1] can foretell with ease;
Not naming persons, and confounding times,
One casual truth supports a thousand lying rhymes.

Th' advice was true but fear had seized the most,
And all good counsel is on cowards lost.
The question crudely put, to shun delay,
'Twas carried by the major part to stay.

His point thus gained, Sir Martin dated thence
His pow'r, and from a priest become a prince.
He ordered all things with a busy care,
And cells and refectories did prepare
And large provisions laid of winter fare.
But now and then let fall a word or two
Of hope that heav'n some miracle might show
And, for their sakes, the sun should backward go,
Against the laws of nature upward climb
And, mounted on the Ram, renew the prime;
For which two proofs in sacred story lay,
Of Ahaz' dial and of Joshua's day.
In expectation of such times as these,
A chapel housed 'em, truly called of ease;
For Martin much devotion did not ask,
They prayed sometimes and that was all their task.

It happened (as beyond the reach of wit
Blind prophecies may have a lucky hit)

1. Nostradamus (1503–66), the French astrologer.

That this accomplished, or at least in part,
Gave great repute to their new Merlin's art.
Some Swifts, the giants of the Swallow kind,[1]
Large-limbed, stout-hearted, but of stupid mind
(For Swisses or for Gibeonites designed),
These lubbers, peeping through a broken pane
To suck fresh air, surveyed the neighbouring plain
And saw (but scarcely could believe their eyes)
New blossoms flourish and new flow'rs arise,
As God had been abroad and walking there
Had left his foot-steps and reformed the year.
The sunny hills from far were seen to glow
With glittering beams, and in the meads below
The burnished brooks appeared with liquid gold to
    flow.
At last they heard the foolish Cuckoo sing,
Whose note proclaimed the holy-day of spring.

*Otherwise
called
Martlets.*

No longer doubting, all prepare to fly
And repossess their patrimonial sky.
The priest before 'em did his wings display;
And, that good omens might attend their way,
As luck would have it, 'twas St Martin's day.

Who but the Swallow now triumphs alone,
The canopy of heaven is all her own;
Her youthful offspring to their haunts repair,
And glide along in glades, and skim in air,
And dip for insects in the purling springs,
And stoop on rivers to refresh their wings.
Their mothers think a fair provision made,
That ev'ry son can live upon his trade,
And now the careful charge is off their hands
Look out for husbands and new nuptial bands.

1. A reference to the Irish Roman Catholics.

The youthful widow longs to be supplied,
But first the lover is by lawyers tied
To settle jointure-chimneys on the bride.
So thick they couple, in so short a space,
That Martin's marriage offerings rise apace.
Their ancient houses, running to decay,
Are furbished up and cemented with clay;
They teem already; store of eggs are laid
And brooding mothers call Lucina's aid.
Fame spreads the news, no foreign fowls appear
In flocks to greet the new returning year,
To bless the founder and partake the cheer.
    And now 'twas time (so fast their numbers rise)
To plant abroad, and people colonies.
The youth drawn forth, as Martin had desired
(For so their cruel destiny required),
Were sent far off on an ill-fated day;
The rest would need conduct 'em on their way,
And Martin went because he feared alone to stay.
    So long they flew with inconsiderate haste
That now their afternoon began to waste,
And, what was ominous, that very morn
The sun was entered into Capricorn,
Which, by their bad astronomer's account,
That week the virgin balance should remount;
An infant moon eclipsed him in his way
And hid the small remainders of his day.
The crowd amazed pursued no certain mark,
But birds met birds and justled in the dark;
Few mind the public in a panic fright,
And fear increased the horror of the night.
Night came, but unattended with repose,
Alone she came, no sleep their eyes to close,
Alone and black she came, no friendly stars arose.

What should they do, beset with dangers round,
No neighb'ring dorp, no lodging to be found,
But bleaky plains and bare unhospitable ground.
The latter brood, who just began to fly,
Sick-feathered and unpractised in the sky,
For succour to their helpless mother call.
She spread her wings; some few beneath 'em crawl,
She spread 'em wider yet but could not cover all.
T' augment their woes, the winds began to move
Debate in air for empty fields above,
Till Boreas got the skies and poured amain
His rattling hail-stones mixed with snow and rain.
    The joyless morning late arose and found
A dreadful desolation reign around.
Some buried in the snow, some frozen to the ground;
The rest were struggling still with death and lay
The crows' and ravens' rights, an undefended prey.
Excepting Martin's race, for they and he
Had gained the shelter of a hollow tree,
But soon discover'd by a sturdy clown,
He headed all the rabble of a town
And finished 'em with bats or polled 'em down.
Martin himself was caught alive and tried
For treas'nous crimes, because the laws provide
No martin there in winter shall abide.
High on an oak, which never leaf shall bear,
He breathed his last, exposed to open air;
And there his corpse, unblessed, are hanging still
To show the change of winds with his prophetic bill.

MR OLDHAM[1]

FAREWELL, too little and too lately known,
Whom I began to think and call my own;
For sure our souls were near allied, and thine
Cast in the same poetic mould with mine.
One common note on either lyre did strike,
And knaves and fools we both abhorred alike.
To the same goal did both our studies drive;
The last set out the soonest did arrive.
Thus Nisus fell upon the slippery place,
While his young friend performed and won the race.
O early ripe! to thy abundant store
What could advancing age have added more?
It might (what nature never gives the young)
Have taught the numbers of thy native tongue;
But satire needs not those, and wit will shine
Through the harsh cadence of a rugged line.
A noble error, and but seldom made
When poets are by too much force betrayed.
Thy generous fruits though gathered ere their prime
Still showed a quickness; and maturing time
But mellows what we write to the dull sweets of rhyme.
Once more, hail and farewell! farewell thou young
But ah! too short Marcellus of our tongue.
Thy brows with ivy and with laurels bound;
But Fate and gloomy night encompass thee around.

1. John Oldham (1653–83), the satirist. His *Satires on the Jesuits*, published in 1679, made him famous.

MR CONGREVE

WELL then, the promised hour is come at last;
The present age of wit obscures the past.
Strong were our sires; and as they fought they writ,
Conqu'ring with force of arms and dint of wit.
Theirs was the giant race before the Flood;
And thus, when Charles returned, our empire stood.
Like Janus he the stubborn soil manured,
With rules of husbandry the rankness cured;
Tamed us to manners when the stage was rude,
And boisterous English wit with art endued.
Our age was cultivated thus at length;
But what we gained in skill we lost in strength.
Our builders were with want of genius cursed;
The second temple was not like the first:
Till you, the best Vitruvius, come at length,
Our beauties equal but excel our strength.
Firm doric pillars found your solid base;
The fair corinthian crowns the higher space;
Thus all below is strength and all above is grace.
In easy dialogue is Fletcher's praise;
He moved the mind but had not power to raise.
Great Jonson did by strength of judgement please;
Yet doubling Fletcher's force, he wants his ease.
In differing talents both adorned their age;
One for the study, t'other for the stage.
But both to Congreve justly shall submit,
One matched in judgement, both o'er-matched in wit.
In him all beauties of this age we see;
Etherege his courtship, Southerne's purity,
The satire, wit, and strength of manly Wycherley.

All this in blooming youth you have achieved,
Nor are your foiled contemporaries grieved;
So much the sweetness of your manners move,
We cannot envy you because we love.
Fabius might joy in Scipio when he saw
A beardless consul made against the law,
And join his suffrage to the votes of Rome,
Though he with Hannibal was overcome.
Thus old Romano bowed to Raphael's fame,
And scholar to the youth he taught became.

Oh, that your brows my laurel had sustained,
Well had I been deposed if you had reigned!
The father had descended for the son,
For only you are lineal to the throne.
Thus when the state one Edward did depose,
A greater Edward in his room arose.
But now not I but poetry is cursed,
For Tom the second reigns like Tom the first;[1]
But let 'em not mistake my patron's part,
Nor call his charity their own desert.
Yet this I prophesy; thou shalt be seen
(Tho' with some short parenthesis between)
High on the throne of wit, and seated there
Not mine (that's little) but thy laurel wear.
Thy first attempt an early promise made;
That early promise this has more than paid.
So bold yet so judiciously you dare
That your least praise is to be regular.
Time, place, and action, may with pains be wrought,
But genius must be born and never can be taught.

1. Thomas Shadwell, the hero of *Mac Flecknoe*, who succeeded
Dryden as Poet Laureate and Historiographer Royal, died in
1692. He was succeeded as Poet Laureate by Nahum Tate and
as Historiographer by Thomas Rymer (1641–1713), the author
of a poor tragedy, to whom Dryden refers in this line.

This is your portion, this your native store.
Heav'n, that but once was prodigal before,
To Shakespeare gave as much; she could not give him
  more.
 Maintain your post. That's all the fame you need;
For 'tis impossible you should proceed.
Already I am worn with cares and age,
And just abandoning th' ungrateful stage;
Unprofitably kept at heav'n's expense,
I live a rent-charge on His providence;
But you, whom ev'ry muse and grace adorn,
Whom I foresee to better fortune born,
Be kind to my remains, and oh, defend
Against your judgement your departed friend!
Let not the insulting foe my fame pursue,
But shade those laurels which descend to you;
And take for tribute what these lines express:
You merit more, nor could my love do less.

TO MY HONOURED KINSMAN

JOHN DRIDEN

OF CHESTERTON IN THE COUNTY OF HUNTINGDON
ESQUIRE

How blessed is he who leads a country life,
Unvexed with anxious cares and void of strife!
Who studying peace and shunning civil rage
Enjoyed his youth and now enjoys his age.
All who deserve his love, he makes his own,
And to be loved himself needs only to be known.
 Just, good, and wise, contending neighbours come
From your award to wait their final doom,
And, foes before, return in friendship home.

Without their cost you terminate the cause,
And save th' expense of long litigious laws;
Where suits are traversed, and so little won
That he who conquers is but last undone.
Such are not your decrees, but so designed
The sanction leaves a lasting peace behind;
Like your own soul, serene; a pattern of your mind.
　　Promoting concord and composing strife,
Lord of yourself, uncumbered with a wife;
Where, for a year, a month, perhaps a night,
Long penitence succeeds a short delight.
Minds are so hardly matched that ev'n the first,
Though paired by heav'n in Paradise, were cursed;
For man and woman though in one they grow
Yet, first or last, return again to two.
He to God's image, she to his was made;
So farther from the fount the stream at random strayed.
How could he stand when, put to double pain,
He must a weaker than himself sustain!
Each might have stood perhaps, but each alone;
Two wrestlers help to pull each other down.
Not that my verse would blemish all the fair;
But yet if some be bad 'tis wisdom to beware,
And better shun the bait than struggle in the snare.
Thus have you shunned, and shun the married state,
Trusting as little as you can to Fate.
　　No porter guards the passage of your door
T' admit the wealthy and exclude the poor;
For God, who gave the riches, gave the heart
To sanctify the whole by giving part.
Heav'n, who foresaw the will, the means has wrought,
And to the second son a blessing brought;
The first-begotten had his father's share,
But you, like Jacob, are Rebecca's heir.

So may your stores and fruitful fields increase,
And ever be you blessed who live to bless.
As Ceres sowed where'er her chariot flew,
As heav'n in deserts rained the bread of dew,
So free to many, to relations most,
You feed with manna your own Israel-host.

   With crowds attended of your ancient race,
You seek the champaign-sports or sylvan-chase.
With well-breathed beagles you surround the
    wood;
Ev'n then industrious of the common good.
And often have you brought the wily fox
To suffer for the firstlings of the flocks;
Chased ev'n amid the folds and made to bleed,
Like felons, where they did the murd'rous deed.
This fiery game your active youth maintained;
Not yet by years extinguished, though restrained,
You season still with sports your serious hours,
For age but tastes of pleasures, youth devours.
The hare in pastures or in plains is found,
Emblem of human life, who runs the round
And, after all his wand'ring ways are done,
His circle fills and ends where he begun
Just as the setting meets the rising sun.

   Thus princes ease their cares. But happier he,
Who seeks not pleasure thro' necessity,
Than such as once on slipp'ry thrones were placed,
And chasing, sigh to think themselves are chased.

   So lived our sires, e'er doctors learned to kill,
And multiplied with theirs the weekly bill.
The first physicians by debauch were made;
Excess began and sloth sustains the trade.
Pity the gen'rous kind their cares bestow
To search forbidden truths (a sin to know);

To which, if human science could attain,
The doom of death, pronounced by God, were vain.
In vain the leech would interpose delay;
Fate fastens first and vindicates the prey.
What help from art's endeavours can we have!
Guibbons[1] but guesses nor is sure to save;
But Maurus[2] sweeps whole parishes and peoples ev'ry
    grave,
And no more mercy to mankind will use
Than when he robbed and murdered Maro's muse.
Would'st thou be soon dispatched and perish whole?
Trust Maurus with thy life, and Milbourne[3] with thy
    soul.

  By chase our long-lived fathers earned their food,
Toil strung the nerves and purified the blood;
But we, their sons, a pampered race of men,
Are dwindled down to threescore years and ten.
Better to hunt in fields for health unbought,
Than fee the doctor for a nauseous draught.
The wise, for cure, on exercise depend;
God never made his work for man to mend.
The Tree of Knowledge, once in Eden placed,
Was easy found but was forbid the taste;
O, had our grandsire walked without his wife,
He first had sought the better Plant of Life!
Now, both are lost. Yet, wand'ring in the dark,
Physicians for the Tree have found the bark.
They, lab'ring for relief of human kind,
With sharpened sight some remedies may find;
Th' apothecary-train is wholly blind.

1. Dr Guibbons, a celebrated physician of the day.
2. Sir Richard Blackmore, see *Preface to Fables*, p. 251 n. 2.
3. Luke Milbourne, see *Preface to Fables*, p. 246 n. 1.

From files a random-recipe they take,
And many deaths of one prescription make.
Garth,[1] gen'rous as his muse, prescribes and gives;
The shopman sells, and by destruction lives.
Ungrateful tribe! who, like the viper's brood,
From med'cine issuing, suck their mother's blood!
Let these obey; and let the learn'd prescribe,
That men may die without a double bribe.
Let them but under their superiors kill,
When doctors first have signed the bloody Bill.
He scapes the best who nature to repair
Draws physic from the fields in draughts of vital
    air.
   You hoard not health for your own private use
But on the public spend the rich produce,
When, often urged, unwilling to be great,
Your country calls you from your loved Retreat
And sends to Senates charged with common care,
Which none more shuns, and none can better bear.
Where could they find another formed so fit
To poise with solid sense a spritely wit!
Were these both wanting (as they both abound),
Where could so firm integrity be found?
Well-born and wealthy, wanting no support,
You steer betwixt the Country and the Court;
Nor gratify whate'er the great desire,
Nor grudging give what public needs require.
Part must be left, a fund when foes invade,
And part employed to roll the watery trade;
Ev'n Canaan's happy land, when worn with toil,
Required a sabbath-year to mend the meagre soil.

1. Sir Samuel Garth (1661–1719), poet and physician. His well-known poem of *The Dispensary* appeared in 1699.

Good senators (and such are you) so give
That kings may be supplied, the people thrive;
And he, when want requires, is truly wise
Who slights not foreign aids nor over-buys,
But on our native strength in time of need relies.
Munster was bought, we boast not the success;[1]
Who fights for gain, for greater makes his peace.
Our foes, compelled by need, have peace embraced —
The peace both parties want is like to last —
Which if secure, securely we may trade,
Or not secure, should never have been made.
Safe in ourselves, while on ourselves we stand,
The sea is ours and that defends the land.
Be, then, the naval stores the nation's care,
New ships to build and battered to repair.
Observe the war, in ev'ry annual course;
What has been done was done with British force.
Namur subdued is England's palm alone;
The rest besieged but we constrained the town.[2]
We saw th' event that followed our success;
France, though pretending arms, pursued the peace,
Obliged by one sole treaty to restore
What twenty years of war had won before.
Enough for Europe has our Albion fought;
Let us enjoy the peace our blood has bought.
When once the Persian King was put to flight,
The weary Macedons refused to fight;
Themselves their own mortality confessed
And left the son of Jove to quarrel for the rest.

1. The Bishop of Munster was subsidized by England to invade the
   Dutch provinces, but when France entered the war on the side
   of the Dutch in 1666, the Bishop withdrew his forces and con-
   cluded a separate peace.
2. William III took Namur in 1695 after a siege of one month.

Ev'n victors are by victories undone;
Thus Hannibal, with foreign laurels won,
To Carthage was recalled too late to keep his own.
While sore of battle, while our wounds are green,
Why should we tempt the doubtful dye agen?
In wars renewed, uncertain of success;
Sure of a share as umpires of the peace.

A patriot both the king and country serves,
Prerogative and privilege preserves;
Of each, our laws the certain limit show,
One must not ebb nor t' other overflow.
Betwixt the prince and Parliament we stand,
The barriers of the state on either hand;
May neither overflow, for then they drown the land.
When both are full they feed our blessed abode,
Like those that watered once the Paradise of God.
Some overpoise of sway by turns they share;
In peace the people, and the prince in war.
Consuls of mod'rate pow'r in calms were made;
When the Gauls came one sole dictator swayed.
Patriots in peace assert the people's right,
With noble stubbornness resisting might;
No lawless mandates from the Court receive,
Nor lend by force but in a body give.
Such was your gen'rous grandsire; free to grant
In Parliaments that weighed their prince's want,
But so tenacious of the common cause
As not to lend the king against his laws;
And, in a loathsome dungeon doomed to lie,
In bonds retained his birthright, liberty,
And shamed oppression till it set him free.[1]

1. Sir Erasmus Driden (*d.* 1632), the common grandfather of the
poet and John Driden, was imprisoned for resisting an illegal levy
of Charles I.

O true descendant of a patriot line,
Who, while thou shar'st their lustre, lend'st 'em thine,
Vouchsafe this picture of thy soul to see;
'Tis so far good as it resembles thee.
The beauties to th' original I owe,
Which, when I miss, my own defects I show.
Nor think the kindred-muses thy disgrace;
A poet is not born in ev'ry race.
Two of a house, few ages can afford;
One to perform, another to record.
Praise-worthy actions are by thee embraced,
And 'tis my praise to make thy praises last.
For ev'n when death dissolves our human frame,
The soul returns to heav'n from whence it came;
Earth keeps the body, verse preserves the fame.

THE TEMPEST

As when a tree's cut down the secret root
Lives under ground, and thence new branches shoot,
So from old Shakespeare's honoured dust this day
Springs up and buds a new reviving play.
Shakespeare, who (taught by none) did first impart
To Fletcher wit, to labouring Jonson art.
He monarch-like gave those his subjects law,
And is that nature which they paint and draw.
Fletcher reached that which on his heights did grow,
Whilst Jonson crept and gathered all below.
This did his love, and this his mirth digest;
One imitates him most, the other best.
If they have since out-writ all other men,
'Tis with the drops which fell from Shakespeare's pen
The storm which vanished on the neighb'ring shore,
Was taught by Shakespeare's Tempest first to roar.
That innocence and beauty which did smile
In Fletcher, grew on this Enchanted Isle.
But Shakespeare's magic could not copied be,
Within that circle none durst walk but he.
I must confess 'twas bold, nor would you now
That liberty to vulgar wits allow,
Which works by magic supernatural things;
But Shakespeare's pow'r is sacred as a king's.
Those legends from old priesthood were received,
And he then writ as people then believed.

But, if for Shakespeare we your grace implore,
We for our theatre shall want it more;
Who by our dearth of youths are forced t' employ
One of our women to present a boy;
And that's a transformation you will say
Exceeding all the magic in the play.
Let none expect in the last act to find
Her sex transformed from man to womankind.
Whate'er she was before the play began,
All you shall see of her is perfect man.
Or if your fancy will be farther led
To find her woman, it must be abed.

EPILOGUE TO

TYRANNIC LOVE

OR

THE ROYAL MARTYR

[Spoken by Mrs ELLEN,[1] *when she was to be carried off
dead by the bearers]*

To the bearer: HOLD, are you mad? you damned confounded
dog,
I am to rise and speak the Epilogue.
To the audience: I come, kind gentlemen, strange news to
tell ye,
I am the ghost of poor departed Nelly.
Sweet ladies, be not frighted, I'll be civil,
I'm what I was, a little harmless devil.
For after death we sprights have just such natures,
We had for all the world when human creatures;

1. The famous Nell Gwyn. She played the part of Valeria in the play
and, having stabbed herself at the close, as she was about to be
carried dead off the stage, she rose to deliver this Epilogue.

And therefore I, that was an actress here,
Play all my tricks in hell, a goblin there,
Gallants, look to 't, you say there are no sprights,
But I'll come dance about your beds at nights;
And faith you'll be in a sweet kind of taking
When I surprise you between sleep and waking.
To tell you true, I walk because I die
Out of my calling in a tragedy.
O poet, damned dull poet, who could prove
So senseless to make Nelly die for love!
Nay, what's yet worse, to kill me in the prime
Of Easter Term, in tart and cheesecake time!
I'll fit the fop; for I'll not one word say
T' excuse his godly out of fashion play:
A play which if you dare but twice sit out,
You'll all be slandered and be thought devout.
But farewell gentlemen, make haste to me,
I'm sure ere long to have your company.
As for my epitaph when I am gone,
I'll trust no poet but will write my own:
Here Nelly lies, who though she lived a slattern,
Yet died a princess, acting in St Cather'n.[1]

EPILOGUE TO

THE SECOND PART OF

THE CONQUEST OF GRANADA

THEY who have best succeeded on the stage,
Have still conformed their genius to their age.
Thus Jonson did mechanic humour show,
When men were dull and conversation low.

1. St Catherine was 'the Royal Martyr' of the play.

Then comedy was faultless, but 'twas coarse;
Cobb's tankard was a jest, and Otter's horse.[1]
And as their comedy, their love was mean;
Except, by chance, in some one laboured scene,
Which must atone for an ill-written play.
They rose; but at their height could seldom stay.
Fame then was cheap, and the first comer sped;
And they have kept it since, by being dead.
But were they now to write, when critics weigh
Each line and ev'ry word throughout a play,
None of 'em, no, not Jonson in his height,
Could pass without allowing grains for weight.
Think it not envy that these truths are told,
Our poet's not malicious, though he's bold.
'Tis not to brand 'em that their faults are shown,
But by their errors to excuse his own.
If love and honour now are higher raised,
'Tis not the poet but the age is praised.
Wit's now arrived to a more high degree;
Our native language more refined and free.
Our ladies and our men now speak more wit
In conversation than those poets writ.
Then, one of these is, consequently, true:
That what this poet writes comes short of you,
And imitates you ill (which most he fears),
Or else his writing is not worse than theirs.
Yet, though you judge (as sure the critics will)
That some before him writ with greater skill,
In this one praise he has their fame surpassed,
To please an age more gallant than the last.

1. *Cobb*, the water-bearer in Ben Jonson's *Every Man in his Humour*, and *Captain Otter*, who called his tankards, Horse, Bull, and Bear, in his *Epicene, or, the Silent Woman*.

THE UNIVERSITY OF OXFORD

1673

AT THE ACTING OF BEN JONSON'S
'THE SILENT WOMAN'

WHAT Greece, when learning flourished, only knew,
(Athenian judges) you this day renew.
Here too are annual Rites to Pallas done,
And here poetic prizes lost or won.
Methinks I see you crowned with olives sit,
And strike a sacred horror from the pit.
A day of doom is this of your decree,
Where even the best are but by mercy free;
A day which none but Jonson durst have wished to see.
Here they who long have known the useful stage
Come to be taught themselves to teach the age.
As your commissioners our poets go,
To cultivate the virtue which you sow;
In your Lycaeum first themselves refined,
And delegated thence to human kind.
But as ambassadors, when long from home,
For new instructions to their princes come;
So poets, who your precepts have forgot,
Return and beg they may be better taught.
Follies and faults elsewhere by them are shown,
But by your manners they correct their own.
Th' illiterate writer, empiric-like, applies
To minds diseased, unsafe, chance remedies;
The learned in schools, where knowledge first began,
Studies with care th' anatomy of man;
Sees virtue, vice, and passions in their cause,
And fame from science, not from fortune, draws.

So poetry, which is in Oxford made
An art, in London only is a trade.
There haughty dunces, whose unlearned pen
Could ne'er spell grammar, would be reading men.
Such build their poems the Lucretian way,
So many huddled atoms make a play;
And if they hit in order by some chance,
They call that nature which is ignorance.
To such a fame let mere town-wits aspire,
And their gay nonsense their own cits admire.
Our poet, could he find forgiveness here,
Would wish it rather than a plaudit there.
He owns no crown from those Praetorian bands,
But knows *that* right is in this Senate's hands.
Not impudent enough to hope your praise,
Low at the muses' feet his wreath he lays,
And, where he took it up, resigns his bays.
Kings make their poets whom themselves think fit;
But 'tis your suffrage makes authentic wit.

PROLOGUE TO

THE SPANISH FRIAR

Now luck for us and a kind hearty pit;
For he who pleases never fails of wit.
Honour is yours:
And you like kings at City treats bestow it;
The writer kneels and is bid rise a poet.
But you are fickle sovereigns to our sorrow,
You dub to-day and hang a man to-morrow;
You cry the same sense up and down again,
Just like brass money once a year in Spain.
Take you i' th' mood, whate'er base metal come,

You coin as fast as groats at Bromingam;[1]
Though 'tis no more like sense in ancient plays
Than Rome's religion like St Peter's days.
In short, so swift your judgements turn and wind,
You cast our fleetest wits a mile behind.
'Twere well your judgements but in plays did range,
But ev'n your follies and debauches change
With such a whirl, the poets of your age
Are tired and cannot score 'em on the stage,
Unless each vice in short-hand they indite,
Ev'n as notched prentices whole sermons write.[2]
The heavy Hollanders no vices know
But what they used a hundred years ago;
Like honest plants, where they were stuck they
        grow;
They cheat, but still from cheating sires they come;
They drink, but they were christ'ned first in
        mum.
Their patrimonial sloth the Spaniards keep,
And Philip first taught Philip how to sleep.
The French and we still change, but here's the
        curse,
They change for better and we change for worse;
They take up our old trade of conquering,
And we are taking theirs, to dance and sing.
Our fathers did for change to France repair,
And they for change will try our English air.
As children when they throw one toy away,
Straight a more foolish gewgaw comes in play;
So we, grown penitent on serious thinking,
Leave whoring and devoutly fall to drinking.

1. Birmingham was notorious for its counterfeit coins.
2. Apprentices were often required by their masters to take notes
   of the sermon.

Scouring the Watch grows out of fashion wit;
Now we set up for tilting in the pit,
Where 'tis agreed by bullies, chicken-hearted,
To fright the ladies first and then be parted.
A fair attempt has twice or thrice been made
To hire night murd'rers and make death a trade.
When murder's out, what vice can we advance?
Unless the new found pois'ning trick of France;
And when their art of rats-bane we have got,
By way of thanks, we'll send 'em o'er our Plot.

PROLOGUE AND EPILOGUE TO

THE UNIVERSITY OF OXFORD

1674

PROLOGUE

[Spoken by Mr HART*]*

POETS, your subjects, have their parts assigned
T' unbend and to divert their sovereign's mind.
When tired with following nature, you think fit
To seek repose in the cool shades of wit,
And from the sweet retreat with joy survey
What rests and what is conquered of the way;
Here free yourselves from envy, care and strife,
You view the various turns of human life;
Safe in our scene through dangerous courts you go
And, undebauched, the vice of cities know.
Your theories are here to practice brought,
As in mechanic operations wrought;

And man, the little world, before you set,
As once the sphere of crystal showed the great.
Blest sure are you above all mortal kind;
If to your fortunes you can suit your mind.
Content to see and shun those ills we show,
And crimes on theatres alone to know.
With joy we bring what our dead authors writ,
And beg from you the value of their wit.
That Shakespeare's, Fletcher's, and great Jonson's claim
May be renewed from those who gave them fame.
None of our living poets dare appear;
For muses so severe are worshipped here,
That conscious of their faults they shun the eye
And, as profane, from sacred places fly
Rather than see th' offended god, and die.
We bring no imperfections but our own,
Such faults as made are by the makers shown;
And you have been so kind, that we may boast
The greatest judges still can pardon most.
Poets must stoop when they would please our pit,
Debased even to the level of their wit.
Disdaining that which yet they know will take,
Hating themselves what their applause must make;
But when to praise from you they would aspire,
Though they like eagles mount, your Jove is higher.
So far your knowledge all their pow'r transcends,
As what *should* be beyond what *is* extends.

EPILOGUE

[*Spoken by Mrs* BOUTELL]

OFT has our poet wished this happy seat
Might prove his fading muses' last retreat.

I wondered at his wish, but now I find
He sought for quiet and content of mind;
Which noiseful towns and courts can never know,
And only in the shades like laurels grow.
Youth, ere it sees the world, here studies rest,
And age returning thence concludes it best.
What wonder if we court that happiness
Yearly to share, which hourly you possess;
Teaching ev'n you (while the vexed world we show)
Your peace to value more and better know?
'Tis all we can return for favours past,
Whose holy memory shall ever last,
For patronage from him whose care presides
O'er every noble art, and every science guides:
Bathurst, a name the learned with reverence know,
And scarcely more to his own Virgil owe. [1]
Whose age enjoys but what his youth deserved,
To rule those muses whom before he served.
His learning and untainted manners too
We find (Athenians) are derived to you;
Such ancient hospitality there rests
In yours as dwelt in the first Grecian breasts,
Whose kindness was religion to their guests.
Such modesty did to our sex appear
As had there been no laws we need not fear,
Since each of you was our protector here.
Converse so chaste, and so strict virtue shown,
As might Apollo with the muses own.
Till our return we must despair to find
Judges so just, so knowing, and so kind.

1. Ralph Bathurst (1620–1704), president of Trinity College, 1664,
was vice-chancellor of the University in 1674. He was an accom-
plished poet in both Latin and English.

DON SEBASTIAN[1]

Spoken by a Woman

THE Judge removed, though he's no more My Lord,
May plead at bar or at the Council-Board:
So may cast poets write; there's no pretension
To argue loss of wit from loss of pension.
Your looks are cheerful; and in all this place
I see not one that wears a damning face.
The British nation is too brave to show
Ignoble vengeance on a vanquished foe;
At least be civil to the wretch imploring,
And lay your paws upon him without roaring.
Suppose our poet was your foe before;
Yet now the bus'ness of the field is o'er;
'Tis time to let your civil wars alone
When troops are into winter-quarters gone.
Jove was alike to Latian and to Phrygian;
And you well know a play's of no religion.
Take good advice and please yourselves this day;
No matter from what hands you have the play.
Among good fellows ev'ry health will pass
That serves to carry round another glass:
When with full bowls of burgundy you dine,
Though at the mighty monarch you repine,
You grant him still most christian in his wine.
    Thus far the poet, but his brains grow addle;
And all the rest is purely from this noddle.

1. *Don Sebastian*, 1690, was the first play to be written by Dryden
   after the Glorious Revolution, when he was in disgrace on
   account of his politics and religion and had lost his places and
   pension.

You've seen young ladies at the senate door
Prefer petitions and your grace implore;
However grave the legislators were,
Their cause went ne'er the worse for being fair.
Reasons as weak as theirs perhaps I bring,
But I could bribe you with as good a thing.
I heard him make advances of good nature,
That he for once would sheath his cutting satire;
Sign but his peace, he vows he'll ne'er again
The sacred names of fops and beaus profane.
Strike up the bargain quickly; for I swear,
As times go now, he offers very fair.
Be not too hard on him with statutes neither;
Be kind, and do not set your teeth together
To stretch the laws, as cobblers do their leather.
Horses by papists are not to be ridden;
But sure the muses' horse was ne'er forbidden.
For in no rate-book it was ever found
That Pegasus was valued at five pound.[1]
Fine him to daily drudging and inditing;
And let him pay his taxes out, in writing.

1. An allusion to the Act forbidding Roman Catholics to keep a
   horse of more than £5 in value.

THEODORE AND HONORIA

FROM

FABLES

ANCIENT AND MODERN

FROM BOCCACE

O F all the cities in Romanian lands,
The chief and most renowned Ravenna stands;
Adorned in ancient times with arms and arts,
And rich inhabitants with generous hearts.
But Theodore the brave, above the rest
With gifts of fortune and of nature blessed,
The foremost place for wealth and honour held,
And all in feats of chivalry excelled.
  This noble youth to madness loved a dame
Of high degree, Honoria was her name.
Fair as the fairest but of haughty mind,
And fiercer than became so soft a kind;
Proud of her birth (for equal she had none);
The rest she scorned, but hated him alone.
His gifts, his constant courtship, nothing gained;
For she, the more he loved, the more disdained.
He lived with all the pomp he could devise,
At tilts and tournaments obtained the prize,
But found no favour in his lady's eyes.
Relentless as a rock, the lofty maid
Turned all to poison that he did or said.
Nor pray'rs nor tears nor offered vows could move
The work went backward; and the more he strove
T' advance his suit, the farther from her love.

Wearied at length, and wanting remedy,
He doubted oft and oft resolved to die.
But pride stood ready to prevent the blow,
For who would die to gratify a foe?
His generous mind disdained so mean a fate;
That passed, his next endeavour was to hate.
But vainer that relief than all the rest,
The less he hoped with more desire possessed;
Love stood the siege and would not yield his
    breast.
Change was the next, but change deceived his care,
He sought a fairer but found none so fair.
He would have worn her out by slow degrees,
As men by fasting starve th' untamed disease;
But present love required a present ease.
Looking he feeds alone his famished eyes,
Feeds ling'ring death, but looking not he dies.
Yet still he chose the longest way to fate,
Wasting at once his life, and his estate.
His friends beheld and pitied him in vain,
For what advice can ease a lover's pain!
Absence, the best expedient they could find,
Might save the fortune if not cure the mind:
This means they long proposed but little gained,
Yet after much pursuit at length obtained.
Hard, you may think it was, to give consent,
But struggling with his own desires he went:
With large expense, and with a pompous train
Provided, as to visit France or Spain,
Or for some distant voyage o'er the main.
But love had clipped his wings and cut him short,
Confined within the purlieus of his court.
Three miles he went, nor farther could retreat;
His travels ended at his country-seat.

To Chassis' pleasing plains he took his way,
There pitched his tents and there resolved to stay.

  The Spring was in the prime; the neighb'ring grove
Supplied with birds, the choristers of love;
Music unbought, that ministered delight,
The morning-walks, and lulled his cares by night.
There he discharged his friends, but not th' expense
Of frequent treats and proud magnificence.
He lived as kings retire, though more at large
From public business, yet with equal charge;
With house and heart still open to receive;
As well content as love would give him leave.
He would have lived more free, but many a guest,
Who could forsake the friend, pursued the feast.

  It happed one morning, as his fancy led,
Before his usual hour he left his bed
To walk within a lonely lawn, that stood
On ev'ry side surrounded by the wood.
Alone he walked to please his pensive mind,
And sought the deepest solitude to find.
'Twas in a grove of spreading pines he strayed;
The winds within the quiv'ring branches played,
And dancing-trees a mournful music made.
The place itself was suiting to his care,
Uncouth and savage as the cruel fair.
He wandered on unknowing where he went,
Lost in the wood and all on love intent.
The day already half his race had run,
And summoned him to due repast at noon,
But love could feel no hunger but his own.
While list'ning to the murm'ring leaves he stood,
More than a mile immersed within the wood,
At once the wind was laid; the whisp'ring sound
Was dumb; a rising earthquake rocked the ground;

With deeper brown the grove was overspread;
A sudden horror seized his giddy head,
And his ears tinkled, and his colour fled.
Nature was in alarm; some danger nigh
Seemed threatened, though unseen to mortal eye.
Unused to fear, he summoned all his soul
And stood collected in himself and whole;
Not long: for soon a whirlwind rose around,
And from afar he heard a screaming sound
As of a dame distressed, who cried for aid
And filled with loud laments the secret shade.
A thicket close beside the grove there stood
With briars and brambles choked and dwarfish wood;
From thence the noise; which now approaching near
With more distinguished notes invades his ear.
He raised his head and saw a beauteous maid,
With hair dishevelled, issuing through the shade;
Stripped of her clothes, and e'en those parts revealed
Which modest nature keeps from sight concealed.
Her face, her hands, her naked limbs were torn
With passing through the brakes and prickly thorn;
Two mastiffs, gaunt and grim, her flight pursued
And oft their fastened fangs in blood imbrued;
Oft they came up and pinched her tender side,
'Mercy, O mercy, heav'n,' she ran and cried;
When heav'n was named they loosed their hold
    again,
Then sprung she forth, they followed her amain.
Not far behind, a knight of swarthy face,
High on a coal-black steed pursued the chase;
With flashing flames his ardent eyes were filled,
And in his hands a naked sword he held.
He cheered the dogs to follow her who fled,
And vowed revenge on her devoted head.

As Theodore was born of noble kind,
The brutal action roused his manly mind.
Moved with unworthy usage of the maid,
He, though unarmed, resolved to give her aid.
A sapling pine he wrenched from out the ground,
The readiest weapon that his fury found.
Thus furnished for offence, he crossed the way
Betwixt the graceless villain and his prey.
The knight came thund'ring on, but from afar
Thus in imperious tone forbad the war:
'Cease, Theodore, to proffer vain relief,
Nor stop the vengeance of so just a grief;
But give me leave to seize my destined prey,
And let eternal justice take the way.
I but revenge my fate; disdained, betrayed,
And suff'ring death for this ungrateful maid.'
He said, at once dismounting from the steed;
For now the hell-hounds with superior speed
Had reached the dame, and fast'ning on her side,
The ground with issuing streams of purple dyed.
Stood Theodore surprised in deadly fright,
With chatt'ring teeth and bristling hair upright;
Yet armed with inborn worth, 'Whate'er,' said he,
'Thou art, who know'st me better than I thee;
Or prove thy rightful cause, or be defied.'
The spectre, fiercely staring, thus replied:
'Know, Theodore, thy ancestry I claim,
And Guido Cavalcanti was my name.
One common sire our fathers did beget,
My name and story some remember yet.
Thee, then a boy, within my arms I laid,
When for my sins I loved this haughty maid;
Not less adored in life, nor served by me,
Than proud Honoria now is loved by thee.

What did I not her stubborn heart to gain?
But all my vows were answered with disdain;
She scorned my sorrows and despised my pain.
Long time I dragged my days in fruitless care,
Then loathing life, and plunged in deep despair,
To finish my unhappy life, I fell
On this sharp sword, and now am damned in hell.
Short was her joy; for soon th' insulting maid
By heav'n's decree in the cold grave was laid,
And as in unrepenting sin she died,
Doomed to the same bad place is punished for her
    pride;
Because she deemed I well deserved to die,
And made a merit of her cruelty.
There, then, we met; both tried and both were cast,
And this irrevocable sentence pass'd;
That she whom I so long pursued in vain,
Should suffer from my hands a ling'ring pain.
Renewed to life that she might daily die,
I daily doomed to follow, she to fly;
No more a lover but a mortal foe,
I seek her life (for love is none below).
As often as my dogs with better speed
Arrest her flight, is she to death decreed;
Then with this fatal sword on which I died,
I pierce her opened back or tender side,
And tear that hardened heart from out her breast,
Which, with her entrails, makes my hungry hounds a
    feast.
Nor lies she long but, as her fates ordain,
Springs up to life and, fresh to second pain,
Is saved to-day, to-morrow to be slain.'
This, versed in death, th' infernal knight relates,
And then for proof fulfilled their common fates;

Her heart and bowels through her back he drew,
And fed the hounds that helped him to pursue.
Stern looked the fiend, as frustrate of his will,
Not half sufficed and greedy yet to kill.
And now the soul expiring through the wound,
Had left the body breathless on the ground,
When thus the grisly spectre spoke again:
'Behold the fruit of ill-rewarded pain.
As many months as I sustained her hate,
So many years is she condemned by fate
To daily death; and ev'ry several place
Conscious of her disdain and my disgrace
Must witness her just punishment; and be
A scene of triumph and revenge to me.
As in this grove I took my last farewell,
As on this very spot of earth I fell,
As Friday saw me die, so she my prey
Becomes ev'n here on this revolving day.'
Thus while he spoke, the virgin from the ground
Upstarted fresh, already closed the wound,
And unconcerned for all she felt before
Precipitates her flight along the shore.
The hell-hounds, as ungorged with flesh and blood,
Pursue their prey and seek their wonted food;
The fiend remounts his courser, mends his pace,
And all the vision vanished from the place.

Long stood the noble youth oppressed with awe,
And stupid at the wond'rous things he saw
Surpassing common faith, transgressing nature's law.
He would have been asleep and wished to wake,
But dreams, he knew, no long impression make,
Though strong at first. If vision, to what end,
But such as must his future state portend?
His love the damsel, and himself the fiend.

But yet reflecting that it could not be
From heav'n, which cannot impious acts decree,
Resolved within himself to shun the snare
Which hell for his destruction did prepare;
And as his better genius should direct
From an ill cause to draw a good effect.
Inspired from heav'n he homeward took his way,
Nor palled his new design with long delay;
But of his train a trusty servant sent
To call his friends together at his tent.
They came; and usual salutations paid,
With words premeditated thus he said:
'What you have often counselled, to remove
My vain pursuit of unregarded love;
By thrift my sinking fortune to repair,
Though late, yet is at last become my care.
My heart shall be my own; my vast expense
Reduced to bounds by timely providence.
This only I require; invite for me
Honoria, with her father's family,
Her friends and mine; the cause I shall display,
On Friday next, for that's th' appointed day.'
　　Well pleased were all his friends, the task was light;
The father, mother, daughter they invite;
Hardly the dame was drawn to this repast,
But yet resolved, because it was the last.
The day was come; the guests invited came,
And, with the rest, th' inexorable dame.
A feast prepared with riotous expense,
Much cost, more care, and most magnificence.
The place ordained was in that haunted grove
Where the revenging ghost pursued his love.
The tables in a proud pavilion spread,
With flow'rs below, and tissue overhead.

The rest in rank; Honoria chief in place,
Was artfully contrived to set her face
To front the thicket and behold the chase.
The feast was served; the time so well forecast
That just when the dessert and fruits were placed
The fiend's alarm began; the hollow sound
Sung in the leaves, the forest shook around;
Air blacken'd; rolled the thunder; groaned the ground.
Nor long before the loud laments arise
Of one distressed, and mastiffs' mingled cries;
And first the dame came rushing through the wood,
And next the famished hounds that sought their food
And gripped her flanks and oft essayed their jaws
    in blood.
Last came the felon on the sable steed,
Armed with his naked sword, and urged his dogs to
    speed.
She ran and cried; her flight directly bent
(A guest unbidden) to the fatal tent,
The scene of death and place ordained for punish-
    ment.
Loud was the noise, aghast was every guest,
The women shrieked, the men forsook the feast;
The hounds at nearer distance hoarsely bayed;
The hunter close pursued the visionary maid;
She rent the heav'n with loud laments, imploring
    aid.
The gallants to protect the ladies right,
Their fauchions brandished at the grisly spright;
High on his stirrups, he provoked the fight.
Then on the crowd he cast a furious look,
And withered all their strength before he strook.
'Back on your lives; let be,' said he, 'my prey,
And let my vengeance take the destined way.

Vain are your arms, and vainer your defence,
Against th' eternal doom of providence.
Mine is th' ungrateful maid by heav'n designed:
Mercy she would not give, nor mercy shall she
    find.'
At this the former tale again he told
With thund'ring tone, and dreadful to behold.
Sunk were their hearts with horror of the crime,
Nor needed to be warned a second time
But bore each other back; some knew the face,
And all had heard the much lamented case
Of him who fell for love, and this the fatal place.
And now th' infernal minister advanced,
Seized the due victim, and with fury lanced
Her back, and piercing through her inmost heart
Drew backward, as before, th' offending part.
The reeking entrails next he tore away,
And to his meagre mastiffs made a prey.
The pale assistants on each other stared
With gaping mouths for issuing words prepared;
The still-born sounds upon the palate hung,
And died imperfect on the falt'ring tongue.
The fright was general; but the female band
(A helpless train) in more confusion stand;
With horror shudd'ring, on a heap they run,
Sick at the sight of hateful justice done;
For conscience rung th' alarm, and made the case
    their own.
So spread upon a lake with upward eye
A plump of fowl behold their foe on high;
They close their trembling troop, and all attend
On whom the sowsing eagle will descend.
But most the proud Honoria feared th' event,
And thought to her alone the vision sent.

Her guilt presents to her distracted mind
Heav'n's justice, Theodore's revengeful kind,
And the same fate to the same sin assigned;
Already sees herself the monster's prey,
And feels her heart and entrails torn away.
'Twas a mute scene of sorrow, mixed with fear.
Still on the table lay th' unfinished cheer,
The knight and hungry mastiffs stood around,
The mangled dame lay breathless on the ground;
When on a sudden reinspired with breath,
Again she rose, again to suffer death;
Nor stayed the hell-hounds, nor the hunter stayed,
But followed as before the flying maid.
Th' avenger took from earth th' avenging sword
And, mounting light as air, his sable steed he spurred.
The clouds dispelled, the sky resumed her light,
And nature stood recovered of her fright.
    But fear, the last of ills, remained behind,
And horror heavy sat on ev'ry mind.
Nor Theodore encourag'd more his feast,
But sternly looked, as hatching in his breast
Some deep design, which when Honoria viewed,
The fresh impulse her former fright renewed.
She thought herself the trembling dame who fled,
And him the grisly ghost that spurred th' infernal steed;
The more dismayed, for when the guests withdrew,
Their courteous host, saluting all the crew,
Regardless passed her o'er, nor graced with kind adieu.
That sting enfixed within her haughty mind,
The downfall of her empire she divined;
And her proud heart with secret sorrow pined.
Home as they went, the sad discourse renewed
Of the relentless dame to death pursued,
And of the sight obscene so lately viewed.

None durst arraign the righteous doom she bore,
Ev'n they who pitied most yet blamed her more.
The parallel they needed not to name,
But in the dead they damned the living dame.
At ev'ry little noise she looked behind,
For still the knight was present to her mind;
And anxious oft she started on the way
And thought the horseman-ghost came thund'ring for
    his prey.
Returned she took her bed with little rest,
But in short slumbers dreamt the funeral feast;
Awaked she turned her side, and slept again,
The same black vapours mounted in her brain,
And the same dreams returned with double pain.
Now forced to wake because afraid to sleep,
Her blood all fevered, with a furious leap
She sprung from bed, distracted in her mind,
And feared at every step a twitching spright behind.
Darkling and desp'rate with a stagg'ring pace,
Of death afraid and conscious of disgrace;
Fear, pride, remorse, at once her heart assailed,
Pride put remorse to flight but fear prevailed.
Friday, the fatal day, when next it came,
Her soul forethought the fiend would change his
    game,
And her pursue; or Theodore be slain,
And two ghosts join their packs to hunt her o'er the
    plain.
This dreadful image so possessed her mind,
That desp'rate any succour else to find,
She ceased all farther hope; and now began
To make reflection on th' unhappy man.
Rich, brave, and young, who past expression loved,
Proof to disdain, and not to be removed.

Of all the men respected and admired,
Of all the dames, except herself, desired.
Why not of her? preferred above the rest
By him with knightly deeds and open love pro-
    fessed?
So had another been, where he his vows addressed.
This quelled her pride, yet other doubts remained,
That once disdaining she might be disdained.
The fear was just but greater fear prevailed;
Fear of her life by hellish hounds assailed.
He took a low'ring leave; but who can tell
What outward hate might inward love conceal?
Her sex's arts she knew, and why not then
Might deep dissembling have a place in men?
Here hope began to dawn; resolved to try,
She fixed on this her utmost remedy;
Death was behind but hard it was to die.
'Twas time enough at last on death to call,
The precipice in sight; a shrub was all
That kindly stood betwixt to break the fatal fall.
One maid she had, beloved above the rest,
Secure of her the secret she confessed;
And now the cheerful light her fears dispelled,
She with no winding turns the truth concealed
But put the woman off and stood revealed;
With faults confessed commission'd her to go,
If pity yet had place, and reconcile her foe.
The welcome message made, was soon received;
'Twas what he wished and hoped but scarce believed
Fate seemed a fair occasion to present,
He knew the sex, and feared she might repent
Should he delay the moment of consent.
There yet remained to gain her friends (a care
The modesty of maidens well might spare),

But she with such a zeal the cause embraced
(As women where they will are all in haste),
The father, mother, and the kin beside,
Were overborne by fury of the tide.
With full consent of all, she changed her state,
Resistless in her love as in her hate.
　By her example warned, the rest beware;
More easy, less imperious, were the fair;
And that one hunting which the devil designed
For one fair female, lost him half the kind.

SONGS AND ODES

1

Aʜ fading joy, how quickly art thou past!
     Yet we thy ruin haste.
As if the cares of human life were few,
     We seek out new;
And follow fate that does too fast pursue.

See how on every bough the birds express
     In the sweet notes their happiness;
    They all enjoy and nothing spare,
    But on their mother nature lay their care.
Why then should man, the lord of all below,
     Such troubles choose to know
As none of all his subjects undergo?

    Hark, hark, the waters fall, fall, fall;
    And with a murmuring sound
    Dash, dash, upon the ground,
     To gentle slumbers call.

2

I ꜰᴇᴇᴅ a flame within which so torments me,
That it both pains my heart and yet contents me;
'Tis such a pleasing smart, and I so love it,
That I had rather die than once remove it.

Yet he for whom I grieve shall never know it,
My tongue does not betray, nor my eyes show it;
Not a sigh nor a tear my pain discloses,
But they fall silently like dew on roses.

Thus to prevent my love from being cruel,
My heart's the sacrifice as 'tis the fuel;
And while I suffer this to give him quiet,
My faith rewards my love though he deny it.

On his eyes will I gaze, and there delight me;
While I conceal my love, no frown can fright me;
To be more happy I dare not aspire;
Nor can I fall more low, mounting no higher.

3

You charmed me not with that fair face,
    Though it was all divine;
To be another's is the grace
    That makes me wish you mine.
The gods and fortune take their part
    Who like young monarchs fight;
And boldly dare invade that heart
    Which is another's right.
First mad with hope we undertake
    To pull up every bar;
But once possessed, we faintly make
    A dull defensive war.
Now every friend is turned a foe
    In hope to get our store;
And passion makes us cowards grow,
    Which made us brave before.

4

Wherever I am, and whatever I do,
　　My Phillis is still in my mind.
When angry I mean not to Phillis to go,
　　My feet of themselves the way find;
Unknown to myself I am just at her door,
And when I would rail, I can bring out no more
　　Than 'Phillis too fair and unkind!'

When Phillis I see, my heart bounds in my breast,
　　And the love I would stifle is shown;
But asleep or awake I am never at rest
　　When from my eyes Phillis is gone!
Sometimes a sad dream does delude my sad mind,
But, alas, when I wake and no Phillis I find,
　　How I sigh to myself all alone.

Should a king be my rival in her I adore,
　　He should offer his treasure in vain;
O let me alone to be happy and poor,
　　And give me my Phillis again.
Let Phillis be mine and but ever be kind,
I could to a desert with her be confined,
　　And envy no monarch his reign.

Alas, I discover too much of my love,
　　And she too well knows her own power!
She makes me each day a new martyrdom prove,
　　And makes me grow jealous each hour.
But let her each minute torment my poor mind,
I had rather love Phillis both false and unkind,
　　Than ever be freed from her pow'r.

5

FAREWELL fair Arminda, my joy and my grief,
In vain I have loved you and hope no relief;
Undone by your virtue, too strict and severe,
Your eyes gave me love and you gave me despair.
Now called by my honour, I seek with content
The fate which in pity you would not prevent;
To languish in love were to find by delay
A death that's more welcome the speediest way.

On seas and in battles, in bullets and fire,
The danger is less than in hopeless desire;
My death's-wound you gave me though far off I bear
My fall from your sight, not to cost you a tear.
But if the kind flood on a wave should convey
And under your window my body would lay,
The wound on my breast when you happen to see,
You'll say with a sigh – 'it was given by me.'

6

CAN life be a blessing,
Or worth the possessing,
Can life be a blessing if love were away?
Ah no! though our love all night keep us waking,
And though he torment us with cares all the day,
Yet he sweetens, he sweetens our pains in the taking;
There's an hour at the last, there's an hour to repay.

In every possessing,
The ravishing blessing,
In every possessing the fruit of our pain,
Poor lovers forget long ages of anguish,
Whate'er they have suffered and done to obtain;
'Tis a pleasure, a pleasure to sigh and to languish,
When we hope, when we hope to be happy again.

7

FAREWELL ungrateful traitor,
　　Farewell my perjured swain;
Let never injured creature
　　Believe a man again.
The pleasure of possessing
Surpasses all expressing,
But 'tis too short a blessing,
　　And love too long a pain.

'Tis easy to deceive us
　　In pity of our pain,
But when we love you leave us
　　To rail at you in vain.
Before we have descried it
There is no bliss beside it,
But she that once has tried it
　　Will never love again.

The passion you pretended
　　Was only to obtain,
But when the charm is ended
　　The charmer you disdain.
Your love by ours we measure,
Till we have lost our treasure;
But dying is a pleasure,
　　When living is a pain.

8

A SONG OF THE RIVER THAMES

OLD Father Ocean calls my tide;
Come away, come away;
The barks upon the billows ride,
The master will not stay;

The merry bo'sun from his side
His whistle takes to check and chide
The ling'ring lads delay;
And all the crew aloud has cried,
Come away, come away.

See the god of seas attends thee,
Nymphs divine, a beauteous train:
All the calmer gales befriend thee
In thy passage o'er the main.
Every maid her locks is binding,
Every Triton's horn is winding,
Welcome to the wat'ry plain.

9

Go tell Amynta, gentle swain,
I would not die nor dare complain;
Thy tuneful voice with numbers join,
Thy words will more prevail than mine.
To souls oppressed and dumb with grief,
The gods ordain this kind relief;
That music should in sounds convey,
What dying lovers dare not say.

A sigh or tear perhaps she'll give,
But love on pity cannot live.
Tell her that hearts for hearts were made,
And love with love is only paid.
Tell her my pains so fast increase,
That soon they will be past redress;
But ah! the wretch that speechless lies,
Attends but death to close his eyes.

10

FAIREST isle, all isles excelling,
 Seat of pleasures and of loves;
Venus here will choose her dwelling,
 And forsake her Cyprian groves.

Cupid, from his fav'rite nation,
 Care and envy will remove;
Jealousy, that poisons passion,
 And despair that dies for love.

Gentle murmurs, sweet complaining,
 Sighs that blow the fire of love;
Soft repulses, kind disdaining,
 Shall be all the pains you prove.

Every swain shall pay his duty,
 Grateful every nymph shall prove;
And as these excel in beauty,
 Those shall be renowned for love.

11

How happy the lover,
 How easy his chain,
 How pleasing his pain!
How sweet to discover
 He sighs not in vain.
For love every creature
Is formed by his nature;
No joys are above
The pleasures of love.

In vain are our graces,
   In vain are your eyes,
   If love you despise;
When age furrows faces,
   'Tis time to be wise.
Then use the short blessing,
That flies in possessing;
No joys are above
The pleasures of love.

12

A SONG BY COMUS AND THREE PEASANTS

COMUS: Your hay it is mowed, and your corn is reaped;
   Your barns will be full, and your hovels heaped:
     Come, my boys, come;
     Come, my boys, come;
   And merrily roar out Harvest Home;
     Harvest Home,
     Harvest Home;
   And merrily roar out Harvest Home.

CHORUS: Come, my boys, come, &c.

1 MAN: We ha' cheated the parson, we'll cheat him agen;
   For why should a blockhead ha' one in ten?
     One in ten,
     One in ten;
   For why should a blockhead ha' one in ten?

CHORUS: One in ten,
     One in ten;
   For why should a blockhead ha' one in ten?

2 MAN: For prating so long like a book-learned sot,
        Till pudding and dumpling burn to pot;
          Burn to pot,
          Burn to pot;
        Till pudding and dumpling burn to pot.

CHORUS: Burn to pot, &c.

3 MAN: We'll toss off our ale till we canno' stand,
        And hoigh for the honour of Old England;
          Old England,
          Old England;
        And hoigh for the honour of Old England.

CHORUS: Old England, &c.

13

SONG TO A FAIR YOUNG LADY,
GOING OUT OF THE TOWN IN THE SPRING

Ask not the cause why sullen Spring
    So long delays her flow'rs to bear;
Why warbling birds forget to sing,
    And winter storms invert the year!
Chloris is gone; and fate provides
To make it Spring where she resides.

Chloris is gone, the cruel fair;
    She cast not back a pitying eye,
But left her lover in despair,
    To sigh, to languish, and to die.
Ah, how can those fair eyes endure
To give the wounds they will not cure!

Great god of love, why hast thou made
    A face that can all hearts command,
That all religions can invade,
    And change the laws of ev'ry land?
Where thou hadst placed such pow'r before,
Thou shouldst have made her mercy more.

When Chloris to the temple comes,
    Adoring crowds before her fall;
She can restore the dead from tombs,
    And ev'ry life but mine recall.
I only am by love designed
To be the victim for mankind.

14

THE LADY'S SONG

A CHOIR of bright beauties in spring did appear,
To choose a May-lady to govern the year.
All the nymphs were in white, and the shepherds in green,
The garland was giv'n, and Phillis was Queen;
But Phillis refused it, and sighing did say,
'I'll not wear a garland while Pan is away.'

While Pan and fair Syrinx are fled from our shore,
The graces are banished, and love is no more.
The soft god of pleasure that warmed our desires,
Has broken his bow, and extinguished his fires;
And vows that himself and his mother will mourn,
Till Pan and fair Syrinx in triumph return.

Forbear your addresses, and court us no more,
For we will perform what the Deity swore.
But if you dare think of deserving our charms,
Away with your sheephooks and take to your arms;
Then laurels and myrtles your brows shall adorn,
When Pan and his son and fair Syrinx return.

15

FAIR, sweet and young, receive a prize
Reserved for your victorious eyes.
From crowds, whom at your feet you see,
O pity, and distinguish me;
As I from thousand beauties more
Distinguish you, and only you adore.

Your face for conquest was designed,
Your ev'ry motion charms my mind;
Angels, when you your silence break,
Forget their hymns to hear you speak;
But when at once they hear and view,
Are loath to mount and long to stay with you.

No graces can your form improve,
But all are lost, unless you love;
While that sweet passion you disdain,
Your veil and beauty are in vain.
In pity then prevent my fate,
For after dying all reprieve's too late.

A SONG FOR

ST CECILIA'S DAY, 1687

1

FROM harmony, from heav'nly harmony
　　This universal frame began.
　When nature underneath a heap
　　Of jarring atoms lay,
　And could not heave her head,
The tuneful voice was heard from high,
　'Arise ye more than dead.'

Then cold, and hot, and moist, and dry,
 In order to their stations leap,
  And music's pow'r obey.
From harmony, from heav'nly harmony
 This universal frame began;
  From harmony to harmony
Through all the compass of the notes it ran,
The diapason closing full in man.

2

What passion cannot music raise and quell!
 When Jubal struck the corded shell,
 His list'ning brethren stood around
 And wond'ring on their faces fell
 To worship that celestial sound.
Less than a god they thought there could not dwell
 Within the hollow of that shell,
 That spoke so sweetly and so well.
What passion cannot music raise and quell!

3

The trumpet's loud clangour
 Excites us to arms
With shrill notes of anger
 And mortal alarms.
The double double double beat
 Of the thund'ring drum
 Cries hark the foes come!
Charge, charge, 'tis too late to retreat.

4

The soft complaining flute
In dying notes discovers
The woes of hopeless lovers,
Whose dirge is whisper'd by the warbling lute.

5

Sharp violins proclaim
Their jealous pangs and desperation,
Fury, frantic indignation,
Depth of pains and height of passion,
    For the fair, disdainful dame.

6

But oh! what art can teach
    What human voice can reach
The sacred organ's praise?
Notes inspiring holy love,
Notes that wing their heav'nly ways
        To mend the choirs above.

7

Orpheus could lead the savage race,
And trees unrooted left their place,
        Sequacious of the lyre.
But bright Cecilia raised the wonder high'r;
    When to her organ vocal breath was giv'n,
An angel heard and straight appeared
        Mistaking earth for heav'n.

GRAND CHORUS

As from the pow'r of sacred lays
    The spheres began to move,
And sung the great creator's praise
    To all the blessed above;
So when the last and dreadful hour
This crumbling pageant shall devour,
The trumpet shall be heard on high,
The dead shall live, the living die,
And music shall untune the sky.

ALEXANDER'S FEAST

OR THE POWER OF MUSIC

AN ODE
IN HONOUR OF ST CECILIA'S DAY

I

'TWAS at the royal feast, for Persia won,
 By Philip's warlike son:
 Aloft in awful state
 The god-like hero sate
 On his imperial throne;
His valiant peers were placed around,
Their brows with roses and with myrtles bound
 (So should desert in arms be crowned).
The lovely Thais by his side
Sate like a blooming Eastern bride
In flow'r of youth and beauty's pride.
 Happy, happy, happy pair!
  None but the brave,
  None but the brave,
 None but the brave deserves the fair.

CHORUS

 Happy, happy, happy pair!
  None but the brave,
  None but the brave,
 None but the brave deserves the fair.

II

 Timotheus, placed on high
  Amid the tuneful quire,
With flying fingers touched the lyre.
 The trembling notes ascend the sky,
  And heav'nly joys inspire.

The song began from Jove;
Who left his blissful seats above
(Such is the pow'r of mighty love).
A dragon's fiery form belied the god,
Sublime on radiant spires he rode,
    When he to fair Olympia press'd;
      And while he sought her snowy breast,
Then round her slender waist he curled
And stamped an image of himself, a sov'reign of the world.
    The list'ning crowd admire the lofty sound,
      'A present deity,' they shout around;
      'A present deity,' the vaulted roofs rebound.
            With ravished ears
            The monarch hears,
            Assumes the god,
            Affects to nod,
      And seems to shake the spheres.

CHORUS

            With ravished ears
            The monarch hears,
            Assumes the god,
            Affects to nod,
      And seems to shake the spheres.

III

The praise of Bacchus then the sweet musician sung,
    Of Bacchus ever fair and ever young.
        The jolly god in triumph comes;
        Sound the trumpets, beat the drums;
            Flushed with a purple grace
            He shows his honest face;

Now give the hautboys breath; he comes, he comes.
  Bacchus ever fair and young,
   Drinking joys did first ordain.
  Bacchus' blessings are a treasure,
  Drinking is the soldier's pleasure;
   Rich the treasure,
   Sweet the pleasure;
  Sweet is pleasure after pain.

CHORUS

  Bacchus' blessings are a treasure,
  Drinking is the soldier's pleasure;
   Rich the treasure,
   Sweet the pleasure;
  Sweet is pleasure after pain.

IV

  Soothed with the sound the King grew vain;
   Fought all his battles o'er again;
And thrice he routed all his foes, and thrice he slew
  the slain.
  The master saw the madness rise;
  His glowing cheeks, his ardent eyes;
  And while he heav'n and earth defied,
  Changed his hand and checked his pride.
   He chose a mournful muse
   Soft pity to infuse.
  He sung Darius, great and good,
   By too severe a fate
  Fallen, fallen, fallen, fallen,
   Fallen from his high estate
  And welt'ring in his blood.

Deserted at his utmost need
By those his former bounty fed;
On the bare earth exposed he lies,
With not a friend to close his eyes.
With downcast looks the joyless victor sate,
    Revolving in his altered soul
        The various turns of chance below;
    And now and then a sigh he stole,
        And tears began to flow.

CHORUS

    Revolving in his altered soul
        The various turns of chance below;
    And now and then a sigh he stole,
        And tears began to flow.

V

The mighty master smiled to see
That love was in the next degree;
'Twas but a kindred-sound to move,
For pity melts the mind to love.
    Softly sweet, in Lydian measures,
    Soon he soothed his soul to pleasures.
War, he sung, is toil and trouble;
Honour but an empty bubble.
    Never ending, still beginning,
Fighting still, and still destroying,
    If the world be worth thy winning,
Think, O think, it worth enjoying.
    Lovely Thais sits beside thee;
    Take the good the gods provide thee.

The many rend the skies with loud applause;
So love was crowned, but music won the cause.

The Prince, unable to conceal his pain,
    Gazed on the fair
    Who caused his care,
  And sighed and looked, sighed and looked,
  Sighed and looked, and sighed again.
At length, with love and wine at once oppressed,
The vanquished victor sunk upon her breast.

CHORUS

The Prince, unable to conceal his pain,
    Gazed on the fair
    Who caused his care,
  And sighed and looked, sighed and looked,
  Sighed and looked, and sighed again.
At length, with love and wine at once oppressed,
The vanquished victor sunk upon her breast.

VI

Now strike the golden lyre again;
A louder yet and yet a louder strain.
Break his bands of sleep asunder
And rouse him, like a rattling peal of thunder.
  Hark, hark, the horrid sound
    Has raised up his head
    As awaked from the dead,
  And amazed he stares around.
Revenge, revenge, Timotheus cries,
    See the Furies arise!
    See the snakes that they rear,
    How they hiss in their hair,
And the sparkles that flash from their eyes!
    Behold a ghastly band,
    Each a torch in his hand!

Those are Grecian ghosts that in battle were slain,
  And unburied remain
  Inglorious on the plain.
  Give the vengeance due
  To the valiant crew.
Behold how they toss their torches on high,
  How they point to the Persian abodes,
And glitt'ring temples of their hostile gods!
The princes applaud with a furious joy,
And the King seized a flambeau with zeal to destroy;
  Thais led the way
  To light him to his prey
And, like another Helen, fired another Troy.

CHORUS

And the King seized a flambeau with zeal to destroy;
  Thais led the way
  To light him to his prey
And, like another Helen, fired another Troy.

VII

  Thus, long ago,
  Ere heaving bellows learned to blow,
  While organs yet were mute;
  Timotheus, to his breathing flute
  And sounding lyre,
Could swell the soul to rage or kindle soft desire.
  At last divine Cecilia came,
  Invent'ress of the vocal frame.
The sweet enthusiast, from her sacred store,
  Enlarged the former narrow bounds,
  And added length to solemn sounds,
With nature's mother-wit and arts unknown before.

Let old Timotheus yield the prize,
    Or both divide the crown;
He raised a mortal to the skies;
    She drew an angel down.

GRAND CHORUS

At last divine Cecilia came,
Invent'ress of the vocal frame.
The sweet enthusiast, from her sacred store,
    Enlarged the former narrow bounds,
    And added length to solemn sounds,
With nature's mother-wit and arts unknown before.
    Let old Timotheus yield the prize,
        Or both divide the crown;
    He raised a mortal to the skies;
        She drew an angel down.

THE SECULAR MASQUE

[*Enter* JANUS]

JANUS.   Chronos, Chronos, mend thy pace,
          An hundred times the rolling sun
          Around the radiant belt has run
          In his revolving race.
          Behold, behold, the goal in sight,
          Spread thy fans, and wing thy flight.

[*Enter* CHRONOS, *with a scythe in his hand and a great globe on his back, which he sets down at his entrance*]

CHRONOS. Weary, weary of my weight,
          Let me, let me drop my freight,
          And leave the world behind.
          I could not bear
          Another year
          The load of humankind.

[*Enter* MOMUS *laughing*]

MOMUS.   Ha! ha! ha! Ha! ha! ha! well hast thou done
              To lay down thy pack
              And lighten thy back.
          The world was a fool e'er since it begun,
          And since neither Janus nor Chronos nor I
              Can hinder the crimes
              Or mend the bad times,
          'Tis better to laugh than to cry.

CHO. OF ALL 3. 'Tis better to laugh than to cry.

JANUS.   Since Momus comes to laugh below,
              Old Time begin the show,
          That he may see in every scene
          What changes in this age have been.

CHRONOS. Then Goddess of the Silver Bow begin.

[*Horns or hunting music within*]

143

[*Enter* DIANA]

DIANA. With horns and with hounds I waken the day,
And hie to my woodland walks away;
I tuck up my robe, and am buskin'd soon,
And tie to my forehead a waxing moon.
I course the fleet stag, unkennel the fox,
And chase the wild goats o'er summits of rocks;
With shouting and hooting we pierce thro' the sky,
And Echo turns hunter and doubles the cry.

CHO. OF ALL. With shouting and hooting we pierce through the sky,
And Echo turns hunter and doubles the cry.

JANUS. Then our age was in its prime,

CHRONUS. Free from rage,

DIANA. And free from crime.

MOMUS. A very merry, dancing, drinking,
Laughing, quaffing, and unthinking time.

CHO. OF ALL. Then our age was in its prime,
Free from rage, and free from crime,
A very merry, dancing, drinking,
Laughing, quaffing, and unthinking time.

[*Dance of* DIANA's *attendants*]

[*Enter* MARS]

MARS. Inspire the vocal brass, inspire;
The world is past its infant age:
Arms and honour,
Arms and honour,
Set the martial mind on fire,
And kindle manly rage.
Mars has looked the sky to red;
And peace, the lazy good, is fled.

Plenty, peace, and pleasure fly;
    The sprightly green
In woodland-walks no more is seen;
    The sprightly green has drunk the Tyrian dye.

CHO. OF ALL. Plenty, peace, &c.

MARS.   Sound the trumpet, beat the drum,
    Through all the world around;
    Sound a reveille, sound, sound,
    The warrior god is come.

CHO. OF ALL. Sound the trumpet, &c.

MOMUS.   Thy sword within the scabbard keep,
    And let mankind agree;
Better the world were fast asleep
    Than kept awake by thee.
The fools are only thinner,
    With all our cost and care;
But neither side a winner,
    For things are as they were.

CHO. OF ALL. The fools are only, &c.

[*Enter* VENUS]

VENUS.   Calms appear, when storms are past;
Love will have his hour at last:
Nature in my kindly care;
Mars destroys, and I repair;
Take me, take me, while you may,
Venus comes not ev'ry day.

CHO. OF ALL. Take her, take her, &c.

CHRONOS. The world was then so light,
    I scarcely felt the weight;
Joy ruled the day, and love the night.
But since the Queen of Pleasure left the ground,
    I faint, I lag,
    And feebly drag
    The pond'rous orb around.

MOMUS.   All, all, of a piece throughout;

pointing ⎫
to DIANA. ⎬ Thy chase had a beast in view;

to MARS, Thy wars brought nothing about;

to VENUS. Thy lovers were all untrue.

JANUS.   'Tis well an old age is out,

CHRONOS. And time to begin a new.

CHO. OF ALL. All, all, of a piece throughout;
             Thy chase had a beast in view;
             Thy wars brought nothing about;
             Thy lovers were all untrue.
             'Tis well an old age is out,
             And time to begin a new.

Dance of huntsmen, nymphs, warriors and lovers.

AN ESSAY OF
DRAMATIC POESY[1]

Fungar vice cotis, acutum
Reddere quae ferrum valet, exors ipsa secandi.
Horat. De Arte Poet.[2]

IT was that memorable day,[3] in the first summer of the
late war, when our navy engaged the Dutch; a day wherein
the two most mighty and best appointed fleets which any
age had ever seen disputed the command of the greater
half of the globe, the commerce of nations, and the riches
of the universe. While these vast floating bodies on either
side moved against each other in parallel lines, and our
countrymen, under the happy conduct of his Royal High-
ness, went breaking by little and little into the line of the
enemies, the noise of the cannon from both navies reached
our ears about the city; so that all men, being alarmed with
it and in a dreadful suspense of the event which they knew
was then deciding, everyone went following the sound as
his fancy led him; and leaving the town almost empty,
some took towards the park, some cross the river, others
down it; all seeking the noise in the depth of silence.

Among the rest, it was the fortune of Eugenius, Crites,
Lisideius, and Neander,[4] to be in company together; three

1. The text is that of the 2nd edition, 1684.
2. I shall act as a whetstone, which is able to sharpen iron, though
   of itself it cannot cut. (*Ars Poetica* 304–5.)
3. 3 June 1665. The English fleet won a great victory over the
   Dutch on that day.
4. Eugenius, Crites, Lisideius, and Neander: Charles Sackville, Lord
   Buckhurst (1638–1707), to whom *An Essay* was dedicated, Sir
   Robert Howard (1626–98), dramatist and Dryden's brother-in-
   law, Sir Charles Sedley (*c.* 1639–1701), poet and dramatist, and
   Dryden.

of them persons whom their wit and quality have made known to all the town; and whom I have chose to hide under these borrowed names that they may not suffer by so ill a relation as I am going to make of their discourse.

Taking then a barge which a servant of Lisideius had provided for them, they made haste to shoot the bridge and left behind them that great fall of waters which hindered them from hearing what they desired. After which, having disengaged themselves from many vessels which rode at anchor in the Thames, and almost blocked up the passage towards Greenwich, they ordered the watermen to let fall their oars more gently; and then everyone favouring his own curiosity with a strict silence, it was not long ere they perceived the air to break about them like the noise of distant thunder, or of swallows in a chimney: those little undulations of sound, though almost vanishing before they reached them, yet still seeming to retain somewhat of their first horror which they had betwixt the fleets. After they had attentively listened till such time as the sound by little and little went from them, Eugenius, lifting up his head, and taking notice of it, was the first who congratulated to the rest that happy omen of our nation's victory; adding, that we had but this to desire in confirmation of it, that we might hear no more of that noise, which was now leaving the English coast. When the rest had concurred in the same opinion, Crites, a person of a sharp judgement, and somewhat too delicate a taste in wit, which the world has mistaken in him for ill-nature, said, smiling to us, that if the concernment of this battle had not been so exceeding great, he could scarce have wished the victory at the price he knew he must pay for it, in being subject to the reading and hearing of so many ill verses as he was sure would be made on that subject. Adding, that no argument could scape some of those eternal rhymers, who watch a battle with more diligence than the ravens and birds of prey; and the worst of them surest to be first in upon the quarry while the better able, either out of modesty writ not at all, or set that due value upon their poems, as to let them be often desired and long expected! 'There are some of those impertinent people of whom you speak,' answered Lisideius, 'who to my knowledge are already so provided, either way, that they can produce not only a panegyric upon the victory, but, if need be, a funeral elegy on the duke; wherein, after they have crowned his valour with many laurels, they will at last deplore the odds under which he fell, concluding that his courage deserved a better destiny.' All the company smiled at the conceit of Lisideius; but Crites, more eager than before, began to make particular exceptions against some writers, and said the public magistrate ought to send betimes to forbid them; and that it concerned the peace and quiet of all honest people, that ill poets should be as well silenced as seditious preachers. 'In my opinion,' replied Eugenius, 'you pursue your point too far; for as to my own particular, I am so great a lover of poesy, that I could wish them all rewarded who attempt but to do well; at least I would not have them worse used than one of their brethren was by Sylla the Dictator : – *Quem in concione vidimus* (says Tully), *cum ei libellum malus poeta de populo subjecisset, quod epigramma in eum iecisset tantummodo alternis versiculis longiusculis, statim ex iis rebus quas tunc vendebat jubere ei praemium tribuit, sub ea conditione ne quid postea scriberet.*[1] 'I could wish

---

1. We have seen him at a public meeting, when a bad poet, one of the crowd, had simply composed an epigram against him in rather lengthy couplets, order a reward to be paid to the fellow out of the property he was selling at the time – on the condition that he wrote nothing more. (Cicero, *Pro Archia* 25.)

with all my heart,' replied Crites, 'that many whom we know were as bountifully thanked upon the same condition, that they would never trouble us again. For amongst others, I have a mortal apprehension of two poets, whom this victory with the help of both her wings will never be able to escape.' ''Tis easy to guess whom you intend,' said Lisideius; 'and without naming them, I ask you if one of them[1] does not perpetually pay us with clenches upon words, and a certain clownish kind of raillery? if now and then he does not offer at a catachresis or Clevelandism,[2] wresting and torturing a word into another meaning: in fine, if he be not one of those whom the French would call *un mauvais buffon*; one who is so much a well-willer to the satire, that he intends at least to spare no man; and though he cannot strike a blow to hurt any, yet he ought to be punished for the malice of the action, as our witches are justly hanged because they think themselves to be such; and suffer deservedly for believing they did mischief, because they meant it.' 'You have described him', said Crites, 'so exactly that I am afraid to come after you with my other extremity of poetry. He is one of those who, having had some advantage of education and converse, knows better than the other what a poet should be, but puts it into practice more unluckily than any man; his style and matter are everywhere alike: he is the most calm, peaceable writer you ever read: he never disquiets your passions with the least concernment, but still leaves you in as even a temper as he found you; he is a very leveller in poetry, he creeps along with ten little words in every line, and helps out his numbers with

1. Robert Wild (1609–79), a metaphysical poet, whose chief work was *Iter Boreale*, 1660.
2. John Cleveland (1613–58), the most extravagant of the metaphysical poets.

For to, and *Unto*, and all the pretty expletives he can find, till he drags them to the end of another line; while the sense is left tired half way behind it: he doubly starves all his verses, first for want of thought, and then of expression his poetry neither has wit in it, nor seems to have it; like him in Martial:

Pauper videri Cinna vult, et est pauper.[1]

'He affects plainness, to cover his want of imagination: when he writes the serious way, the highest flight of his fancy is some miserable antithesis, or seeming contradiction; and in the comic he is still reaching at some thin conceit, the ghost of a jest, and that too flies before him, never to be caught; these swallows which we see before us on the Thames are the just resemblance of his wit: you may observe how near the water they stoop, how many proffers they make to dip, and yet how seldom they touch it; and when they do, 'tis but the surface: they skim over it but to catch a gnat, and then mount into the air and leave it.'

'Well, gentlemen,' said Eugenius, 'you may speak your pleasure of these authors; but though I and some few more about the town may give you a peaceable hearing, yet assure yourselves, there are multitudes who would think you malicious and them injured: especially him whom you first described; he is the very Withers of the city: they have bought more editions of his works than would serve to lay under all their pies at the lord mayor's Christmas. When his famous poem first came out in the year 1660, I have seen them reading it in the midst of 'Change time; nay, so vehement they were at it, that they

---

1. Cinna wishes to seem poor, and poor he is, in fact. (*Epigrams* 8. 19.)

lost their bargain by the candles' ends;[1] but what will you say, if he has been received amongst great persons? I can assure you he is, this day, the envy of one who is lord in the art of quibbling; and who does not take it well, that any man should intrude so far into his province.' 'All I would wish,' replies Crites, 'is, that they who love his writings, may still admire him, and his fellow poet, *qui Bavium non odit, &c.*[2] is curse sufficient.' 'And farther,' added Lisideius, 'I believe there is no man who writes well, but would think he had hard measure, if their admirers should praise anything of his: *Nam quos contemnimus eorum quoque laudes contemnimus.*'[3] 'There are so few who write well in this age,' says Crites, 'that methinks any praises should be welcome; they neither rise to the dignity of the last age, nor to any of the ancients: and we may cry out of the writers of this time, with more reason than Petronius of his, *Pace vestrâ liceat dixisse, primi omnium eloquentiam perdidistis:*[4] you have debauched the true old poetry so far, that Nature, which is the soul of it, is not in any of your writings.'

'If your quarrel,' said Eugenius, 'to those who now write, be grounded only on your reverence to antiquity, there is no man more ready to adore those great Greeks and Romans than I am. But on the other side, I cannot think so contemptibly of the age in which I live, or so dishonourably of my own country, as not to judge we equal the ancients in most kinds of poesy, and in some surpass them; neither know I any reason why I may not be as

1. A method of auction; bids could be made as long as the candle burnt.
2. He who hates not Bavius, let him love your poems, Maevius. (Virgil, *Eclogues* 3. 90.)
3. For if we despise a man, we despise his praises too.
4. If you will allow me to say so, you have been the very first to ruin the art of speech. (*Satyricon* 2.)

zealous for the reputation of our age, as we find the
ancients themselves were in reference to those who lived
before them. For you hear your Horace saying,

> *Indignor quidquam reprehendi, non quia crassè*
> *Compositum illepideve putetur, sed quia nuper.*[1]

And after:

> *Si meliora dies, ut vina, poemata reddit,*
> *Scire velim pretium chartis quotus arroget annus?*[2]

'But I see I am engaging in a wide dispute, where the
arguments are not like to reach close on either side; for
poesy is of so large an extent, and so many both of the
ancients and moderns have done well in all kinds of it, that
in citing one against the other we shall take up more time
this evening than each man's occasions will allow him.
Therefore I would ask Crites to what part of poesy he
would confine his arguments, and whether he would de-
fend the general cause of the ancients against the moderns,
or oppose any age of the moderns against this of ours?'

Crites, a little while considering upon this demand, told
Eugenius that if he pleased he would limit their dispute to
dramatic poesy; in which he thought it not difficult to prove,
either that the ancients were superior to the moderns, or
the last age to this of ours.

Eugenius was somewhat surprised, when he heard
Crites make choice of that subject. 'For aught I see,' said
he, 'I have undertaken a harder province than I imagined;
for though I never judged the plays of the Greek or Roman

1. I think it far from proper that any poem should be censured on
the grounds, not that it is deemed to be written rudely or inele-
gantly, but that it is new. (*Epistles* 2. 1. 76–7.)
2. If lapse of time improves poetry as it does wines, I should like to
know after how many years' end the paper we write on acquires its
value. (*Epistles* 2. 1. 34–5.)

poets comparable to ours, yet, on the other side, those we now see acted come short of many which were written in the last age. But my comfort is if we are overcome it will be only by our own countrymen; and if we yield to them in this one part of poesy, we more surpass them in all the other: for in the epic or lyric way, it will be hard for them to show us one such amongst them as we have many now living, or who lately were. They can produce nothing so courtly writ, or which expresses so much the conversation of a gentleman, as Sir John Suckling; nothing so even, sweet, and flowing, as Mr Waller; nothing so majestic, so correct as Sir John Denham; nothing so elevated, so copious, and full of spirit, as Mr Cowley; as for the Italian, French, and Spanish plays, I can make it evident that those who now write surpass them, and that the drama is wholly ours.'

All of them were thus far of Eugenius his opinion, that the sweetness of English verse was never understood or practised by our fathers; even Crites himself did not much oppose it: and everyone was willing to acknowledge how much our poesy is improved by the happiness of some writers yet living, who first taught us to mould our thoughts into easy and significant words; to retrench the super-fluities of expression, and to make our rhyme so properly a part of the verse that it should never mislead the sense but itself be led and governed by it.

Eugenius was going to continue this discourse, when Lisideius told him that it was necessary, before they pro-ceeded further, to take a standing measure of their con-troversy; for how was it possible to be decided who writ the best plays, before we know what a play should be? But this once agreed on by both parties, each might have recourse to it, either to prove his own advantages or to discover the failings of his adversary.

He had no sooner said this but all desired the favour of him to give the definition of a play; and they were the more importunate because neither Aristotle, nor Horace, nor any other who had writ of that subject, had ever done it.

Lisideius, after some modest denials, at last confessed he had a rude notion of it; indeed, rather a description than a definition, but which served to guide him in his private thoughts when he was to make a judgement of what others writ: that he conceived a play ought to be *A just and lively image of human nature, representing its passions and humours, and the changes of fortune to which it is subject, for the delight and instruction of mankind.*

This definition, though Crites raised a logical objection against it – that it was only *a genere et fine*,[1] and so not altogether perfect – was yet well received by the rest. And after they had given order to the watermen to turn their barge and row softly that they might take the cool of the evening in their return, Crites, being desired by the company to begin, spoke on behalf of the ancients, in this manner:

'If confidence presage a victory, Eugenius, in his own opinion, has already triumphed over the ancients. Nothing seems more easy to him than to overcome those whom it is our greatest praise to have imitated well; for we do not only build upon their foundations, but by their models. Dramatic poesy had time enough, reckoning from Thespis (who first invented it) to Aristophanes, to be born, to grow up, and to flourish in maturity. It has been observed of arts and sciences, that in one and the same century they have arrived to great perfection; and no wonder, since every age has a kind of universal genius, which inclines those that live in it to some particular studies: the work then being pushed on by many hands must of necessity go forward.

1. By genus and purpose.

'Is it not evident, in these last hundred years (when the study of philosophy has been the business of all the virtuosi in Christendom) that almost a new nature has been revealed to us? That more errors of the School have been detected, more useful experiments in philosophy have been made, more noble secrets in optics, medicine, anatomy, astronomy, discovered than in all those credulous and doting ages from Aristotle to us? So true it is that nothing spreads more fast than science when rightly and generally cultivated.

'Add to this, the more than common emulation that was in those times of writing well; which though it be found in all ages and all persons that pretend to the same reputation, yet poesy, being then in more esteem than now it is, had greater honours decreed to the professors of it; and consequently the rivalship was more high between them. They had judges ordained to decide their merit, and prizes to reward it; and historians have been diligent to record of Aeschylus, Euripides, Sophocles, Lycophron, and the rest of them, both who they were that vanquished in these wars of the theatre, and how often they were crowned. While the Asian kings and Grecian commonwealths scarce afforded them a nobler subject than the unmanly luxuries of a debauched court, or giddy intrigues of a factious city. *Alit aemulatio ingenia*, (says Paterculus) *et nunc invidia, nunc admiratio incitationem accendit:* Emulation is the spur of wit; and sometimes envy, sometimes admiration, quickens our endeavours.

'But now, since the rewards of honour are taken away, that virtuous emulation is turned into direct malice; yet so slothful that it contents itself to condemn and cry down others without attempting to do better. 'Tis a reputation too unprofitable to take the necessary pains for it; yet, wishing they had it, that desire is incitement enough to hinder others from it. And this, in short, Eugenius, is the reason why you have now so few good poets, and so many severe judges. Certainly, to imitate the ancients well much labour and long study is required; which pains, I have already shown, our poets would want encouragement to take, if yet they had ability to go through the work. Those ancients have been faithful imitators and wise observers of that nature which is so torn and ill represented in our plays; they have handed down to us a perfect resemblance of her, which we, like ill copiers, neglecting to look on, have rendered monstrous and disfigured. But, that you may know how much you are indebted to those your masters, and be ashamed to have so ill requited them, I must remember you that all the rules by which we practise the drama at this day (either such as relate to the justness and symmetry of the plot; or the episodical ornaments, such as descriptions, narrations, and other beauties, which are not essential to the play) were delivered to us from the observations which Aristotle made of those poets who either lived before him or were his contemporaries. We have added nothing of our own, except we have the confidence to say our wit is better; of which none boast in this our age but such as understand not theirs. Of that book which Aristotle has left us, περὶ τῆς Ποιητικῆς,[1] Horace his *Art of Poetry* is an excellent comment, and, I believe, restores to us that Second Book of his concerning *Comedy*, which is wanting in him.[2]

'Out of these two have been extracted the famous rules, which the French call *Des Trois Unitez*, or, the Three Unities, which ought to be observed in every regular play; namely, of time, place, and action.

'The unity of time they comprehend in twenty-four hours, the compass of a natural day, or as near as it can be

1. The *Poetics*.
2. Aristotle discussed Comedy in the *Poetics*, but this Section of his work is not extant.

contrived; and the reason of it is obvious to every one, that the time of the feigned action, or fable of the play, should be proportioned as near as can be to the duration of that time in which it is represented. Since, therefore, all plays are acted at the theatre in the space of time much within the compass of twenty-four hours, that play is to be thought the nearest imitation of nature whose plot or action is confined within that time. And, by the same rule which concludes this general proportion of time, it follows that all the parts of it are (as near as may be) to be equally subdivided; namely, that one act take not up the supposed time of half a day, which is out of proportion to the rest, since the other four are then to be straitened within the compass of the remaining half. For it is unnatural that one act, which being spoke or written is not longer than the rest, should be supposed longer by the audience; 'tis therefore the poet's duty to take care that no act should be imagined to exceed the time in which it is represented on the stage, and that the intervals and inequalities of time be supposed to fall out between the acts.

'This rule of time, how well it has been observed by the ancients, most of their plays will witness. You see them in their tragedies (wherein to follow this rule is certainly most difficult) from the very beginning of their plays falling close into that part of the story which they intend for the action or principal object of it, leaving the former part to be delivered by narration; so that they set the audience, as it were, at the post where the race is to be concluded, and, saving them the tedious expectation of seeing the poet set out and ride the beginning of the course, they suffer you not to behold him till he is in sight of the goal and just upon you.

'For the second unity, which is that of place, the ancients meant by it that the scene ought to be continued through the play in the same place where it was laid in the beginning; for the stage on which it is represented being but one and the same place, it is unnatural to conceive it many, and those far distant from one another. I will not deny but by the variation of painted scenes the fancy (which in these cases will contribute to its own deceit) may sometimes imagine it several places with some appearance of probability; yet it still carries the greater likelihood of truth if those places be supposed so near each other as in the same town or city, which may all be comprehended under the larger denomination of one place; for a greater distance will bear no proportion to the shortness of time which is allotted in the acting to pass from one of them to another. For the observation of this, next to the ancients, the French are to be most commended. They tie themselves so strictly to the unity of place that you never see in any of their plays a scene changed in the middle of an act. If the act begins in a garden, a street, or chamber, 'tis ended in the same place; and that you may know it to be the same, the stage is so supplied with persons that it is never empty all the time: he who enters second has business with him who was on before, and before the second quits the stage a third appears who has business with him.

'This Corneille calls *la liaison des scenes*, the continuity or joining of the scenes; and 'tis a good mark of a well-contrived play, when all the persons are known to each other, and every one of them has some affairs with all the rest.

'As for the third unity which is that of action, the ancients meant no other by it than what the logicians do by their *finis*, the end or scope of any action: that which is the first in intention and last in execution. Now the poet is to aim at one great and complete action, to the carrying on of which all things in his play, even the very obstacles, are to be subservient; and the reason of this is as evident as any of the former.

'For two actions equally laboured and driven on by the writer would destroy the unity of the poem; it would be no longer one play but two. Not but that there may be many actions in a play, as Ben Jonson has observed in his *Discoveries*; but they must be all subservient to the great one, which our language happily expresses in the name of under-plots: such as in Terence's *Eunuch* is the difference and reconcilement of Thais and Phaedria, which is not the chief business of the play but promotes the marriage of Chaerea and Chremes's sister, principally intended by the poet. There ought to be but one action, says Corneille, that is, one complete action, which leaves the mind of the audience in a full repose; but this cannot be brought to pass but by many other imperfect actions which conduce to it, and hold the audience in a delightful suspense of what will be.

'If by these rules (to omit many other drawn from the precepts and practice of the ancients) we should judge our modern plays, 'tis probable that few of them would endure the trial: that which should be the business of a day takes up in some of them an age; instead of one action they are the epitomes of a man's life; and for one spot of ground (which the stage should represent) we are sometimes in more countries than the map can show us.

'But if we allow the ancients to have contrived well, we must acknowledge them to have written better. Questionless we are deprived of a great stock of wit in the loss of Menander among the Greek poets, and of Caecilius, Afranius, and Varius, among the Romans; we may guess at Menander's excellency by the plays of Terence, who translated some of them; and yet wanted so much of him that he was called by C. Caesar the half-Menander; and may judge of Varius, by the testimonies of Horace, Martial, and Velleius Paterculus. 'Tis probable that these, could they be recovered, would decide the controversy; but so long as Aristophanes and Plautus are extant; while the tragedies of Euripides, Sophocles, and Seneca are in our hands, I can never see one of those plays which are now written but it increases my admiration of the ancients. And yet I must acknowledge further, that to admire them as we ought, we should understand them better than we do. Doubtless many things appear flat to us, the wit of which depended on some custom or story which never came to our knowledge; or perhaps on some criticism in their language, which being so long dead and only remaining in their books, 'tis not possible they should make us understand perfectly. To read Macrobius, explaining the propriety and elegancy of many words in Virgil, which I had before passed over without consideration as common things, is enough to assure me that I ought to think the same of Terence; and that in the purity of his style (which Tully so much valued that he ever carried his works about him) there is yet left in him great room for admiration, if I knew but where to place it. In the meantime I must desire you to take notice that the greatest man of the last age (Ben Jonson) was willing to give place to them in all things. He was not only a professed imitator of Horace but a learned plagiary of all the others; you track him everywhere in their snow. If Horace, Lucan, Petronius Arbiter, Seneca, and Juvenal, had their own from him, there are few serious thoughts which are new in him; you will pardon me therefore if I presume he loved their fashion when he wore their clothes. But since I have other- wise a great veneration for him, and you, Eugenius, prefer him above all other poets, I will use no farther argument to you than his example: I will produce before you Father Ben dressed in all the ornaments and colours of the ancients; you will need no other guide to our party, if you follow

F   161

him; and whether you consider the bad plays of our age, or regard the good plays of the last, both the best and worst of the modern poets will equally instruct you to admire the ancients.'

Crites had no sooner left speaking but Eugenius, who had waited with some impatience for it, thus began:

'I have observed in your speech that the former part of it is convincing as to what the moderns have profited by the rules of the ancients, but in the latter you are careful to conceal how much they have excelled them. We own all the helps we have from them, and want neither veneration nor gratitude while we acknowledge that to overcome them we must make use of the advantages we have received from them; but to these assistances we have joined our own industry; for, had we sat down with a dull imitation of them, we might then have lost somewhat of the old perfection but never acquired any that was new. We draw not therefore after their lines, but those of nature; and having the life before us, besides the experience of all they knew, it is no wonder if we hit some airs and features which they have missed. I deny not what you urge of arts and sciences, that they have flourished in some ages more than others; but your instance in philosophy makes for me. For if natural causes be more known now than in the time of Aristotle, because more studied, it follows that poesy and other arts may with the same pains arrive still nearer to perfection, and, that granted, it will rest for you to prove that they wrought more perfect images of human life than we; which, seeing in your discourse you have avoided to make good, it shall now be my task to show you some part of their defects and some few excellencies of the moderns. And I think there is none among us can imagine I do it enviously, or with purpose to detract from them; for what interest of fame or profit can the living lose by the reputation of the dead? On the other side, it is a great truth which Velleius Paterculus affirms: *Audita visis libentius laudamus; et praesentia invidia, praeterita admiratione prosequimur; et his nos obrui, illis instrui credimus:*[1] that praise or censure is certainly the most sincere which unbribed posterity shall give us.

'Be pleased then in the first place to take notice, that the Greek poesy, which Crites has affirmed to have arrived to perfection in the reign of the old comedy, was so far from it that the distinction of it into acts was not known to them; or if it were, it is yet so darkly delivered to us that we cannot make it out.

'All we know of it is from the singing of their chorus, and that too is so uncertain that in some of their plays we have reason to conjecture they sung more than five times. Aristotle indeed divides the integral parts of a play into four. First, the *Protasis*, or entrance, which gives light only to the characters of the persons and proceeds very little into any part of the action. Secondly, the *Epitasis*, or working up of the plot where the play grows warmer – the design or action of it is drawing on and you see something promising that it will come to pass. Thirdly, the *Catastasis*, called by the Romans, *Status*, the height and full growth of the play: we may call it properly the counter-turn, which destroys that expectation, imbroils the action in new difficulties, and leaves you far distant from that hope in which it found you, as you may have observed in a violent stream resisted by a narrow passage; it runs round to an eddy, and carries back the waters with more swiftness than it brought them on. Lastly, the *Catastrophe*, which the Grecians called λύσις,[2]

---

1. We are readier to praise things we have heard of than things we have seen; upon those of the present we bestow malice, on those of the past, admiration; and we consider ourselves to be oppressed by the former, but instructed by the latter. (2. 92.)
2. Literally, 'untying'.

the French *le dénouement*, and we the discovery or un-
ravelling of the plot. There you see all things settling
again upon their first foundations, and the obstacles which
hindered the design or action of the play once removed, it
ends with that resemblance of truth and nature that the
audience are satisfied with the conduct of it. Thus this great
man delivered to us the image of a play, and I must confess
it is so lively, that from thence much light has been derived
to the forming it more perfectly into acts and scenes. But
what poet first limited to five the number of the acts, I
know not; only we see it so firmly established in the time
of Horace that he gives it for a rule in comedy, — *Neu brevior
quinto, neu sit productior actu.*[1] So that you see the Grecians
cannot be said to have consummated this art; writing rather
by entrances than by acts, and having rather a general
indigested notion of a play than knowing how and where
to bestow the particular graces of it.

'But since the Spaniards at this day allow but three acts,
which they call *Jornadas*, to a play, and the Italians in many
of theirs follow them, when I condemn the ancients I declare
it is not altogether because they have not five acts to every
play, but because they have not confined themselves to one
certain number; 'tis building an house without a model;
and when they succeeded in such undertakings, they ought
to have sacrificed to Fortune, not to the Muses.

'Next for the plot, which Aristotle called τὸ μυθός[2], and
often τῶν πραγμάτων σύνθεσις,[3] and from him the Romans
Fabula, it has already been judiciously observed by a late
writer, that in their tragedies it was only some tale derived
from Thebes or Troy, or at least something that happened
in those two ages; which was worn so threadbare by the

---

1. Let it not be shorter than five acts, nor yet prolonged beyond that
number. (*Ars Poetica* 189.)
2. The plot.   3. The composition of the story.

pens of all the epic poets, and even by tradition itself of the talkative Greeklings (as Ben Jonson calls them) that before it came upon the stage it was already known to all the audience. And the people, so soon as ever they heard the name of Oedipus, knew as well as the poet that he had killed his father by a mistake and committed incest with his mother before the play; that they were now to hear of a great plague, an oracle, and the ghost of Laius; so that they sat with a yawning kind of expectation till he was to come with his eyes pulled out, and speak a hundred or more verses in a tragic tone in complaint of his misfortunes. But one Oedipus, Hercules, or Medea, had been tolerable. Poor people, they scaped not so good cheap; they had still the *chapon bouillé* set before them till their appetites were cloyed with the same dish, and, the novelty being gone the pleasure vanished; so that one main end of dramatic poesy in its definition, which was to cause delight, was of consequence destroyed.

'In their comedies, the Romans generally borrowed their plots from the Greek poets; and theirs was commonly a little girl stolen or wandered from her parents, brought back unknown to the city, there got with child by some lewd young fellow, who, by the help of his servant, cheats his father; and when her time comes to cry *Juno Lucina fer opem*[1], one or other sees a little box or cabinet which was carried away with her, and so discovers her to her friends, if some god do not prevent it by coming down in a machine and taking the thanks of it to himself.

'By the plot you may guess much of the characters of the persons. An old father, who would willingly before he dies see his son well married; his debauched son, kind in his nature to his mistress, but miserably in want of money; a servant or slave, who has so much wit to strike in with

1. Juno, goddess of childbirth, lend thine aid!

him and help to dupe his father; a braggadocio captain, a parasite, and a lady of pleasure.

'As for the poor honest maid, on whom the story is built and who ought to be one of the principal actors in the play, she is commonly a mute in it. She has the breeding of the old Elizabeth way, which was for maids to be seen and not to be heard; and it is enough you know she is willing to be married when the fifth act requires it.

'These are plots built after the Italian mode of houses, you see through them all at once. The characters are indeed the imitations of nature, but so narrow as if they had imitated only an eye or an hand and did not dare to venture on the lines of a face, or the proportion of a body.

'But in how strait a compass soever they have bounded their plots and characters, we will pass it by if they have regularly pursued them and perfectly observed those three unities of time, place, and action: the knowledge of which you say is derived to us from them. But in the first place give me leave to tell you that the unity of place, however it might be practised by them, was never any of their rules. We neither find it in Aristotle, Horace, or any who have written of it, till in our age the French poets first made it a precept of the stage. The unity of time even Terence himself (who was the best and most regular of them) has neglected. His *Heautontimoroumenos*, or Self-Punisher, takes up visibly two days, says Scaliger; the two first acts concluding the first day, the three last the day ensuing. And Euripides, in tying himself to one day, has committed an absurdity never to be forgiven him; for in one of his tragedies he has made Theseus go from Athens to Thebes, which was about forty English miles, under the walls of it to give battle, and appear victorious in the next act; and yet from the time of his departure to the return of the Nuntius, who gives the relation of his victory, Aethra and the Chorus have but thirty-six verses, which is not for every mile a verse.

'The like error is as evident in Terence his *Eunuch*, when Laches, the old man, enters by mistake into the house of Thais, where betwixt his exit and the entrance of Pythias, who comes to give ample relation of the disorders he has raised within, Parmeno, who was left upon the stage, has not above five lines to speak. *C'est bien employer un temps si court*, says the French poet, who furnished me with one of the observations; and almost all their tragedies will afford us examples of the like nature.

''Tis true they have kept the continuity or, as you called it, *liaison des scenes* somewhat better: two do not perpetually come in together, talk, and go out together, and other two succeed them and do the same throughout the act, which the English call by the name of single scenes. But the reason is because they have seldom above two or three scenes, properly so called, in every act; for it is to be accounted a new scene not only every time the stage is empty, but every person who enters, though to others, makes it so because he introduces a new business. Now the plots of their plays being narrow and the persons few, one of their acts was written in a less compass than one of our well-wrought scenes; and yet they are often deficient even in this. To go no further than Terence, you find in the *Eunuch* Antipho entering single in the midst of the third act, after Chremes and Pythias were gone off. In the same play you have likewise Dorias beginning the fourth act alone; and after she has made a relation of what was done at the Soldier's entertainment (which by the way was very inartificial, because she was presumed to speak directly to the audience, and to acquaint them with what was necessary to be known, but yet should have been so contrived by the poet as to have been told by persons of the drama to one another, and so by them to have come to the knowledge of the people), she quits the stage, and Phaedria enters next, alone likewise. He also gives you an account of himself, and of his returning from the country, in monologue, to which unnatural way of narration Terence is subject in all his plays. In his *Adelphi*, or Brothers, Syrus and Demea enter after the scene was broken by the departure of Sostrata, Geta, and Canthara; and indeed you can scarce look into any of his comedies, where you will not presently discover the same interruption.

'But as they have failed both in laying of their plots and in the management, swerving from the rules of their own art by misrepresenting nature to us, in which they have ill satisfied one intention of a play, which was delight, so in the instructive part they have erred worse. Instead of punishing vice and rewarding virtue, they have often shown a prosperous wickedness and an unhappy piety. They have set before us a bloody image of revenge in Medea, and given her dragons to convey her safe from punishment. A Priam and Astyanax murdered, and Cassandra ravished, and the lust and murder ending in the victory of him who acted them. In short, there is no indecorum in any of our modern plays which, if I would excuse, I could not shadow with some authority from the ancients.

'And one further note of them let me leave you. Tragedies and comedies were not writ then as they are now, promiscuously, by the same person; but he who found his genius bending to the one never attempted the other way. This is so plain that I need not instance to you that Aristophanes, Plautus, Terence, never any of them writ a tragedy. Aeschylus, Euripides, Sophocles, and Seneca, never meddled with comedy. The sock and buskin were not worn by the same poet. Having then so much care to excel in one kind, very little is to be pardoned them if they miscarried in it; and this would lead me to the consideration of their wit had not Crites given me sufficient warning not to be too bold in my judgement of it; because the languages being dead, and many of the customs and little accidents on which it depended lost to us, we are not competent judges of it. But though I grant that here and there we may miss the application of a proverb or a custom, yet a thing well said will be wit in all languages; and though it may lose something in the translation, yet to him who reads it in the original, 'tis still the same. He has an idea of its excellency, though it cannot pass from his mind into any other expression or words than those in which he finds it. When Phaedria – in the *Eunuch* – had a command from his mistress to be absent two days and, encouraging himself to go through with it, said: *Tandem ego non illa caream, si opus sit, vel totum triduum?*[1] Parmeno, to mock the softness of his master, lifting up his hands and eyes, cries out as it were in admiration: *Hui! universum triduum!*[2] the elegancy of which *universum*, though it cannot be rendered in our language, yet leaves an impression on our souls. But this happens seldom in him, in Plautus oftener, who is infinitely too bold in his metaphors and coining words; out of which many times his wit is nothing, which questionless was one reason why Horace falls upon him so severely in those verses:

> *Sed proavi nostri Plautinos et numeros, et*
> *Laudavere sales, nimium patienter utrumque*
> *Ne dicam stolide.*[3]

1. Wouldn't I be prepared to be without her for a whole weekend, even, if necessary? (Terence, *Eunuchus* 2. 1. 17.)
2. What! An entire weekend! (*Ibid.* 2. 1. 18.)
3. But our great-grandfathers praised Plautus' verse-rhythms and his wit; in both cases too complacently – not to say with excessive stupidity. (*Ars Poetica* 270–2.)

For Horace himself was cautious to obtrude a new word on his readers, and makes custom and common use the best measure of receiving it into our writings:

> *Multa renascentur quae nunc cecidere, cadentque;*
> *Quae nunc sunt honore in vocabula, si volet usus,*
> *Quem penes, arbitrium est, et jus, et norma loquendi.*[1]

'The not observing this rule is that which the world has blamed in our satirist, Cleveland; to express a thing hard and unnaturally is his new way of elocution. 'Tis true, no poet but may sometimes use a catachresis; Virgil does it:

> *Mistaque ridenti colocasia fundet acantho*[2]

in his eclogue of Pollio; and in his seventh Aeneid,

> *mirantur et undae,*
> *Miratur nemus, insuetum fulgentia longe,*
> *Scuta virum fluvio, pictasque; innare carinas.*[3]

And Ovid once so modestly, that he asks leave to do it:

> *Si verbo audacia detur*
> *Haud metuam summi dixisse Palatia coeli.*[4]

calling the court of Jupiter by the name of Augustus his palace, though in another place he is more bold, where he says, *et longas visent Capitolia pompas.*[5] But to do this

1. Many words which have now fallen out of use will be reborn, and many now prominent will disappear, if usage (which owns the right to decide, and the law, and the canons of speech) so choose. (*Ars Poetica* 70–2.)
2. The earth will yield, together and in profusion, the bean and the smiling acanthus. (*Eclogues* 4. 20.)
3. The waves, and the woods too, wonder at the unaccustomed sight of men's shields flashing far over the stream, and man-made craft afloat thereon. (*Aeneid* 8. 91–3.)
4. If I may speak so boldly, I should not hesitate to call it the Palace of the highest heaven. (*Metamorphoses* 1. 176.)
5. And the Capitol shall behold long processions. (*Metamorphoses* 1. 561.)

always and never be able to write a line without it, though it may be admired by some few pedants, will not pass upon those who know that wit is best conveyed to us in the most easy language; and is most to be admired when a great thought comes dressed in words so commonly received that it is understood by the meanest apprehensions, as the best meat is the most easily digested. But we cannot read a verse of Cleveland's without making a face at it, as if every word were a pill to swallow; he gives us many times a hard nut to break our teeth without a kernel for our pains. So that there is this difference betwixt his Satires and Doctor Donne's: that the one gives us deep thoughts in common language though rough cadence; the other gives us common thoughts in abstruse words. 'Tis true, in some places his wit is independent of his words, as in that of the Rebel Scot:

Had Cain been Scot God would have changed his doom:
Not forced him wander but confined him home.

Si sic omnia dixisset![1] This is wit in all languages: 'tis like Mercury, never to be lost or killed. And so that other:

For beauty, like white powder, makes no noise,
And yet the silent hypocrite destroys.

You see the last line is highly metaphorical, but it is so soft and gentle, that it does not shock us as we read it.

'But, to return from whence I have digressed, to the consideration of the ancients' writing and their wit (of which by this time you will grant us in some measure to be fit judges). Though I see many excellent thoughts in Seneca, yet he of them who had a genius most proper for the stage was Ovid; he had a way of writing so fit to stir up a pleasing admiration and concernment, which are the objects of

1. Had he but expressed everything thus!

a tragedy, and to show the various movements of a soul combating betwixt two different passions, that, had he lived in our age, or in his own could have writ with our advantages, no man but must have yielded to him; and therefore I am confident the *Medea* is none of his: for, though I esteem it for the gravity and sententiousness of it, which he himself concludes to be suitable to a tragedy, *Omne genus scripti gravitate tragedia vincit,*[1] yet it moves not my soul enough to judge that he, who in the epic way wrote things so near the drama as the story of Myrrha, of Caunus and Biblis, and the rest, should stir up no more concernment where he most endeavoured it. The masterpiece of Seneca I hold to be that scene in the *Troades*, where Ulysses is seeking for Astyanax to kill him. There you see the tenderness of a mother so represented in Andromache that it raises compassion to a high degree in the reader, and bears the nearest resemblance of any thing in the tragedies of the ancients to the excellent scenes of passion in Shakespeare, or in Fletcher: for love-scenes you will find few among them. Their tragic poets dealt not with that soft passion, but with lust, cruelty, revenge, ambition, and those bloody actions they produced, which were more capable of raising horror than compassion in an audience: leaving love untouched, whose gentleness would have tempered them; which is the most frequent of all the passions, and which, being the private concernment of every person, is soothed by viewing its own image in a public entertainment.

'Among their comedies, we find a scene or two of tenderness, and that where you would least expect it, in Plautus; but to speak generally, their lovers say little, when they see each other, but *anima mea, vita mea*;[2] Ζωὴ καὶ ψυχῆ,[3] as

1. Of all kinds of literature, Tragedy is the most solemn and elevated. (Ovid, *Tristia* 2. 381.)
2. My soul; my life.   3. Life and Soul. (Juvenal 6. 195.)

the women in Juvenal's time used to cry out in the fury of their kindness. Any sudden gust of passion (as an ecstasy of love in an unexpected meeting) cannot better be expressed than in a word and a sigh, breaking one another. Nature is dumb on such occasions, and to make her speak, would be to represent her unlike herself. But there are a thousand other concernments of lovers, as jealousies, complaints, contrivances, and the like, where not to open their minds at large to each other, were to be wanting to their own love, and to the expectation of the audience; who watch the movements of their minds, as much as the changes of their fortunes. For the imaging of the first is properly the work of a poet, the latter he borrows from the historian.'

Eugenius was proceeding in that part of his discourse, when Crites interrupted him. 'I see,' said he, 'Eugenius and I are never like to have this question decided betwixt us; for he maintains the moderns have acquired a new perfection in writing; I can only grant they have altered the mode of it. Homer described his heroes men of great appetites, lovers of beef broiled upon the coals, and good fellows; contrary to the practice of the French Romances, whose heroes neither eat, nor drink, nor sleep, for love. Virgil makes Aeneas a bold avower of his own virtues:

Sum pius Aeneas, fama super aethera notus;[1]

which, in the civility of our poets, is the character of a fanfaron or Hector: for with us the knight takes occasion to walk out, or sleep, to avoid the vanity of telling his own story, which the trusty squire is ever to perform for him. So in their love-scenes, of which Eugenius spoke last, the ancients were more hearty, we more talkative: they writ love as it was then the mode to make it; and I will grant

1. I am Aeneas the Dutiful, known by repute even beyond the skies. (*Aeneid* 1. 378–9.)

thus much to Eugenius, that perhaps one of their poets, had he lived in our age,

Si foret hoc nostrum fato delapsus in aevum,[1]

(as Horace says of Lucilius) he had altered many things; not that they were not natural before, but that he might accommodate himself to the age in which he lived. Yet in the meantime, we are not to conclude anything rashly against those great men, but preserve to them the dignity of masters, and give that honour to their memories, *quos Libitina sacravit,*[2] part of which we expect may be paid to us in future times.'

This moderation of Crites, as it was pleasing to all the company, so it put an end to that dispute; which Eugenius, who seemed to have the better of the argument, would urge no farther: but Lisideius, after he had acknowledged himself of Eugenius his opinion concerning the ancients, yet told him he had forborne till his discourse were ended to ask him why he preferred the English plays above those of other nations? and whether we ought not to submit our stage to the exactness of our next neighbours?

'Though,' said Eugenius, 'I am at all times ready to defend the honour of my country against the French, and to maintain we are as well able to vanquish them with our pens as our ancestors have been with their swords, yet, if you please,' added he, looking upon Neander, 'I will commit this cause to my friend's management; his opinion of our plays is the same with mine: and besides, there is no reason that Crites and I, who have now left the stage, should re-enter so suddenly upon it; which is against the laws of comedy.'

1. If he had been fated to come down to this age of ours. (*Satires* 1. 10. 68.)
2. Consecrated by decease. (Horace, *Epistles* 2. 1. 49.)

'If the question had been stated,' replied Lisideius, 'who had writ best, the French or English, forty years ago, I should have been of your opinion, and adjudged the honour to our own nation; but since that time,' said he, turning towards Neander, 'we have been so long together bad Englishmen that we had not leisure to be good poets. Beaumont, Fletcher, and Jonson (who were only capable of bringing us to that degree of perfection which we have) were just then leaving the world; as if in an age of so much horror, wit and those milder studies of humanity had no farther business among us. But the muses, who ever follow peace, went to plant in another country. It was then that the great Cardinal of Richelieu began to take them into his protection, and that, by his encouragement, Corneille and some other Frenchmen reformed their theatre, which before was as much below ours as it now surpasses it and the rest of Europe. But because Crites in his discourse for the ancients has prevented me, by observing many rules of the stage which the moderns have borrowed from them, I shall only, in short, demand of you whether you are not convinced that of all nations the French have best observed them? In the unity of time you find them so scrupulous that it yet remains a dispute among their poets whether the artificial day of twelve hours more or less be not meant by Aristotle, rather than the natural one of twenty-four; and consequently, whether all plays ought not to be reduced into that compass? This I can testify, that in all their dramas writ within these last twenty years and upwards, I have not observed any that have extended the time to thirty hours. In the unity of place they are full as scrupulous, for many of their critics limit it to that very spot of ground where the play is supposed to begin; none of them exceed the compass of the same town or city.

'The unity of action in all their plays is yet more conspicuous, for they do not burden them with underplots as the English do; which is the reason why many scenes of our tragi-comedies carry on a design that is nothing of kin to the main plot; and that we see two distinct webs in a play, like those in ill-wrought stuffs; and two actions, that is two plays carried on together to the confounding of the audience, who, before they are warm in their concernments for one part, are diverted to another, and by that means espouse the interest of neither. From hence likewise it arises that the one half of our actors are not known to the other. They keep their distances as if they were Montagues and Capulets, and seldom begin an acquaintance till the last scene of the fifth act, when they are all to meet upon the stage. There is no theatre in the world has anything so absurd as the English tragi-comedy. 'Tis a drama of our own invention, and the fashion of it is enough to proclaim it so; here a course of mirth, there another of sadness and passion, and a third of honour and a duel. Thus in two hours and a half we run through all the fits of Bedlam. The French affords you as much variety on the same day, but they do it not so unseasonably, or *mal à propos*, as we. Our poets present you the play and the farce together; and our stages still retain somewhat of the original civility of the Red Bull[1]:

Atque ursum et pugiles media inter carmina poscunt.[2]

'The end of tragedies or serious plays, says Aristotle, is to beget admiration, compassion or concernment; but are not mirth and compassion things incompatible? and is it not evident that the poet must of necessity destroy the former by intermingling of the latter? that is, he must ruin

1. The *Red Bull* in St John's Street, Clerkenwell, was used for plays, drolls, and other diversions.
2. And in the middle of a poetic play, call for boxers and a bear. (Horace, *Epistles* 2. 1. 186.)

the sole end and object of his tragedy to introduce some-
what that is forced into it and is not of the body of it.
Would you not think that physician mad who having pre-
scribed a purge should immediately order you to take
restringents?

'But to leave our plays and return to theirs: I have noted
one great advantage they have had in the plotting of their
tragedies; that is they are always grounded upon some
known history, according to that of Horace, *Ex noto fictum
carmen sequar*,[1] and in that they have so imitated the
ancients that they have surpassed them. For the ancients,
as was observed before, took for the foundation of their
plays some poetical fiction such as under that consideration
could move but little concernment in the audience because
they already knew the event of it. But the French goes
farther:

> *Atque ita mentitur; sic veris falsa remiscet,*
> *Primo ne medium, medio ne discrepet imum.*[2]

He so interweaves truth with probable fiction, that he puts
a pleasing fallacy upon us, mends the intrigues of fate and
dispenses with the severity of history to reward that virtue
which has been rendered to us there unfortunate. Some-
times the story has left the success so doubtful that the
writer is free, by the privilege of a poet, to take that
which of two or more relations will best suit with his
design, as, for example, in the death of Cyrus, whom
Justin and some others report to have perished in the
Scythian war but Xenophon affirms to have died in his bed
of extreme old age. Nay more, when the event is past

1. I should pursue my poetic invention upon a basis of known themes.
   (*Ars Poetica* 240.)
2. And thus he spins fictions; so does he mingle the false with the
   true, that the middle may not clash with the beginning, nor the
   end with the middle. (*Ars Poetica* 151–2.)

dispute even then we are willing to be deceived, and the poet, if he contrives it with appearance of truth, has all the audience of his party, at least during the time his play is acting; so naturally we are kind to virtue, when our own interest is not in question, that we take it up as the general concernment of mankind. On the other side, if you consider the historical plays of Shakespeare, they are rather so many chronicles of kings, or the business many times of thirty or forty years, cramped into a representation of two hours and a half, which is not to imitate or paint nature but rather to draw her in miniature; to take her in little; to look upon her through the wrong end of a perspective, and receive her images not only much less but infinitely more imperfect than the life. This, instead of making a play delightful, renders it ridiculous.

Quodcunque ostendis mihi sic, incredulus odi.[1]

For the spirit of man cannot be satisfied but with truth, or at least verisimility; and a poem is to contain, if not τὰ ἔτυμα,[2] yet ἐτύμοισιν ὁμοῖα,[3] as one of the Greek poets has expressed it.

'Another thing in which the French differ from us and from the Spaniards is that they do not embarrass or cumber themselves with too much plot; they only represent so much of a story as will constitute one whole and great action sufficient for a play; we, who undertake more, do but multiply adventures: which, not being produced from one another, as effects from causes, but barely following, constitute many actions in the drama, and consequently make it many plays.

1. I disbelieve and loathe whatever is exhibited to me in this fashion. (Horace, *Ars Poetica* 188.)
2. The truth.
3. Things similar to the truth.

'But by pursuing closely one argument, which is not cloyed with many turns, the French have gained more liberty for verse, in which they write; they have leisure to dwell on a subject which deserves it; and to represent the passions (which we have acknowledged to be the poet's work) without being hurried from one thing to another, as we are in the plays of Calderon, which we have seen lately upon our theatres, under the name of Spanish plots.[1] I have taken notice but of one tragedy of ours, whose plot has that uniformity and unity of design in it which I have commended in the French; and that is *Rollo*[2], or rather, under the name of Rollo, the Story of Bassianus and Geta in Herodian; there indeed the plot is neither large nor intricate, but just enough to fill the minds of the audience, not to cloy them. Besides, you see it founded upon the truth of history, only the time of the action is not reduceable to the strictness of the rules; and you see in some places a little farce mingled, which is below the dignity of the other parts. And in this all our poets are extremely peccant: even Ben Jonson himself, in *Sejanus* and *Catiline* has given us this oleo of a play, this unnatural mixture of comedy and tragedy, which to me sounds just as ridiculously as the history of David with the merry humours of Golia's. In *Sejanus* you may take notice of the scene betwixt Livia and the physician, which is a pleasant satire upon the artificial helps of beauty: in *Catiline* you may see the parliament of women; the little envies of them to one another; and all that passes betwixt Curio and Fulvia: scenes admirable in their kind, but of an ill mingle with the rest.

1. Sir Samuel Tuke's comedy of *The Adventures of Five Hours*, 1663, and the Earl of Bristol's *Elvira, or the Worst not always True*, 1667, were both adaptations from plays by Calderon.
2. John Fletcher's tragedy of *The Bloody Brother, or, Rollo, Duke of Normandy*, 1616 (?).

'But I return again to the French writers who, as I have said, do not burden themselves too much with plot, which has been reproached to them by an ingenious person of our nation as a fault, for he says they commonly make but one person considerable in a play; they dwell on him and his concernments while the rest of the persons are only subservient to set him off. If he intends this by it, that there is one person in the play who is of greater dignity than the rest, he must tax not only theirs but those of the ancients and, which he would be loath to do, the best of ours; for 'tis impossible but that one person must be more conspicuous in it than any other, and consequently the greatest share in the action must devolve on him. We see it so in the management of all affairs. Even in the most equal aristocracy the balance cannot be so justly poised but someone will be superior to the rest, either in parts, fortune, interest, or the consideration of some glorious exploit, which will reduce the greatest part of business into his hands.

'But if he would have us to imagine that in exalting one character the rest of them are neglected, and that all of them have not some share or other in the action of the play, I desire him to produce any of Corneille's tragedies wherein every person (like so many servants in a well-governed family) has not some employment, and who is not necessary to the carrying on of the plot, or at least to your understanding it.

'There are indeed some protatic persons[1] in the ancients whom they make use of in their plays either to hear or give the relation; but the French avoid this with great address, making their narrations only to or by such who are some way interested in the main design. And now I am speaking of relations, I cannot take a fitter opportunity to add this

1. Characters who appear only in the introductory part of a play.

in favour of the French, that they often use them with better judgement and more *à propos* than the English do. Not that I commend narrations in general, but there are two sorts of them. One, of those things which are antecedent to the play, and are related to make the conduct of it more clear to us. But 'tis a fault to choose such subjects for the stage as will force us on that rock, because we see they are seldom listened to by the audience, and that is many times the ruin of the play; for, being once let pass without attention, the audience can never recover themselves to understand the plot; and indeed it is somewhat unreasonable that they should be put to so much trouble, as, that to comprehend what passes in their sight, they must have recourse to what was done, perhaps, ten or twenty years ago.

'But there is another sort of relations, that is of things happening in the action of the play and supposed to be done behind the scenes. And this is many times both convenient and beautiful, for by it the French avoid the tumult to which we are subject in England, by representing duels, battles, and the like, which renders our stage too like the theatres where they fight prizes. For what is more ridiculous than to represent an army with a drum and five men behind it, all which the hero of the other side is to drive in before him; or to see a duel fought and one slain with two or three thrusts of the foils, which we know are so blunted that we might give a man an hour to kill another in good earnest with them.

'I have observed that in all our tragedies the audience cannot forbear laughing when the actors are to die; 'tis the most comic part of the whole play. All *passions* may be lively represented on the stage if to the well-writing of them the actor supplies a good commanded voice, and limbs that move easily and without stiffness; but there are many *actions* which can never be imitated to a just height. Dying especially is a thing which none but a Roman gladiator could naturally perform on the stage when he did not imitate or represent but do it; and therefore it is better to omit the representation of it.

'The words of a good writer which describe it lively will make a deeper impression of belief in us than all the actor can insinuate into us when he seems to fall dead before us; as a poet in the description of a beautiful garden, or a meadow, will please our imagination more than the place itself can please our sight. When we see death represented we are convinced it is but fiction, but when we hear it related, our eyes (the strongest witnesses) are wanting, which might have undeceived us; and we are all willing to favour the sleight when the poet does not too grossly impose on us. They, therefore, who imagine these relations would make no concernment in the audience are deceived by confounding them with the other, which are of things antecedent to the play. Those are made often in cold blood (as I may say) to the audience; but these are warmed with our concernments, which were before awakened in the play. What the philosophers say of motion, that when it is once begun it continues of itself and will do so to eternity without some stop put to it, is clearly true on this occasion; the soul being already moved with the characters and fortunes of those imaginary persons continues going of its own accord, and we are no more weary to hear what becomes of them when they are not on the stage than we are to listen to the news of an absent mistress. But it is objected, that if one part of the play may be related then why not all? I answer, some parts of the action are more fit to be represented, some to be related. Corneille says judiciously, that the poet is not obliged to expose to view all particular actions which conduce to the principal. He ought to select such of them to be seen which will appear with the greatest beauty, either by the magnificence of the show, or the vehemence of passions which they produce, or some other charm which they have in them, and let the rest arrive to the audience by narration. 'Tis a great mistake in us to believe the French present no part of the action on the stage: every alteration or crossing of a design, every new-sprung passion, and turn of it, is a part of the action, and much the noblest, except we conceive nothing to be action till the players come to blows; as if the painting of the hero's mind were not more properly the poet's work than the strength of his body. Nor does this anything contradict the opinion of Horace, where he tells us,

> *Segnius irritant animos demissa per aurem*
> *Quam quae sunt oculis subjecta fidelibus.*[1]

For he says immediately after,

> *Non tamen intus*
> *Digna geri promes in scenam, multaque tolles*
> *Ex oculis, quae nox narret facundia praesens.*[2]

Among which many he recounts some:

> *Nec pueros coram populo Medea trucidet,*
> *Aut in avem Procne mutetur, Cadmus in anguem; &c.*[3]

That is, those actions which by reason of their cruelty will cause aversion in us, or by reason of their impossibility

1. That which we hear instilled into the ears arouses our minds more slowly than what is presented before our eyes, which we trust. (*Ars Poetica* 180–1.)
2. Yet you will not bring upon the scene actions that ought to be performed behind the scenes, and you will remove from sight many things which can be presently related by the eloquence of a witness. (*Ibid.* 182–3.)
3. Nor must Medea slay her children in the sight of the audience, or Procne be changed to a bird thus, or Cadmus to a serpent. (*Ibid.* 185, 187.)

unbelief, ought either wholly to be avoided by a poet, or only delivered by narration. To which we may have leave to add such as to avoid tumult (as was before hinted) or to reduce the plot into a more reasonable compass of time, or for defect of beauty in them, are rather to be related than presented to the eye. Examples of all these kinds are frequent, not only among all the ancients, but in the best received of our English poets. We find Ben Jonson using them in his *Magnetic Lady*, where one comes out from dinner, and relates the quarrels and disorders of it to save the undecent appearance of them on the stage, and to abbreviate the story; and this in express imitation of Terence, who had done the same before him in his *Eunuch*, where Pythias makes the like relation of what had happened within at the Soldier's entertainment. The relations likewise of Sejanus's death, and the prodigies before it, are remarkable; the one of which was hid from sight to avoid the horror and tumult of the representation; the other to shun the introducing of things impossible to be believed. In that excellent play, *The King and no King*, Fletcher goes yet farther; for the whole unravelling of the plot is done by narration in the fifth act, after the manner of the ancients; and it moves great concernment in the audience, though it be only a relation of what was done many years before the play. I could multiply other instances, but these are sufficient to prove that there is no error in choosing a subject which requires this sort of narrations; in the ill management of them, there may.

'But I find I have been too long in this discourse since the French have many other excellencies not common to us; as that you never see any of their plays end with a conversion, or simple change of will, which is the ordinary way which our poets use to end theirs. It shows little art in the conclusion of a dramatic poem when they who have hindered the felicity during the four acts desist from it in the fifth without some powerful cause to take them off their design; and though I deny not but such reasons may be found, yet it is a path that is cautiously to be trod, and the poet is to be sure he convinces the audience that the motive is strong enough. As for example, the conversion of the usurer in *The Scornful Lady* seems to me a little forced; for being an usurer, which implies a lover of money to the highest degree of covetousness (and such the poet has represented him) the account he gives for the sudden change is, that he has been duped by the wild young fellow, which in reason might render him more wary another time, and make him punish himself with harder fare and coarser clothes to get up again what he had lost: but that he should look on it as a judgement and so repent, we may expect to hear in a sermon, but I should never endure it in a play.

'I pass by this. Neither will I insist on the care they take that no person after his first entrance shall ever appear but the business which brings him upon the stage shall be evident; which rule, if observed, must needs render all the events in the play more natural. For there you see the probability of every accident in the cause that produced it, and that which appears chance in the play will seem so reasonable to you that you will there find it almost necessary; so that in the exit of the actor you have a clear account of his purpose and design in the next entrance (though, if the scene be well wrought, the event will commonly deceive you). For there is nothing so absurd, says Corneille, as for an actor to leave the stage only because he has no more to say.

'I should now speak of the beauty of their rhyme, and the just reason I have to prefer that way of writing in tragedies before ours in blank verse; but because it is partly received by us, and therefore not altogether peculiar to them, I will say no more of it in relation to their plays. For our own, I doubt not but it will exceedingly beautify them, and I can see but one reason why it should not generally obtain, that is because our poets write so ill in it. This indeed may prove a more prevailing argument than all others which are used to destroy it, and therefore I am only troubled when great and judicious poets, and those who are acknowledged such, have writ or spoke against it; as for others they are to be answered by that one sentence of an ancient author: *Sed ut primo ad conse-quendos eos quos priores ducimus accendimur, ita ubi aut praeteriri, aut aequari eos posse desperavimus, studium cum spe senescit: quod, scilicet, assequi non potest, sequi desinit; praeteritoque eo in quo eminere non possumus, aliquid in quo nitamur, conquirimus.'* [1]

Lisideius concluded in this manner; and Neander after a little pause thus answered him:

'I shall grant Lisideius without much dispute a great part of what he has urged against us; for I acknowledge that the French contrive their plots more regularly, and observe the laws of comedy and decorum of the stage (to speak generally) with more exactness than the English. Farther, I deny not but he has taxed us justly in some irregularities of ours which he has mentioned; yet, after all, I am of opinion that neither our faults nor their virtues are considerable enough to place them above us.

'For the lively imitation of nature being in the definition

1. But as at the beginning we are fired to follow those whom we take to be the leaders, so, when we have despaired of the possibility of outrunning or even drawing level with them, our enthusiasm fades along with our hopes; what plainly cannot be overtaken ceases even to be followed; and forgoing that in which we are unable to distinguish ourselves, we look for something else to strive at. (*Velleius Paterculus* 1. 17.)

of a play, those which best fulfil that law ought to be esteemed superior to the others. 'Tis true, those beauties of the French poesy are such as will raise perfection higher where it is, but are not sufficient to give it where it is not. They are indeed the beauties of a statue, but not of a man because not animated with the soul of poesy, which is imitation of humour and passions; and this Lisideius himself, or any other, however biased to their party, cannot but acknowledge if he will either compare the humours of our comedies or the characters of our serious plays with theirs. He who will look upon theirs which have been written till these last ten years or thereabouts will find it a hard matter to pick out two or three passable humours amongst them. Corneille himself, their arch-poet, what has he produced except *The Liar*? and you know how it was cried up in France; but when it came upon the English stage, though well translated, and that part of Dorant acted to so much advantage as I am confident it never received in its own country, the most favourable to it would not put it in competition with many of Fletcher's or Ben Jonson's. In the rest of Corneille's comedies you have little humour; he tells you himself his way is first to show two lovers in good intelligence with each other; in the working up of the play to embroil them by some mistake, and in the latter end to clear it, and reconcile them.

'But of late years Molière, the younger Corneille, Quinault, and some others, have been imitating afar off the quick turns and graces of the English stage. They have mixed their serious plays with mirth like our tragi-come-dies, since the death of Cardinal Richelieu, which Lisideius and many others not observing have commended that in them for a virtue which they themselves no longer practise. Most of their new plays are like some of ours derived from the Spanish novels. There is scarce one of them without a veil, and a trusty Diego, who drolls much after the rate of *The Adventures*[1]. But their humours, if I may grace them with that name, are so thin-sown that never above one of them comes up in any play. I dare take upon me to find more variety of them in some one play of Ben Jonson's than in all theirs together; as he who has seen *The Alchemist*, *The Silent Woman*, or *Bartholomew Fair*, cannot but acknowledge with me.

'I grant the French have performed what was possible on the groundwork of the Spanish plays; what was pleasant before, they have made regular; but there is not above one good play to be writ on all those plots; they are too much alike to please often, which we need not the experience of our own stage to justify. As for their new way of mingling mirth with serious plot, I do not with Lisideius condemn the thing, though I cannot approve their manner of doing it. He tells us we cannot so speedily recollect ourselves after a scene of great passion and concernment as to pass to another of mirth and humour and to enjoy it with any relish; but why should he imagine the soul of man more heavy than his senses? Does not the eye pass from an unpleasant object to a pleasant in a much shorter time than is required to this? and does not the unpleasantness of the first commend the beauty of the latter? The old rule of logic might have convinced him that contraries when placed near set off each other. A continued gravity keeps the spirit too much bent; we must refresh it sometimes, as we bait in a journey, that we may go on with greater ease. A scene of mirth mixed with tragedy has the same effect upon us which our music has betwixt the acts, which we find a relief to us from the best plots and language of the stage if the discourses have been long. I must therefore have

1. See above, p. 179, n. 1.

stronger arguments ere I am convinced that compassion and mirth in the same subject destroy each other, and in the meantime cannot but conclude, to the honour of our nation, that we have invented, increased, and perfected a more pleasant way of writing for the stage than was ever known to the ancients or moderns of any nation, which is tragi-comedy.

'And this leads me to wonder why Lisideius and many others should cry up the barrenness of the French plots above the variety and copiousness of the English. Their plots are single; they carry on one design which is pushed forward by all the actors, every scene in the play contributing and moving towards it. Our plays, besides the main design, have under-plots, or by-concernments of less considerable persons, and intrigues which are carried on with the motion of the main plot; as they say the orb of the fixed stars and those of the planets, though they have motions of their own, are whirled about by the motion of the *primum mobile* in which they are contained. That similitude expresses much of the English stage; for if contrary motions may be found in nature to agree; if a planet can go east and west at the same time, one way by virtue of his own motion, the other by the force of the first mover; it will not be difficult to imagine how the under-plot, which is only different not contrary to the great design, may naturally be conducted along with it.

'Eugenius has already shown us from the confession of the French poets, that the unity of action is sufficiently preserved if all the imperfect actions of the play are conducing to the main design. But when those petty intrigues of a play are so ill ordered that they have no coherence with the other, I must grant that Lisideius has reason to tax that want of due connexion; for co-ordination in a play is as dangerous and unnatural as in a state. In the meantime he must acknowledge our variety, if well ordered, will afford a greater pleasure to the audience.

'As for his other argument, that by pursuing one single theme they gain an advantage to express and work up the passions, I wish any example he could bring from them would make it good; for I confess their verses are to me the coldest I have ever read. Neither indeed is it possible for them, in the way they take, so to express passion as that the effects of it should appear in the concernment of an audience, their speeches being so many declamations which tire us with the length; so that instead of persuading us to grieve for their imaginary heroes, we are concerned for our own trouble, as we are in tedious visits of bad company; we are in pain till they are gone. When the French stage came to be reformed by Cardinal Richelieu those long harangues were introduced to comply with the gravity of a churchman. Look upon the *Cinna* and the *Pompey*; they are not so properly to be called plays as long discourses of reason of state; and *Polyeucte* in matters of religion is as solemn as the long stops upon our organs.[1] Since that time it is grown into a custom, and their actors speak by the hourglass like our parsons; nay, they account it the grace of their parts, and think themselves disparaged by the poet if they may not twice or thrice in a play entertain the audience with a speech of an hundred lines. I deny not but this may suit well enough with the French; for as we, who are a more sullen people, come to be diverted at our plays, so they who are of an airy and gay temper come thither to make themselves more serious. And this I conceive to be one reason why comedies are more pleasing to us and tragedies to them. But to speak generally, it cannot be denied that short speeches and replies are more apt to move

1. These three plays, *Cinna*, 1643, *La Mort de Pompée*, 1644, and *Polyeucte Martyr*, 1643, were by Pierre Corneille.

the passions and beget concernment in us than the other; for it is unnatural for any one in a gust of passion to speak long together, or for another in the same condition to suffer him, without interruption. Grief and passion are like floods raised in little brooks by a sudden rain; they are quickly up, and if the concernment be poured unexpectedly in upon us it overflows us; but a long sober shower gives them leisure to run out as they came in without troubling the ordinary current. As for comedy, repartee is one of its chiefest graces. The greatest pleasure of the audience is a chase of wit kept up on both sides and swiftly managed. And this our forefathers, if not we, have had in Fletcher's plays, to a much higher degree of perfection than the French poets can reasonably hope to reach.

'There is another part of Lisideius his discourse in which he has rather excused our neighbours than commended them; that is, for aiming only to make one person considerable in their plays. 'Tis very true what he has urged, that one character in all plays, even without the poet's care, will have advantage of all the others; and that the design of the whole drama will chiefly depend on it. But this hinders not that there may be more shining characters in the play; many persons of a second magnitude, nay, some so very near, so almost equal to the first, that greatness may be opposed to greatness, and all the persons be made considerable not only by their quality but their action. 'Tis evident that the more the persons are the greater will be the variety of the plot. If then the parts are managed so regularly that the beauty of the whole be kept entire, and that the variety become not a perplexed and confused mass of accidents, you will find it infinitely pleasing to be led in a labyrinth of design, where you see some of your way before you yet discern not the end till you arrive at it. And that all this is practicable, I can produce for examples many of our English plays: as *The Maid's Tragedy*, *The Alchemist*, *The Silent Woman*; I was going to have named *The Fox*, but that the unity of design seems not exactly observed in it; for there appear two actions in the play; the first naturally ending with the fourth act, the second forced from it in the fifth, which yet is the less to be condemned in him, because the disguise of Volpone, though it suited not with his character as a crafty or covetous person, agreed well enough with that of a voluptuary; and by it the poet gained the end at which he aimed, the punishment of vice, and the reward of virtue, both which that disguise produced. So that to judge equally of it, it was an excellent fifth act, but not so naturally proceeding from the former.

'But to leave this, and pass to the latter part of Lisideius his discourse which concerns relations. I must acknowledge with him that the French have reason to hide that part of the action which would occasion too much tumult on the stage, and to choose rather to have it made known by narration to the audience. Farther, I think it very convenient, for the reasons he has given, that all incredible actions were removed; but, whether custom has so insinuated itself into our countrymen, or nature has so formed them to fierceness, I know not, but they will scarcely suffer combats and other objects of horror to be taken from them. And, indeed, the indecency of tumults is all which can be objected against fighting: for why may not our imagination as well suffer itself to be deluded with the probability of it as with any other thing in the play? For my part, I can with as great ease persuade myself that the blows are given in good earnest as I can that they who strike them are kings or princes, or those persons which they represent. For objects of incredibility I would be satisfied from Lisideius, whether we have any so removed from all appearance of truth, as are those of Corneille's *Andromède*?[1] A play which has been frequented the most of any he has writ? If the Perseus, or the son of an heathen god, the Pegasus, and the Monster were not capable to choke a strong belief, let him blame any representation of ours hereafter. Those indeed were objects of delight; yet the reason is the same as to the probability: for he makes it not a ballet or masque, but a play, which is to resemble truth. But for death, that it ought not to be represented, I have besides the arguments alleged by Lisideius the authority of Ben Jonson, who has forborne it in his tragedies; for both the death of Sejanus and Catiline are related: though in the latter I cannot but observe one irregularity of that great poet; he has removed the scene in the same act from Rome to Catiline's army, and from thence again to Rome; and besides, has allowed a very inconsiderable time, after Catiline's speech, for the striking of the battle, and the return of Petreius, who is to relate the event of it to the senate: which I should not animadvert on him, who was otherwise a painful observer of τὸ πρέπον, or the *decorum* of the stage, if he had not used extreme severity in his judgement on the incomparable Shakespeare for the same fault. To conclude on this subject of relations; if we are to be blamed for showing too much of the action, the French are as faulty for discovering too little of it; a mean betwixt both should be observed by every judicious writer, so as the audience may neither be left unsatisfied by not seeing what is beautiful, or shocked by beholding what is either incredible or undecent. I hope I have already proved in this discourse, that though we are not altogether so punctual as the French in observing the laws of comedy, yet our errors are so few and little, and those things wherein we

1. Pierre Corneille's tragedy of *Andromède*, an elaborately staged festival piece, was published in 1651.

excel them so considerable, that we ought of right to be preferred before them. But what will Lisideius say, if they themselves acknowledge they are too strictly bounded by those laws, for breaking which he has blamed the English? I will allege Corneille's words, as I find them in the end of his discourse of the three unities: — *Il est facile aux speculatifs d'être sévères &c.* " 'Tis easy for speculative persons to judge severely; but if they would produce to public view ten or twelve pieces of this nature, they would perhaps give more latitude to the rules than I have done, when by experience they had known how much we are limited and constrained by them, and how many beauties of the stage they banished from it." To illustrate a little what he has said. By their servile observations of the unities of time and place and integrity of scenes they have brought on themselves that dearth of plot, and narrowness of imagination, which may be observed in all their plays. How many beautiful accidents might naturally happen in two or three days which cannot arrive with any probability in the compass of twenty-four hours? There is time to be allowed also for maturity of design, which amongst great and prudent persons, such as are often represented in tragedy, cannot, with any likelihood of truth, be brought to pass at so short a warning. Farther, by tying themselves strictly to the unity of place and unbroken scenes, they are forced many times to omit some beauties which cannot be shown where the act began, but might, if the scene were interrupted and the stage cleared for the persons to enter in another place; and therefore the French poets are often forced upon absurdities. For if the act begins in a chamber all the persons in the play must have some business or other to come thither or else they are not to be shown that act; and sometimes their characters are very unfitting to appear there; as, suppose it were the king's bed-chamber, yet the meanest man in the tragedy must come and dispatch his business there, rather than in the lobby or courtyard (which is fitter for him) for fear the stage should be cleared, and the scenes broken. Many times they fall by it in a greater inconvenience; for they keep their scenes unbroken and yet change the place; as in one of their newest plays,[1] where the act begins in the street. There a gentleman is to meet his friend; he sees him with his man, coming out from his father's house; they talk together, and the first goes out: the second, who is a lover, has made an appointment with his mistress; she appears at the window, and then we are to imagine the scene lies under it. This gentleman is called away, and leaves his servant with his mistress; presently her father is heard from within; the young lady is afraid the servingman should be discovered, and thrusts him into a place of safety, which is supposed to be her closet. After this, the father enters to the daughter, and now the scene is in a house; for he is seeking from one room to another for this poor Philipin, or French Diego, who is heard from within, drolling and breaking many a miserable conceit on the subject of his sad condition. In this ridiculous manner the play goes forward, the stage being never empty all the while: so that the street, the window, the houses, and the closet, are made to walk about, and the persons to stand still. Now what, I beseech you, is more easy than to write a regular French play, or more difficult than to write an irregular English one, like those of Fletcher or of Shakespeare?

'If they content themselves, as Corneille did, with some flat design, which, like an ill riddle, is found out ere it be half proposed, such plots we can make every way regular as easily as they; but whenever they endeavour to rise to any quick turns and counterturns of plot, as some of them

1. Thomas Corneille's comedy of *L'Amour à la Mode*, 1651.

have attempted, since Corneille's plays have been less in vogue, you see they write as irregularly as we, though they cover it more speciously. Hence the reason is perspicuous, why no French plays, when translated, have, or ever can succeed on the English stage. For, if you consider the plots, our own are fuller of variety; if the writing, ours are more quick and fuller of spirit; and therefore 'tis a strange mistake in those who decry the way of writing plays in verse, as if the English therein imitated the French. We have borrowed nothing from them; our plots are weaved in English looms. We endeavour therein to follow the variety and greatness of characters which are derived to us from Shakespeare and Fletcher; the copiousness and well-knitting of the intrigues we have from Jonson; and for the verse itself we have English precedents of elder date than any of Corneille's plays. Not to name our old comedies before Shakespeare, which were all writ in verse of six feet, or Alexandrines, such as the French now use, I can show in Shakespeare many scenes of rhyme together, and the like in Ben Jonson's tragedies: in *Catiline* and *Sejanus* sometimes thirty or forty lines; I mean besides the Chorus, or the monologues, which, by the way, showed Ben no enemy to this way of writing, especially if you read his *Sad Shepherd*, which goes sometimes on rhyme, sometimes on blank verse, like an horse who eases himself on trot and amble. You find him likewise commending Fletcher's pastoral of *The Faithful Shepherdess*; which is for the most part rhyme, though not refined to that purity to which it hath since been brought. And these examples are enough to clear us from a servile imitation of the French.

'But to return whence I have digressed: I dare boldly affirm these two things of the English drama. First, that we have many plays of ours as regular as any of theirs, and which, besides, have more variety of plot and characters.

And secondly, that in most of the irregular plays of Shakespeare or Fletcher (for Ben Jonson's are for the most part regular) there is a more masculine fancy and greater spirit in the writing than there is in any of the French. I could produce even in Shakespeare's and Fletcher's works some plays which are almost exactly formed, as *The Merry Wives of Windsor*, and *The Scornful Lady*. But because (generally speaking) Shakespeare, who writ first, did not perfectly observe the laws of comedy, and Fletcher, who came nearer to perfection, yet through carelessness made many faults, I will take the pattern of a perfect play from Ben Jonson, who was a careful and learned observer of the dramatic laws; and from all his comedies I shall select *The Silent Woman*, of which I will make a short examen, according to those rules which the French observe.'

As Neander was beginning to examine *The Silent Woman*, Eugenius, earnestly regarding him: 'I beseech you, Neander,' said he, 'gratify the company, and me in particular so far as before you speak of the play to give us a character of the author; and tell us frankly your opinion, whether you do not think all writers, both French and English, ought to give place to him?'

'I fear,' replied Neander, 'that in obeying your commands I shall draw some envy on myself. Besides, in performing them, it will be first necessary to speak somewhat of Shakespeare and Fletcher, his rivals in poesy; and one of them, in my opinion, at least his equal, perhaps his superior.

'To begin then with Shakespeare. He was the man who of all modern, and perhaps ancient poets, had the largest and most comprehensive soul. All the images of nature were still present to him, and he drew them not laboriously but luckily; when he describes anything, you more than see it, you feel it too. Those who accuse him to have wanted learning give him the greater commendation: he was naturally learned; he needed not the spectacles of books to read nature; he looked inwards and found her there. I cannot say he is everywhere alike; were he so, I should do him injury to compare him with the greatest of mankind. He is many times flat, insipid; his comic wit degenerating into clenches, his serious swelling into bombast. But he is always great when some great occasion is presented to him. No man can say he ever had a fit subject for his wit and did not then raise himself as high above the rest of poets:

> *Quantum lenta solent inter viburna cupressi.*[1]

The consideration of this made Mr Hales[2] of Eton say that there was no subject of which any poet ever writ but he would produce it much better done in Shakespeare. And however others are now generally preferred before him, yet the age wherein he lived, which had contemporaries with him Fletcher and Jonson, never equalled them to him in their esteem. And in the last king's court, when Ben's reputation was at highest, Sir John Suckling, and with him the greater part of the courtiers, set our Shakespeare far above him.

'Beaumont and Fletcher, of whom I am next to speak, had with the advantage of Shakespeare's wit, which was their precedent, great natural gifts, improved by study. Beaumont especially being so accurate a judge of plays that Ben Jonson while he lived submitted all his writings to his censure and, 'tis thought, used his judgement in correcting if not contriving all his plots. What value he had for him appears by the verses he writ to him; and therefore

1. As the cypresses are wont to tower above the yielding osiers. (Virgil, *Eclogues* 1. 26.)
2. John Hales (1584–1656), a Fellow of Eton.

I need speak no farther of it. The first play that brought Fletcher and him in esteem was their *Philaster*, for before that they had written two or three very unsuccessfully; as the like is reported of Ben Jonson before he writ *Every Man in his Humour*. Their plots were generally more regular than Shakespeare's, especially those which were made before Beaumont's death; and they understood and imitated the conversation of gentlemen much better, whose wild debaucheries, and quickness of wit in repartees, no poet before them could paint as they have done. Humour, which Ben Jonson derived from particular persons, they made it not their business to describe. They represented all the passions very lively, but above all love. I am apt to believe the English language in them arrived to its highest perfection; what words have since been taken in are rather superfluous than ornamental. Their plays are now the most pleasant and frequent entertainments of the stage; two of theirs being acted through the year for one of Shakespeare's or Jonson's. The reason is because there is a certain gaiety in their comedies and pathos in their more serious plays which suits generally with all men's humours. Shakespeare's language is likewise a little obsolete, and Ben Jonson's wit comes short of theirs.

'As for Jonson, to whose character I am now arrived, if we look upon him while he was himself (for his last plays were but his dotages), I think him the most learned and judicious writer which any theatre ever had. He was a most severe judge of himself as well as others. One cannot say he wanted wit but rather that he was frugal of it. In his works you find little to retrench or alter. Wit and language, and humour also, in some measure we had before him; but something of art was wanting to the drama till he came. He managed his strength to more advantage than any who preceded him. You seldom find him making love in any of his scenes, or endeavouring to move the passions; his genius was too sullen and saturnine to do it gracefully, especially when he knew he came after those who had performed both to such an height. Humour was his proper sphere, and in that he delighted most to represent mechanic people. He was deeply conversant in the ancients, both Greek and Latin, and he borrowed boldly from them; there is scarce a poet or historian among the Roman authors of those times whom he has not translated in *Sejanus* and *Catiline*. But he has done his robberies so openly that one may see he fears not to be taxed by any law. He invades authors like a monarch, and what would be theft in other poets is only victory in him. With the spoils of these writers he so represents old Rome to us, in its rites, ceremonies, and customs, that if one of their poets had written either of his tragedies we had seen less of it than in him. If there was any fault in his language, 'twas that he weaved it too closely and laboriously, in his comedies especially. Perhaps too he did a little too much romanize our tongue, leaving the words which he translated almost as much Latin as he found them; wherein, though he learnedly followed their language, he did not enough comply with the idiom of ours. If I would compare him with Shakespeare, I must acknowledge him the more correct poet but Shakespeare the greater wit. Shakespeare was the Homer, or father of our dramatic poets; Jonson was the Virgil, the pattern of elaborate writing. I admire him, but I love Shakespeare. To conclude of him, as he has given us the most correct plays, so in the precepts which he has laid down in his *Discoveries* we have as many and profitable rules for perfecting the stage as any wherewith the French can furnish us.

'Having thus spoken of the author, I proceed to the examination of his comedy, *The Silent Woman*.

EXAMEN OF THE SILENT WOMAN

'To begin first with the length of the action, it is so far from exceeding the compass of a natural day, that it takes not up an artificial one. 'Tis all included in the limits of three hours and an half, which is no more than is required for the presentment on the stage. A beauty perhaps not much observed, if it had, we should not have looked on the Spanish translation of *Five Hours*[1] with so much wonder. The scene of it is laid in London; the latitude of place is almost as little as you can imagine; for it lies all within the compass of two houses, and after the first act, in one. The continuity of scenes is observed more than in any of our plays, except his own *Fox* and *Alchemist*. They are not broken above twice or thrice at most in the whole comedy; and in the two best of Corneille's plays, the *Cid* and *Cinna*, they are interrupted once. The action of the play is entirely one; the end or aim of which is the settling Morose's estate on Dauphine. The intrigue of it is the greatest and most noble of any pure unmixed comedy in any language; you see in it many persons of various characters and humours, and all delightful. As first, Morose, or an old man, to whom all noise but his own talking is offensive. Some who would be thought critics, say this humour of his is forced: but to remove that objection, we may consider him first to be naturally of a delicate hearing, as many are to whom all sharp sounds are unpleasant; and secondly, we may attribute much of it to the peevishness of his age, or the wayward authority of an old man in his own house, where he may make himself obeyed; and to this the poet seems to allude in his name Morose. Beside this, I am assured from divers persons, that Ben Jonson was actually acquainted with such a man,

1. See above, p. 179, n. 1.

one altogether as ridiculous as he is here represented. Others say it is not enough to find one man of such an humour; it must be common to more, and the more common the more natural. To prove this, they instance in the best of comical characters, Falstaff. There are many men resembling him; old, fat, merry, cowardly, drunken, amorous, vain, and lying. But to convince these people, I need but tell them, that humour is the ridiculous extravagance of conversation, wherein one man differs from all others. If then it be common, or communicated to many, how differs it from other men's? or what indeed causes it to be ridiculous so much as the singularity of it? As for Falstaff, he is not properly one humour, but a miscellany of humours or images, drawn from so many several men; that wherein he is singular in his wit, or those things he says *praeter expectatum*[1], unexpected by the audience; his quick evasions when you imagine him surprised, which as they are extremely diverting of themselves so receive a great addition from his person; for the very sight of such an unwieldly old debauched fellow is a comedy alone. And here, having a place so proper for it, I cannot but enlarge somewhat upon this subject of humour into which I am fallen. The ancients had little of it in their comedies; for the τό γελοῖον[2] of the old comedy, of which Aristophanes was chief, was not so much to imitate a man, as to make the people laugh at some odd conceit, which had commonly somewhat of unnatural or obscene in it. Thus, when you see Socrates brought upon the stage, you are not to imagine him made ridiculous by the imitation of his actions, but rather by making him perform something very unlike himself; something so childish and absurd, as by comparing it with the gravity of the true Socrates, makes a ridiculous object for the spectators. In their new comedy

1. Contrary to expectation.   2. The ridiculous.

which succeeded, the poets sought indeed to express the
ἦθος,[1] as in their tragedies the πάθος[2] of mankind. But
this ἦθος contained only the general characters of men
and manners; as old men, lovers, serving-men, courtesans,
parasites, and such other persons as we see in their
comedies; all which they made alike: that is, one old man
or father, one lover, one courtesan, so like another, as if
the first of them had begot the rest of every sort: *ex
homine hunc natum dicas.*[3] The same custom they observed
likewise in their tragedies. As for the French, though they
have the word *humeur* among them, yet they have small
use of it in their comedies or farces; they being but ill
imitations of the *ridiculum*, or that which stirred up
laughter in the old comedy. But among the English 'tis
otherwise; where by humour is meant some extravagant
habit, passion, or affection, particular (as I said before) to
some one person; by the oddness of which he is imme-
diately distinguished from the rest of men; which being
lively and naturally represented, most frequently begets
that malicious pleasure in the audience which is testified by
laughter; as all things which are deviations from common
customs are ever the aptest to produce it: though by the
way this laughter is only accidental, as the person repre-
sented is fantastic or bizarre; but pleasure is essential to
it, as the imitation of what is natural. The description of
these humours, drawn from the knowledge and observa-
tion of particular persons, was the peculiar genius and
talent of Ben Jonson; to whose play I now return.

'Besides Morose, there are at least nine or ten different
characters and humours in *The Silent Woman*, all which
persons have several concernments of their own yet are
all used by the poet to the conducting of the main design

1. Character.   2. Experience.
3. One would say this fellow was born of a human being.

to perfection. I shall not waste time in commending the writing of this play, but I will give you my opinion, that there is more wit and acuteness of fancy in it than in any of Ben Jonson's. Besides, that he has here described the conversation of gentlemen in the persons of True-Wit and his friends with more gaiety, air, and freedom, than in the rest of his comedies. For the contrivance of the plot, 'tis extreme elaborate, and yet withal easy; for the λύσις, or untying of it, 'tis so admirable that when it is done, no one of the audience would think the poet could have missed it; and yet it was concealed so much before the last scene that any other way would sooner have entered into your thoughts. But I dare not take upon me to commend the fabric of it, because it is altogether so full of art that I must unravel every scene in it to commend it as I ought. And this excellent contrivance is still the more to be admired, because 'tis comedy where the persons are only of common rank, and their business private, not elevated by passions or high concernments as in serious plays. Here everyone is a proper judge of all he sees; nothing is represented but that with which he daily converses: so that by consequence all faults lie open to discovery, and few are pardonable. 'Tis this which Horace has judiciously observed:

> Creditur ex medio quia res arcessit habere
> Sudoris minimum, sed habet Comedia tanto
> Plus oneris, quanto veniae minus.[1]

But our poet who was not ignorant of these difficulties, has made use of all advantages; as he who designs a large leap takes his rise from the highest ground. One of these

---

1. Comedy is thought to involve least effort, since it draws its plots from ordinary life; but in fact it involves a heavier responsibility in proportion as it is allowed less indulgence. (*Epistles* 2. 1. 169.)

advantages is that which Corneille has laid down as the greatest which can arrive to any poem, and which he himself could never compass above thrice in all his plays, *viz*. the making choice of some signal and long-expected day whereon the action of the play is to depend. This day was that designed by Dauphine for the settling of his uncle's estate upon him; which to compass he contrives to marry him. That the marriage had been plotted by him long beforehand is made evident by what he tells True-Wit in the second act, that in one moment he had destroyed what he had been raising many months.

'There is another artifice of the poet, which I cannot here omit, because by the frequent practice of it in his comedies he has left it to us almost as a rule, that is, when he has any character or humour wherein he would show a *coup de maître*, or his highest skill, he recommends it to your observation by a pleasant description of it before the person first appears. Thus in *Bartholomew Fair* he gives you the pictures of Numps and Cokes, and in this those of Daw, Lafoole, Morose, and the Collegiate Ladies; all which you hear described before you see them. So that before they come upon the stage you have a longing expectation of them, which prepares you to receive them favourably; and when they are there, even from their first appearance you are so far acquainted with them that nothing of their humour is lost to you.

'I will observe yet one thing further of this admirable plot; the business of it rises in every act. The second is greater than the first; the third than the second; and so forward to the fifth. There too you see, till the very last scene, new difficulties arising to obstruct the action of the play; and when the audience is brought into despair that the business can naturally be effected, then, and not before, the discovery is made. But that the poet might entertain you with more variety all this while, he reserves some new characters to show you, which he opens not till the second and third act. In the second Morose, Daw, the Barber, and Otter; in the third the Collegiate Ladies: all which he moves afterwards in by-walks, or under-plots, as diversions to the main design, lest it should grow tedious, though they are still naturally joined with it, and somewhere or other subservient to it. Thus, like a skilful chess-player, by little and little he draws out his men, and makes his pawns of use to his greater persons.

'If this comedy and some others of his, were translated into French prose (which would now be no wonder to them since Molière has lately given them plays out of verse which have not displeased them) I believe the controversy would soon be decided betwixt the two nations, even making them the judges. But we need not call our heroes to our aid. Be it spoken to the honour of the English, our nation can never want in any age such who are able to dispute the empire of wit with any people in the universe. And though the fury of a civil war, and power for twenty years together abandoned to a barbarous race of men, enemies of all good learning, had buried the muses under the ruins of monarchy; yet, with the restoration of our happiness, we see revived poesy lifting up its head and already shaking off the rubbish which lay so heavy on it. We have seen since his majesty's return many dramatic poems which yield not to those of any foreign nation, and which deserve all laurels but the English. I will set aside flattery and envy: it cannot be denied but we have had some little blemish either in the plot or writing of all those plays which have been made within these seven years; (and perhaps there is no nation in the world so quick to discern them, or so difficult to pardon them, as ours): yet if we can persuade ourselves to use the candour of that poet, who (though the most severe of critics) has left us this caution by which to moderate our censures:

> *ubi plura nitent in carmine non ego paucis*
> *Offendar maculis.*[1]

If in consideration of their many and great beauties, we can wink at some slight and little imperfections; if we, I say, can be thus equal to ourselves, I ask no favour from the French. And if I do not venture upon any particular judgement of our late plays, 'tis out of the consideration which an ancient writer gives me: *vivorum, ut magna admiratio, ita censura difficilis*[2]: betwixt the extremes of admiration and malice, 'tis hard to judge uprightly of the living. Only I think it may be permitted me to say, that as it is no lessening to us to yield to some plays, and those not many of our own nation in the last age, so can it be no addition to pronounce of our present poets that they have far surpassed all the ancients, and the modern writers of other countries.'

This was the substance of what was then spoke on that occasion; and Lisideius, I think, was going to reply when he was prevented thus by Crites: 'I am confident,' said he, 'that the most material things that can be said have been already urged on either side; if they have not, I must beg of Lisideius that he will defer his answer till another time; for I confess I have a joint quarrel to you both because you have concluded, without any reason given for it, that rhyme is proper for the stage. I will not dispute how ancient it hath been among us to write this way: perhaps our ancestors knew no better till Shakespeare's time. I will

1. Where in a poem there are several excellences, I am not one to be offended at a few blemishes. (Horace, *Ars Poetica* 351–2.)
2. Living writers are highly admired and correspondingly hard to judge. (Velleius Paterculus 2. 36).

grant it was not altogether left by him, and that Fletcher and Ben Jonson used it frequently in their pastorals, and sometimes in other plays. Farther, I will not argue whether we received it originally from our own country-men or from the French; for that is an inquiry of as little benefit as theirs who in the midst of the great plague were not so solicitous to provide against it as to know whether we had it from the malignity of our own air, or by trans-portation from Holland. I have, therefore, only to affirm that it is not allowable in serious plays; for comedies, I find you already concluding with me. To prove this, I might satisfy myself to tell you how much in vain it is for you to strive against the stream of the people's inclination; the greatest part of which are prepossessed so much with those excellent plays of Shakespeare, Fletcher, and Ben Jonson (which have been written out of rhyme), that except you could bring them such as were written better in it, and those too by persons of equal reputation with them, it will be impossible for you to gain your cause with them, who will still be judges. This it is to which in fine all your reasons must submit. The unanimous consent of an audience is so powerful, that even Julius Caesar (as Macrobius reports of him) when he was perpetual dictator, was not able to balance it on the other side. But when Laberius, a Roman Knight, at his request contended in the *Mime* with another poet, he was forced to cry out, *Etiam favente me victus es, Laberi.*[1] But I will not on this occasion take the advantage of the greater number, but only urge such reasons against rhyme as I find in the writings of those who have argued for the other way. First, then, I am of opinion that rhyme is unnatural in a play because dialogue there is presented as the effect of sudden thought.

1. You were worsted, Laberius, even though you had my support. (*Saturnalia* 2. 7. 8.)

For a play is the imitation of nature, and since no man without premeditation speaks in rhyme, neither ought he to do it on the stage. This hinders not but the fancy may be there elevated to an higher pitch of thought than it is in ordinary discourse, for there is a probability that men of excellent and quick parts may speak noble things *extempore*; but those thoughts are never fettered with the numbers or sound of verse without study, and therefore it cannot be but unnatural to present the most free way of speaking in that which is the most constrained. For this reason, says Aristotle, 'tis best to write tragedy in that kind of verse which is the least such, or which is nearest prose; and this amongst the ancients was the iambic, and with us is blank verse, or the measure of verse kept exactly without rhyme. These numbers therefore are fittest for a play; the others for a paper of verses or a poem. Blank verse being as much below them as rhyme is improper for the drama. And if it be objected that neither are blank verses made *extempore*, yet, as nearest nature they are still to be preferred. But there are two particular exceptions which many besides myself have had to verse, by which it will appear yet more plainly how improper it is in plays. And the first of them is grounded on that very reason for which some have commended rhyme; they say the quickness of repartees in argumentative scenes receives an ornament from verse. Now what is more unreasonable than to imagine that a man should not only imagine the wit but the rhyme too upon the sudden? This nicking of him who spoke before both in sound and measure is so great an happiness that you must at least suppose the persons of your play to be born poets: *Arcades omnes, et cantare pares et respondere parati*.[1] They must have arrived

1. Arcadians all, ready to sing and to reply in equal contest. (Cf. Virgil, *Eclogues* 7. 4–5.)

to the degree of *quicquid conabar dicere*[1] to make verses almost whether they will or no. If they are anything below this it will look rather like the design of two than the answer of one; it will appear that your actors hold intelligence together, that they perform their tricks like fortune-tellers by confederacy. The hand of art will be too visible in it against that maxim of all professions: *Ars est celare artem*[2]; that it is the greatest perfection of art to keep itself undiscovered. Nor will it serve you to object that however you manage it 'tis still known to be a play, and, consequently, the dialogue of two persons understood to be the labour of one poet. For a play is still an imitation of nature; we know we are to be deceived and we desire to be so; but no man ever was deceived but with a probability of truth, for who will suffer a gross lie to be fastened on him? Thus we sufficiently understand that the scenes which represent cities and countries to us are not really such but only painted on boards and canvas. But shall that excuse the ill painture or designment of them? nay, rather ought they not to be laboured with so much the more diligence and exactness to help the imagination? since the mind of man does naturally tend to truth; and, therefore, the nearer anything comes to the imitation of it, the more it pleases.

'Thus, you see, your rhyme is uncapable of expressing the greatest thoughts naturally, and the lowest it cannot with any grace: for what is more unbefitting the majesty of verse, than to call a servant, or bid a door be shut in rhyme? And yet you are often forced on this miserable necessity. But verse, you say, circumscribes a quick and

1. Whatever I strove to say was verse ('I lisped in numbers, for the numbers came'). (Cf. Ovid, *Tristia* 4. 10. 26.)
2. To conceal one's art, is art itself. (Cf. *Disticha Catonis* 126. 2: 'sic ars deluditur arte'.)

luxuriant fancy, which would extend itself too far on every subject did not the labour which is required to well-turned and polished rhyme set bounds to it. Yet this argument, if granted, would only prove that we may write better in verse but not more naturally. Neither is it able to evince that; for he who wants judgement to confine his fancy in blank verse may want it as much in rhyme, and he who has it will avoid errors in both kinds. Latin verse was as great a confinement to the imagination of those poets as rhyme to ours, and yet you find Ovid saying too much on every subject. *Nescivit* (says Seneca) *quod bene cessit relinquere*:[1] of which he gives you one famous instance in his description of the deluge:

> *Omnia pontus erat, deerant quoque litora ponto.*

Now all was sea, nor had that sea a shore. Thus Ovid's fancy was not limited by verse, and Virgil needed not verse to have bounded his.

'In our own language we see Ben Jonson confining himself to what ought to be said, even in the liberty of blank verse; and yet Corneille, the most judicious of the French poets, is still varying the same sense an hundred ways, and dwelling eternally on the same subject, though confined by rhyme. Some other exceptions I have to verse, but since these I have named are for the most part already public, I conceive it reasonable they should first be answered.'

'It concerns me less than any,' said Neander (seeing he had ended), 'to reply to this discourse; because when I should have proved that verse may be natural in plays, yet I should always be ready to confess that those which I have written in this kind come short of that perfection which is required. Yet since you are pleased I should

---

1. He knew not how to let alone a thing done well enough already. (Seneca the Elder, *Controversiae* 28.)

undertake this province, I will do it, though with all imaginable respect and deference, both to that person from whom you have borrowed your strongest arguments and to whose judgement, when I have said all, I finally submit. But before I proceed to answer your objections, I must first remember you that I exclude all comedy from my defence; and next that I deny not but blank verse may be also used, and content myself only to assert, that in serious plays where the subject and characters are great and the plot unmixed with mirth, which might allay or divert these concernments which are produced, rhyme is there as natural and more effectual than blank verse.

'And now having laid down this as a foundation, to begin with Crites, I must crave leave to tell him, that some of his arguments against rhyme reach no farther than from the faults or defects of ill rhyme to conclude against the use of it in general. May not I conclude against blank verse by the same reason? If the words of some poets who write in it are either ill chosen or ill placed (which makes not only rhyme but all kind of verse in any language unnatural), shall I, for their vicious affectation, condemn those excellent lines of Fletcher which are written in that kind? Is there anything in rhyme more constrained than this line in blank verse, *I heaven invoke, and strong resistance make*? where you see both the clauses are placed unnaturally; that is, contrary to the common way of speaking, and that without the excuse of a rhyme to cause it. Yet you would think me very ridiculous if I should accuse the stubbornness of blank verse for this, and not rather the stiffness of the poet. Therefore, Crites, you must either prove that words, though well chosen and duly placed, yet render not rhyme natural in itself; or that however natural and easy the rhyme may be, yet it is not proper for a play. If you insist on the former part, I would ask you what other conditions are required to make rhyme natural in itself besides an election of apt words and a right disposition of them? For the due choice of your words expresses your sense naturally, and the due placing them adapts the rhyme to it. If you object that one verse may be made for the sake of another, though both the words and rhyme be apt, I answer it cannot possibly so fall out; for either there is a dependence of sense betwixt the first line and the second, or there is none. If there be that connexion, then in the natural position of the words the latter line must of necessity flow from the former; if there be no dependence, yet still the due ordering of words makes the last line as natural in itself as the other. So that the necessity of a rhyme never forces any but bad or lazy writers to say what they would not otherwise. 'Tis true, there is both care and art required to write in verse. A good poet never establishes the first line till he has sought out such a rhyme as may fit the sense, already prepared to heighten the second; many times the close of the sense falls into the middle of the next verse or farther off, and he may often prevail himself of the same advantages in English which Virgil had in Latin: he may break off in the hemistich, and begin another line. Indeed, the not observing these two last things makes plays which are writ in verse so tedious; for though most commonly the sense is to be confined to the couplet, yet nothing that does *perpetuo tenore fluere*, run in the same channel, can please always. 'Tis like the murmuring of a stream, which not varying in the fall, causes at first attention, at last drowsiness. Variety of cadences is the best rule, the greatest help to the actors and refreshment to the audience.

'If then verse may be made natural in itself, how becomes it unnatural in a play? You say the stage is the representation of nature, and no man in ordinary conversation speaks in rhyme. But you foresaw when you said this that it might be answered, neither does any man speak in blank verse, or in measure without rhyme. Therefore you concluded, that which is nearest nature is still to be preferred. But you took no notice that rhyme might be made as natural as blank verse by the well placing of the words, &c. All the difference between them, when they are both correct, is the sound in one, which the other wants; and if so, the sweetness of it and all the advantage resulting from it, which are handled in the Preface to *The Rival Ladies*,[1] will yet stand good. As for that place of Aristotle where he says plays should be writ in that kind of verse which is nearest prose, it makes little for you, blank verse being properly but measured prose. Now measure alone in any modern language does not constitute verse; those of the ancients in Greek and Latin consisted in quantity of words, and a determinate number of feet. But when by the inundation of the Goths and Vandals into Italy new languages were introduced and barbarously mingled with the Latin (of which the Italian, Spanish, French, and ours – made out of them and the Teutonic – are dialects) a new way of poesy was practised; new, I say, in those countries, for in all probability it was that of the conquerors in their own nations. At least we are able to prove that the eastern people have used it from all antiquity, *vid. Dan. his Defence of Rhyme*.[2] This new way consisted in measure or number of feet and rhyme. The sweetness of rhyme and observation of accent supplying the place of quantity in words, which could neither exactly be observed by those barbarians who knew not the rules of it; neither was it suitable

1. *The Rival Ladies*, 1664, was the first of Dryden's plays to be printed.
2. The reference is to Samuel Daniel's (1552–1619) *Defence of Rhyme*, 1602.

to their tongues as it had been to the Greek and Latin. No man is tied in modern poesy to observe any farther rule in the feet of his verse but that they be dissyllables; whether spondee, trochee, or iambic, it matters not; only he is obliged to rhyme. Neither do the Spanish, French, Italian, or Germans acknowledge at all, or very rarely, any such kind of poesy as blank verse amongst them. Therefore at most 'tis but a poetic prose, a *sermo pedestris*[1]; and as such most fit for comedies, where I acknowledge rhyme to be improper. Farther, as to that quotation of Aristotle, our couplet verses may be rendered as near prose as blank verse itself by using those advantages I lately named, as breaks in an hemistich, or running the sense into another line, thereby making art and order appear as loose and free as nature: or not tying ourselves to couplets strictly, we may use the benefit of the pindaric way practised in *The Siege of Rhodes*[2], where the numbers vary, and the rhyme is disposed carelessly and far from often chiming. Neither is that other advantage of the ancients to be despised, of changing the kind of verse when they please with the change of the scene or some new entrance; for they confine not themselves always to iambics, but extend their liberty to all lyric numbers, and sometimes even to hexameter. But I need not go so far to prove that rhyme, as it succeeds to all other offices of Greek and Latin verse, so especially to this of plays, since the custom of nations at this day confirms it; the French, Italian, and Spanish tragedies are generally writ in it; and sure the universal consent of the most civilized parts of the world ought in this, as it doth in other customs, to include the rest.

'But perhaps you may tell me I have proposed such a way to make rhyme natural, and consequently proper to

1. Prose discourse.
2. Sir William Davenant's *The Siege of Rhodes*, 1656.

plays, as is unpracticable; and that I shall scarce find six or eight lines together in any play, where the words are so placed and chosen as is required to make it natural. I answer, no poet need constrain himself at all times to it. It is enough he makes it his general rule; for I deny not but sometimes there may be a greatness in placing the words otherwise, and sometimes they may sound better; sometimes also the variety itself is excuse enough. But if, for the most part, the words be placed as they are in the negligence of prose, it is sufficient to denominate the way practicable; for we esteem that to be such which in the trial oftener succeeds than misses. And thus far you may find the practice made good in many plays; where you do not, remember still that if you cannot find six natural rhymes together it will be as hard for you to produce as many lines in blank verse, even among the greatest of our poets, against which I cannot make some reasonable exception.

'And this, Sir, calls to my remembrance the beginning of your discourse, where you told us we should never find the audience favourable to this kind of writing till we could produce as good plays in rhyme as Ben Jonson, Fletcher, and Shakespeare had writ out of it. But it is to raise envy to the living to compare them with the dead. They are honoured, and almost adored by us, as they deserve; neither do I know any so presumptuous of themselves as to contend with them. Yet give me leave to say thus much, without injury to their ashes, that not only we shall never equal them but they could never equal themselves were they to rise and write again. We acknowledge them our fathers in wit, but they have ruined their estates themselves before they came to their children's hands. There is scarce an humour, a character, or any kind of plot, which they have not used. All comes sullied or wasted to us; and were they to entertain this age, they could not now make so plenteous treatments out of such decayed fortunes. This therefore will be a good argument to us either not to write at all, or to attempt some other way. There is no bays to be expected in their walks: *tentanda via est, quà me quoque possum tollere humo.*[1]

This way of writing in verse they have only left free to us; our age is arrived to a perfection in it which they never knew; and which, if we may guess by what of theirs we have seen in verse (as *The Faithful Shepherdess* and *Sad Shepherd*)[2] 'tis probable they never could have reached. For the genius of every age is different; and though ours excel in this, I deny not but that to imitate nature in that perfection which they did in prose is a greater commendation than to write in verse exactly. As for what you have added, that the people are not generally inclined to like this way; if it were true, it would be no wonder that betwixt the shaking off an old habit and the introducing of a new there should be difficulty. Do we not see them stick to Hopkins and Sternhold's psalms[3] and forsake those of David, I mean Sandys his translation of them?[4] If by the people you understand the multitude, the οἱ πολλοί,[5] 'tis no matter what they think. They are sometimes in the right, sometimes in the wrong. Their judgement is a mere lottery. *Est ubi plebs recte putat, est ubi peccat:*[6] Horace says it of the

---

1. I must try some way to raise myself from the earth, like these. (Virgil, *Georgics* 3. 8.)
2. John Fletcher's pastoral play, *The Faithful Shepherdess*, 1610; Ben Johnson's unfinished pastoral play, *The Sad Shepherd*, 1641.
3. John Hopkins (*d.* 1549) and Thomas Sternhold's (*d.* 1570) famous collection of versified psalms first appeared in 1549.
4. George Sandys's (1578–1644) *Paraphrase upon the Psalmes*, 1636.
5. The many.
6. There are times when the common people is right in its opinions, times when it errs. (*Epistles* 2. 1. 63.)

vulgar, judging poesy. But if you mean the mixed audience of the populace and the noblesse, I dare confidently affirm that a great part of the latter sort are already favourable to verse, and that no serious plays written since the king's return have been more kindly received by them than *The Siege of Rhodes*, the *Mustapha*, *The Indian Queen*, and *The Indian Emperor*.[1]

'But I come now to the inference of your first argument. You said that the dialogue of plays is presented as the effect of sudden thought, but no man speaks suddenly or *extempore* in rhyme. And you inferred from thence that rhyme, which you acknowledge to be proper to epic poesy, cannot equally be proper to dramatic, unless we could suppose all men born so much more than poets that verses should be made in them, not by them.

'It has been formerly urged by you, and confessed by me, that since no man spoke any kind of verse *extempore* that which was nearest nature was to be preferred. I answer you, therefore, by distinguishing betwixt what is nearest to the nature of comedy, which is the imitation of common persons and ordinary speaking, and what is nearest the nature of a serious play: this last is indeed the representation of nature, but 'tis nature wrought up to an higher pitch. The plot, the characters, the wit, the passions, the descriptions, are all exalted above the level of common converse, as high as the imagination of the poet can carry them, with proportion to verisimility. Tragedy we know is wont to image to us the minds and fortunes of noble persons and to portray these exactly. Heroic rhyme is nearest nature as being the noblest kind of modern verse.

1. Roger Boyle's – Earl of Orrery (1621–79) – heroic play, *Mustapha*, 1665. Dryden's *The Indian Queen*, 1664, and *The Indian Emperor*, 1665; the first was written in collaboration with Sir Robert Howard.

Indignatur enim privatis, et prope socco,
Dignis carminibus, narrari coena Thyestae[1] –

says Horace: and in another place,

Effutire leves indigna tragoedia versus[2] –.

Blank verse is acknowledged to be too low for a poem; nay more, for a paper of verses; but if too low for an ordinary sonnet, how much more for tragedy, which is by Aristotle in the dispute betwixt the epic poesy and the dramatic, for many reasons he there alleges, ranked above it?

'But setting this defence aside, your argument is almost as strong against the use of rhyme in poems as in plays; for the epic way is everywhere interlaced with dialogue or discoursive scenes; and therefore you must either grant rhyme to be improper there, which is contrary to your assertion, or admit it into plays by the same title which you have given it to poems. For though tragedy be justly preferred above the other, yet there is a great affinity between them, as may easily be discovered in that definition of a play which Lisideius gave us. The genus of them is the same, a just and lively image of human nature in its actions, passions, and traverses of fortune; so is the end, namely for the delight and benefit of mankind. The characters and persons are still the same, *viz.* the greatest of both sorts, only the manner of acquainting us with those actions, passions, and fortunes is different. Tragedy performs it *viva voce*, or by action, in dialogue, wherein it excels the epic poem which does it chiefly by narration, and therefore is not so lively an image of human nature. However, the agreement betwixt them is such, that if rhyme be proper for one it

1. For the tale of Thyestes' banquet cannot be told adequately in verses of a humdrum sort, fit almost for comedy. (*Ars Poetica* 90–1.)
2. Tragedy is unfitted to prate in frivolous lines. (*Ibid.* 231.)

must be for the other. Verse 'tis true is not the effect of sudden thought; but this hinders not that sudden thought may be represented in verse, since those thoughts are such as must be higher than nature can raise them without premeditation, especially to a continuance of them even out of verse, and consequently you cannot imagine them to have been sudden either in the poet or in the actors. A play, as I have said, to be like nature is to be set above it; as statues which are placed on high are made greater than the life that they may descend to the sight in their just proportion.

'Perhaps I have insisted too long on this objection, but the clearing of it will make my stay shorter on the rest. You tell us, Crites, that rhyme appears most unnatural in repartees or short replies: when he who answers, it being presumed he knew not what the other would say, yet makes up that part of the verse which was left incomplete and supplies both the sound and measure of it. This, you say, looks rather like the confederacy of two than the answer of one.

'This, I confess, is an objection which is in every man's mouth who loves not rhyme; but suppose, I beseech you, the repartee were made only in blank verse, might not part of the same argument be turned against you? for the measure is as often supplied there as it is in rhyme, the latter half of the hemistich as commonly made up or a second line subjoined as a reply to the former; which any one leaf in Jonson's plays will make sufficiently clear to you. You will often find in the Greek tragedians, and in Seneca, that when a scene grows up into the warmth of repartees (which is the close fighting of it) the latter part of the trimeter is supplied by him who answers; and yet it was never observed as a fault in them by any of the ancient or modern critics. The case is the same in our verse as it was in theirs; rhyme to us being in lieu of quantity to them. But if no latitude is to be allowed a poet, you take from him not only his licence of *quidlibet audendi*,[1] but you tie him up in a straighter compass than you would a philosopher. This is indeed *Musas colere severiores*.[2] You would have him follow nature, but he must follow her on foot: you have dismounted him from his Pegasus. But you tell us this supplying the last half of a verse, or adjoining a whole second to the former, looks more like the design of two than the answer of one. Suppose we acknowledge it, how comes this confederacy to be more displeasing to you than in a dance which is well contrived? You see there the united design of many persons to make up one figure; after they have separated themselves in many petty divisions they rejoin one by one into a gross. The confederacy is plain amongst them, for chance could never produce any thing so beautiful; and yet there is nothing in it that shocks your sight. I acknowledge the hand of art appears in repartee, as of necessity it must in all kind of verse. But there is also the quick and poignant brevity of it (which is an high imitation of nature in those sudden gusts of passion) to mingle with it; and this, joined with the cadency and sweetness of the rhyme, leaves nothing in the soul of the hearer to desire. 'Tis an art which appears, but it appears only like the shadowings of painture, which being to cause the rounding of it, cannot be absent; but while that is considered they are lost; so while we attend to the other beauties of the matter, the care and labour of the rhyme is carried from us, or at least drowned in its own sweetness, as bees are sometimes buried in their honey. When a poet has found the repartee, the last perfection he can add to it is to put it into verse. However good the thought may be, however apt the words in which 'tis couched, yet he finds himself at a little unrest

1. Venturing anything he pleases. (*Ars Poetica* 10.)
2. To cultivate the more exacting Muses. (Cf. Horace, *Odes* 2. 1. 9.)

while rhyme is wanting. He cannot leave it till that comes naturally, and then is at ease and sits down contented.

'From replies, which are the most elevated thoughts of verse, you pass to those which are most mean and which are common with the lowest of household conversation. In these, you say, the majesty of verse suffers. You instance in the calling of a servant, or commanding a door to be shut in rhyme. This, Crites, is a good observation of yours, but no argument: for it proves no more but that such thoughts should be waived, as often as may be, by the address of the poet. But suppose they are necessary in the places where he uses them, yet there is no need to put them into rhyme. He may place them in the beginning of a verse, and break it off, as unfit, when so debased, for any other use; or granting the worst, that they require more room than the hemistich will allow; yet still there is a choice to be made of the best words, and least vulgar (provided they be apt) to express such thoughts. Many have blamed rhyme in general for this fault, when the poet, with a little care, might have redressed it. But they do it with no more justice, than if English poesy should be made ridiculous for the sake of the Water Poet's[1] rhymes. Our language is noble, full, and significant; and I know not why he who is master of it may not clothe ordinary things in it as decently as the Latin, if he use the same diligence in his choice of words:

Delectus verborum origo est eloquentiae.[2]

It was the saying of Julius Caesar, one so curious in his, that none of them can be changed but for a worse. One

1. John Taylor (1580–1653), known as the Water Poet, was a Thames waterman with a remarkable gift for writing fluent rhyme. He published his collected works in 1630.
2. Choice of words is the beginning of eloquence. (Julius Caesar, quoted by Cicero, *Brutus* 72. 253.)

would think, *unlock the door*, was a thing as vulgar as could be spoken; and yet Seneca could make it sound high and lofty in his Latin:

> *Reserate clusos regii postes laris.*
> Set wide the palace gates.

'But I turn from this exception, both because it happens not above twice or thrice in any play that those vulgar thoughts are used; and then too (were there no other apology to be made, yet) the necessity of them (which is alike in all kind of writing) may excuse them. For if they are little and mean in rhyme, they are of consequence such in blank verse. Besides that the great eagerness and precipitation with which they are spoken makes us rather mind the substance than the dress; that for which they are spoken, rather than what is spoke. For they are always the effect of some hasty concernment, and something of consequence depends on them.

'Thus, Crites, I have endeavoured to answer your objections. It remains only that I should vindicate an argument for verse, which you have gone about to overthrow. It had formerly been said that the easiness of blank verse renders the poet too luxuriant, but that the labour of rhyme bounds and circumscribes an over-fruitful fancy. The sense there being commonly confined to the couplet, and the words so ordered that the rhyme naturally follows them, not they the rhyme. To this you answered, that it was no argument to the question in hand, for the dispute was not which way a man may write best but which is most proper for the subject on which he writes.

'First, give me leave, Sir, to remember you that the argument against which you raised this objection was only secondary: it was built on this hypothesis, that to write in verse was proper for serious plays. Which supposition being granted (as it was briefly made out in that discourse, by showing how verse might be made natural) it asserted that this way of writing was an help to the poet's judgement, by putting bounds to a wild overflowing fancy. I think, therefore, it will not be hard for me to make good what it was to prove on that supposition. But you add, that were this let pass, yet he who wants judgement in the liberty of his fancy may as well show the defect of it when he is confined to verse; for he who has judgement will avoid errors, and he who has it not will commit them in all kinds of writing.

'This argument, as you have taken it from a most acute person, so I confess it carries much weight in it. But by using the word judgement here indefinitely, you seem to have put a fallacy upon us. I grant he who has judgement, that is, so profound, so strong, or rather so infallible a judgement that he needs no helps to keep it always poised and upright, will commit no faults either in rhyme or out of it. And on the other extreme, he who has a judgement so weak and crazed that no helps can correct or amend it shall write scurvily out of rhyme and worse in it. But the first of these judgements is nowhere to be found, and the latter is not fit to write at all. To speak therefore of judgement as it is in the best poets; they who have the greatest proportion of it want other helps than from it within. As for example, you would be loath to say that he who is endued with a sound judgement has no need of history, geography, or moral philosophy, to write correctly. Judgement is indeed the master-workman in a play; but he requires many subordinate hands, many tools to his assistance; and verse I affirm to be one of these; 'tis a rule and line by which he keeps his building compact and even, which otherwise lawless imagination would raise either irregularly or loosely. At least, if the poet commits errors with this help he would make greater and more without it. 'Tis, in short, a slow and painful but the surest kind of working. Ovid, whom you accuse for luxuriancy in verse, had perhaps been farther guilty of it had he writ in prose. And for your instance of Ben Jonson who, you say, writ exactly without the help of rhyme; you are to remember 'tis only an aid to a luxuriant fancy, which his was not: as he did not want imagination, so none ever said he had much to spare. Neither was verse then refined so much to be an help to that age as it is to ours. Thus then the second thoughts being usually the best, as receiving the maturest digestion from judgement, and the last and most mature product of those thoughts being artful and laboured verse, it may well be inferred that verse is a great help to a luxuriant fancy; and this is what that argument which you opposed was to evince.'

Neander was pursuing this discourse so eagerly that Eugenius had called to him twice or thrice ere he took notice that the barge stood still and that they were at the foot of Somerset Stairs,[1] where they had appointed it to land. The company were all sorry to separate so soon, though a great part of the evening was already spent, and stood awhile looking back on the water upon which the moonbeams played and made it appear like floating quick-silver. At last they went up through a crowd of French people who were merrily dancing in the open air and nothing concerned for the noise of guns which had alarmed the town that afternoon. Walking thence together to the Piazza,[2] they parted there; Eugenius and Lisideius to some pleasant appointment they had made, and Crites and Neander to their several lodgings.

1. Somerset Stairs led from below Somerset House to the river.
2. The Piazza stood in front of Somerset House.

PREFACE

TO

FABLES

ANCIENT AND MODERN

'Tis with a poet as with a man who designs to build, and is very exact, as he supposes, in casting up the cost beforehand; but, generally speaking, he is mistaken in his account, and reckons short of the expense he first intended. He alters his mind as the work proceeds, and will have this or that convenience more, of which he had not thought when he began. So has it happened to me; I have built a house where I intended but a lodge. Yet with better success than a certain nobleman, who beginning with a dog-kennel never lived to finish the palace he had contrived.[1]

From translating the first of Homer's *Iliads* (which I intended as an essay to the whole work) I proceeded to the translation of the twelfth Book of Ovid's *Metamorphoses*, because it contains, among other things, the causes, the beginning, and ending of the Trojan War. Here I ought in reason to have stopped, but the speeches of Ajax and Ulysses lying next in my way, I could not balk 'em. When I had compassed them, I was so taken with the former part of the fifteenth Book (which is the masterpiece of the whole *Metamorphoses*) that I enjoined myself the pleasing task of rendering it into English. And now

---

1. George Villiers, 2nd Duke of Buckingham (1628–87); the unfinished palace was Cliveden. He is the *Zimri* of *Absalom and Achitophel*.

I found, by the number of my verses, that they began to swell into a little volume, which gave me an occasion of looking backward on some beauties of my author in his former books. There occurred to me the *Hunting of the Boar*, *Cinyras and Myrrha*, the good-natured story of *Baucis and Philemon*, with the rest, which I hope I have translated closely enough and given them the same turn of verse which they had in the original; and this, I may say without vanity, is not the talent of every poet. He who has arrived the nearest to it is the ingenious and learned Sandys,[1] the best versifier of the former age; if I may properly call it by that name, which was the former part of this concluding century. For Spenser and Fairfax both flourished in the reign of Queen Elizabeth: great masters in our language, and who saw much farther into the beauties of our numbers than those who immediately followed them. Milton was the poetical son of Spenser, and Mr Waller of Fairfax; for we have our lineal descents and clans as well as other families. Spenser more than once insinuates that the soul of Chaucer was transfused into his body, and that he was begotten by him two hundred years after his decease. Milton has acknowledged to me that Spenser was his original; and many besides myself have heard our famous Waller own that he derived the harmony of his numbers from the *Godfrey of Bulloign*, which was turned into English by Mr Fairfax. But to return: having done with Ovid for this time, it came into my mind that our old English poet Chaucer in many things resembled him, and that with no disadvantage on the side of the modern author, as I shall endeavour to prove when I compare them. And as I am, and always have been studious to promote the honour of my native country, so I soon

1. George Sandys's translation of Ovid's *Metamorphoses* was published in 1626.

resolved to put their merits to the trial by turning some of the *Canterbury Tales* into our language, as it is now refined; for by this means both the poets being set in the same light, and dressed in the same English habit, story to be compared with story, a certain judgement may be made betwixt them by the reader, without obtruding my opinion on him. Or if I seem partial to my countryman, and predecessor in the laurel, the friends of antiquity are not few; and besides many of the learned, Ovid has almost all the *Beaux* and the whole Fair Sex his declared patrons. Perhaps I have assumed somewhat more to myself than they allow me, because I have adventured to sum up the evidence; but the readers are the jury, and their privilege remains entire to decide according to the merits of the cause; or, if they please, to bring it to another hearing before some other court. In the meantime, to follow the thread of my discourse (as thoughts, according to Mr Hobbes, have always some connexion), so from Chaucer I was led to think on Boccace, who was not only his contemporary but also pursued the same studies; wrote novels in prose, and many works in verse; particularly is said to have invented the octave rhyme, or stanza of eight lines, which ever since has been maintained by the practice of all Italian writers, who are, or at least assume the title of, heroic poets. He and Chaucer, among other things, had this in common, that they refined their mother tongues; but with this difference, that Dante had begun to file their language, at least in verse, before the time of Boccace, who likewise received no little help from his master Petrarch. But the reformation of their prose was wholly owing to Boccace himself, who is yet the standard of purity in the Italian tongue, though many of his phrases are become obsolete, as in process of time it must needs happen. Chaucer (as you have formerly been told by our learned Mr Rymer[1]) first adorned and amplified our barren tongue from the Provençal, which was then the most polished of all the modern languages; but this subject has been copiously treated by that great critic, who deserves no little commendation from us his countrymen. For these reasons of time, and resemblance of genius in Chaucer and Boccace, I resolved to join them in my present work; to which I have added some original papers of my own, which whether they are equal or inferior to my other poems, an author is the most improper judge; and therefore I leave them wholly to the mercy of the reader. I will hope the best, that they will not be condemned; but if they should, I have the excuse of an old gentleman, who mounting on horseback before some ladies, when I was present, got up somewhat heavily but desired of the fair spectators that they would count fourscore and eight before they judged him. By the mercy of God, I am already come within twenty years of his number, a cripple in my limbs, but what decays are in my mind, the reader must determine. I think myself as vigorous as ever in the faculties of my soul, excepting only my memory, which is not impaired to any great degree; and if I lose not more of it, I have no great reason to complain. What judgement I had increases rather than diminishes, and thoughts, such as they are, come crowding in so fast upon me that my only difficulty is to choose or to reject, to run them into verse or to give them the other harmony of prose; I have so long studied and practised both that they are grown into a habit and become familiar to me. In short, though I may lawfully plead some part of the old gentleman's excuse, yet I will reserve it till I think I have greater need and

1. Thomas Rymer (1641–1713), critic and historian; he advanced the opinion to which Dryden refers below in his *Short View of Tragedy*, 1692.

ask no grains of allowance for the faults of this my present work but those which are given of course to human frailty. I will not trouble my reader with the shortness of time in which I writ it, or the several intervals of sickness. They who think too well of their own performances are apt to boast in their prefaces how little time their works have cost them, and what other business of more importance interfered, but the reader will be as apt to ask the question, why they allowed not a longer time to make their works more perfect? and why they had so despicable an opinion of their judges as to thrust their indigested stuff upon them, as if they deserved no better?

With this account of my present undertaking, I conclude the first part of this discourse. In the second part, as at a second sitting, though I alter not the draught, I must touch the same features over again and change the dead-colouring of the whole. In general I will only say that I have written nothing which savours of immorality or profaneness; at least, I am not conscious to myself of any such intention. If there happen to be found an irreverent expression, or a thought too wanton, they are crept into my verses through my inadvertency. If the searchers find any in the cargo, let them be staved or forfeited like counterbanded goods; at least, let their authors be answerable for them, as being but imported merchandise and not of my own manufacture. On the other side, I have endeavoured to choose such fables, both ancient and modern, as contain in each of them some instructive moral, which I could prove by induction, but the way is tedious; and they leap foremost into sight, without the reader's trouble of looking after them. I wish I could affirm with a safe conscience that I had taken the same care in all my former writings; for it must be owned, that supposing verses are never so beautiful or pleasing, yet if they contain anything which shocks religion or good manners, they are at best what Horace says of good numbers without good sense, *Versus inopes rerum, nugaeque canorae*.[1] Thus far, I hope, I am right in court, without renouncing to my other right of self-defence where I have been wrongfully accused and my sense wire-drawn into blasphemy or bawdry, as it has often been by a religious lawyer in a late pleading against the stage, in which he mixes truth with falsehood, and has not forgotten the old rule of calumniating strongly that something may remain.[2]

I resume the thread of my discourse with the first of my translations, which was the first *Iliad* of Homer. If it shall please God to give me longer life and moderate health, my intentions are to translate the whole *Ilias*; provided still that I meet with those encouragements from the public which may enable me to proceed in my undertaking with some cheerfulness. And this I dare assure the world beforehand, that I have found by trial Homer a more pleasing task than Virgil (though I say not the translation will be less laborious); for the Grecian is more according to my genius than the Latin poet. In the works of the two authors we may read their manners and natural inclinations, which are wholly different. Virgil was of a quiet, sedate temper; Homer was violent, impetuous, and full of fire. The chief talent of Virgil was propriety of thoughts and ornament of words; Homer was rapid in his thoughts, and took all the liberties both of numbers and of expressions which his language and the age in which he lived allowed him. Homer's invention was more copious, Virgil's more confined; so that if Homer had not led the way, it

1. Lines lacking substance, melodious trifles. (*Ars Poetica* 322.)
2. A reference to Jeremy Collier's (1650–1726) *Short View of the Immorality and Profaneness of the English Stage*, 1698, in which Dryden was criticized.

was not in Virgil to have begun heroic poetry; for nothing can be more evident than that the Roman poem is but the second part of the *Ilias*, a continuation of the same story and the persons already formed. The manners of Aeneas are those of Hector superadded to those which Homer gave him. The adventures of Ulysses in the *Odysseis*, are imitated in the first six Books of Virgil's *Aeneis*; and though the accidents are not the same (which would have argued him of a servile, copying, and total barrenness of invention), yet the seas were the same in which both the heroes wandered; and Dido cannot be denied to be the poetical daughter of Calypso. The six latter Books of Virgil's poem, are the four-and-twenty *Iliads* contracted; a quarrel occasioned by a lady, a single combat, battles fought, and a town besieged. I say not this in derogation to Virgil, neither do I contradict anything which I have formerly said in his just praise; for his episodes are almost wholly of his own invention, and the form which he has given to the telling makes the tale his own, even though the original story had been the same. But this proves, however, that Homer taught Virgil to design; and if invention be the first virtue of an epic poet, then the Latin poem can only be allowed the second place. Mr Hobbes,[1] in the preface to his own bald translation of the *Ilias* (studying poetry as he did mathematics, when it was too late), Mr Hobbes, I say, begins the praise of Homer where he should have ended it. He tells us that the first beauty of an epic poem consists in diction, that is, in the choice of words, and harmony of numbers. Now, the words are the colouring of the work, which in the order of nature is last to be considered. The design, the disposition, the manners, and the thoughts are all before it. Where any of those are

1. Thomas Hobbes (1588–1679), the philosopher, published a translation of Homer in 1676.

wanting or imperfect, so much wants or is imperfect
in the imitation of human life, which is in the very defini-
tion of a poem. Words indeed, like glaring colours, are
the first beauties that arise and strike the sight; but if the
draught be false or lame, the figures ill disposed, the
manners obscure or inconsistent, or the thoughts un-
natural, then the finest colours are but daubing, and the
piece is a beautiful monster at the best. Neither Virgil nor
Homer were deficient in any of the former beauties, but
in this last, which is expression, the Roman poet is at least
equal to the Grecian, as I have said elsewhere; supplying
the poverty of his language by his musical ear and by his
diligence. But to return: our two great poets, being so
different in their tempers; one choleric and sanguine, the
other phlegmatic and melancholic; that which makes them
excel in their several ways is that each of them has
followed his own natural inclination, as well in forming
the design as in the execution of it. The very heroes show
their authors. Achilles is hot, impatient, revengeful,
Impiger, iracundus, inexorabilis, acer, &c.[1] Aeneas patient,
considerate, careful of his people, and merciful to his
enemies; ever submissive to the will of heaven, *quo fata
trahunt retrahuntque, sequamur.*[2] I could please myself with
enlarging on this subject, but am forced to defer it to a
fitter time. From all I have said, I will only draw this
inference, that the action of Homer being more full of
vigour than that of Virgil, according to the temper of the
writer, is of consequence more pleasing to the reader.
One warms you by degrees; the other sets you on fire all
at once, and never intermits his heat. 'Tis the same

1. Energetic, hot-tempered, unyielding and vehement. (*Ars Poetica*
   121.)
2. Where the fates convey us, be it forth or back, let us obey and go.
   (Virgil, *Aeneid* 5. 709.)

difference which Longinus makes betwixt the effects of eloquence in Demosthenes and Tully. One persuades; the other commands. You never cool while you read Homer, even not in the second Book (a graceful flattery to his countrymen); but he hastens from the ships, and concludes not that Book till he has made you an amends by the violent playing of a new machine. From thence he hurries on his action with variety of events, and ends it in less compass than two months. This vehemence of his, I confess, is more suitable to my temper, and therefore I have translated his first Book with greater pleasure than any part of Virgil. But it was not a pleasure without pains. The continual agitations of the spirits must needs be a weakening of any constitution, especially in age; and many pauses are required for refreshment betwixt the heats; the *Iliad* of itself being a third part longer than all Virgil's works together.

This is what I thought needful in this place to say of Homer. I proceed to Ovid and Chaucer; considering the former only in relation to the latter. With Ovid ended the golden age of the Roman tongue; from Chaucer the purity of the English tongue began. The manners of the poets were not unlike; both of them were well-bred, well-natured, amorous, and libertine, at least in their writings, it may be also in their lives. Their studies were the same, philosophy and philology. Both of them were knowing in astronomy, of which Ovid's books of the Roman Feasts, and Chaucer's Treatise of the Astrolabe, are sufficient witnesses. But Chaucer was likewise an astrologer, as were Virgil, Horace, Persius, and Manilius. Both writ with wonderful facility and clearness; neither were great inventors: for Ovid only copied the Grecian fables, and most of Chaucer's stories were taken from his Italian contemporaries, or their predecessors. Boccace his *Decameron* was first published, and from thence our Englishman has borrowed many of his *Canterbury Tales*; yet that of Palamon and Arcite was written in all probability by some Italian wit in a former age, as I shall prove hereafter. The tale of Grizild was the invention of Petrarch; by him sent to Boccace, from whom it came to Chaucer. *Troilus and Cressida* was also written by a Lombard author, but much amplified by our English translator, as well as beautified; the genius of our countrymen in general being rather to improve an invention than to invent themselves, as is evident not only in our poetry but in many of our manufactures. I find I have anticipated already and taken up from Boccace before I come to him, but there is so much less behind, and I am of the temper of most kings, *who love to be in debt*, are all for present money no matter how they pay it afterwards. Besides, the nature of a preface is rambling; never wholly out of the way, nor in it. This I have learned from the practice of honest Montaigne, and return at my pleasure to Ovid and Chaucer, of whom I have little more to say. Both of them built on the inventions of other men; yet since Chaucer had something of his own, as *The Wife of Bath's Tale*, *The Cock and the Fox*, which I have translated, and some others, I may justly give our countryman the precedence in that part, since I can remember nothing of Ovid which was wholly his. Both of them understood the manners; under which name I comprehend the passions and, in a larger sense, the descriptions of persons and their very habits. For an example, I see Baucis and Philemon as perfectly before me as if some ancient painter had drawn them; and all the pilgrims in the *Canterbury Tales*, their humours, their features, and the very dress, as distinctly as if I had supped with them at the Tabard in Southwark. Yet even there too the figures of Chaucer are much more lively and set in a better light; which though I have not time to prove, yet I appeal to the reader, and am sure he will clear me from partiality. The thoughts and words remain to be considered, in the comparison of the two poets, and I have saved myself one-half of that labour by owning that Ovid lived when the Roman tongue was in its meridian; Chaucer, in the dawning of our language. Therefore that part of the comparison stands not on an equal foot, any more than the diction of Ennius and Ovid, or of Chaucer and our present English. The words are given up as a post not to be defended in our poet, because he wanted the modern art of fortifying. The thoughts remain to be considered: and they are to be measured only by their propriety; that is, as they flow more or less naturally from the persons described, on such and such occasions. The vulgar judges, which are nine parts in ten of all nations, who call conceits and jingles wit, who see Ovid full of them, and Chaucer altogether without them, will think me little less than mad for preferring the Englishman to the Roman. Yet, with their leave, I must presume to say that the things they admire are only glittering trifles, and so far from being witty that in a serious poem they are nauseous, because they are unnatural. Would any man who is ready to die for love, describe his passion like Narcissus? Would he think of *inopem me copia fecit*,[1] and a dozen more of such expressions, poured on the neck of one another and signifying all the same thing? If this were wit, was this a time to be witty, when the poor wretch was in the agony of death? This is just John Littlewit in *Bartholomew Fair*, who had a conceit (as he tells you) left him in his misery; a miserable conceit. On these occasions the poet should endeavour to raise pity; but instead of this, Ovid is tickling you to laugh. Virgil never made use of

1. Abundance has rendered me needy. (Ovid, *Metamorphoses* 3. 466.)

such machines when he was moving you to commiserate the death of Dido; he would not destroy what he was building. Chaucer makes Arcite violent in his love, and unjust in the pursuit of it; yet when he came to die, he made him think more reasonably. He repents not of his love, for that had altered his character; but acknowledges the injustice of his proceedings, and resigns Emilia to Palamon. What would Ovid have done on this occasion? He would certainly have made Arcite witty on his death-bed. He had complained he was farther off from possession, by being so near, and a thousand such boyisms, which Chaucer rejected as below the dignity of the subject. They who think otherwise would by the same reason prefer Lucan and Ovid to Homer and Virgil, and Martial to all four of them. As for the turn of words, in which Ovid particularly excels all poets, they are sometimes a fault and sometimes a beauty, as they are used properly or improperly; but in strong passions always to be shunned, because passions are serious and will admit no playing. The French have a high value for them; and I confess they are often what they call delicate, when they are introduced with judgement; but Chaucer writ with more simplicity, and followed nature more closely, than to use them. I have thus far, to the best of my knowledge, been an upright judge betwixt the parties in competition, not meddling with the design nor the disposition of it; because the design was not their own, and in the disposing of it they were equal. It remains that I say somewhat of Chaucer in particular.

In the first place, as he is the father of English poetry, so I hold him in the same degree of veneration as the Grecians held Homer, or the Romans Virgil. He is a perpetual fountain of good sense; learned in all sciences; and therefore speaks properly on all subjects. As he knew what to say, so he knows also when to leave off; a continence which is practised by few writers, and scarcely by any of the ancients, excepting Virgil and Horace. One of our late great poets[1] is sunk in his reputation because he could never forgive any conceit which came in his way, but swept like a drag-net, great and small. There was plenty enough, but the dishes were ill sorted; whole pyramids of sweet-meats, for boys and women, but little of solid meat, for men. All this proceeded not from any want of knowledge, but of judgement; neither did he want that in discerning the beauties and faults of other poets, but only indulged himself in the luxury of writing, and perhaps knew it was a fault but hoped the reader would not find it. For this reason, though he must always be thought a great poet, he is no longer esteemed a good writer. And for ten impressions which his works have had in so many successive years, yet at present a hundred books are scarcely purchased once a twelvemonth; for, as my last Lord Rochester said, though somewhat profanely, *Not being of God, he could not stand.*

Chaucer followed nature everywhere; but was never so bold to go beyond her. And there is a great difference of being *Poeta* and *nimis Poeta*,[2] if we may believe Catullus, as much as betwixt a modest behaviour and affectation. The verse of Chaucer, I confess, is not harmonious to us; but 'tis like the eloquence of one whom Tacitus commends, it was *auribus istius temporis accommodata.*[3] They who lived with him, and some time after him, thought it musical; and it continues so even in our judgement if compared with the numbers of Lydgate and Gower his contemporaries. There is the rude sweetness of a Scotch tune in it, which

1. Abraham Cowley (1618–67).
2. A poet. Poetical to excess.
3. Suited to the ears of that generation. (*Annals* 13. 3.)

is natural and pleasing, though not perfect. 'Tis true, I cannot go so far as he who published the last edition of him;[1] for he would make us believe the fault is in our ears, and that there were really ten syllables in a verse where we find but nine. But this opinion is not worth confuting; 'tis so gross and obvious an error, that common sense (which is a rule in everything but matters of faith and revelation) must convince the reader that equality of numbers in every verse which we call heroic was either not known, or not always practised in Chaucer's age. It were an easy matter to produce some thousands of his verses which are lame for want of half a foot, and sometimes a whole one, and which no pronunciation can make otherwise. We can only say that he lived in the infancy of our poetry, and that nothing is brought to perfection at the first. We must be children before we grow men. There was an Ennius, and in process of time a Lucilius, and a Lucretius, before Virgil and Horace; even after Chaucer there was a Spenser, a Harrington, a Fairfax, before Waller and Denham were in being; and our numbers were in their nonage till these last appeared. I need say little of his parentage, life, and fortunes; they are to be found at large in all the editions of his works. He was employed abroad, and favoured by Edward the Third, Richard the Second, and Henry the Fourth, and was poet, as I suppose, to all three of them. In Richard's time, I doubt, he was a little dipped in the rebellion of the Commons; and being brother-in-law to John of Gaunt, it was no wonder if he followed the fortunes of that family, and was well with Henry the Fourth when he had deposed his predecessor. Neither is it to be admired that Henry, who

1. Thomas Speght's edition of Chaucer appeared in 1597 and 1602. He advanced in his Preface the opinion, to which Dryden here mistakenly objects, that Chaucer's verse could be scanned.

was a wise as well as a valiant prince, who claimed by succession, and was sensible that his title was not sound but was rightfully in Mortimer, who had married the heir of York; it was not to be admired, I say, if that great politician should be pleased to have the greatest wit of those times in his interests, and to be the trumpet of his praises. Augustus had given him the example, by the advice of Maecenas, who recommended Virgil and Horace to him; whose praises helped to make him popular while he was alive, and after his death have made him precious to posterity. As for the religion of our poet, he seems to have some little bias towards the opinions of Wyclif, after John of Gaunt his patron; somewhat of which appears in the tale of *Piers Plowman*. Yet I cannot blame him for inveighing so sharply against the vices of the clergy in his age. Their pride, their ambition, their pomp, their avarice, their worldly interest, deserved the lashes which he gave them, both in that, and in most of his *Canterbury Tales*. Neither has his contemporary Boccace spared them. Yet both those poets lived in much esteem with good and holy men in orders; for the scandal which is given by particular priests, reflects not on the sacred function. Chaucer's Monk, his Canon, and his Friar, took not from the character of his Good Parson. A satirical poet is the check of the laymen on bad priests. We are only to take care that we involve not the innocent with the guilty in the same condemnation. The good cannot be too much honoured, nor the bad too coarsely used; for the corruption of the best becomes the worst. When a clergyman is whipped, his gown is first taken off, by which the dignity of his order is secured. If he be wrongfully accused, he has his action of slander; and 'tis at the poet's peril if he transgress the law. But they will tell us that all kind of satire, though never so well deserved by particular priests, yet brings the whole order into contempt. Is then the peerage of England anything dishonoured when a peer suffers for his treason? If he be libelled, or any way defamed, he has his *scandalum magnatum* to punish the offender. They who use this kind of argument, seem to be conscious to themselves of somewhat which has deserved the poet's lash, and are less concerned for their public capacity, than for their private; at least, there is pride at the bottom of their reasoning. If the faults of men in orders are only to be judged among themselves, they are all in some sort parties; for since they say the honour of their order is concerned in every member of it, how can we be sure that they will be impartial judges? How far I may be allowed to speak my opinion in this case, I know not; but I am sure a dispute of this nature caused mischief in abundance betwixt a king of England and an Archbishop of Canterbury; one standing up for the laws of his land, and the other for the honour (as he called it) of God's Church; which ended in the murder of the prelate, and in the whipping of his Majesty from post to pillar for his penance. The learned and ingenious Dr Drake[1] has saved me the labour of inquiring into the esteem and reverence which the priests have had of old; and I would rather extend than diminish any part of it. Yet I must needs say, that when a priest provokes me without any occasion given him, I have no reason, unless it be the charity of a Christian, to forgive him: *prior laesit* is justification sufficient in the civil law. If I answer him in his own language, self-defence, I am sure, must be allowed me; and if I carry it farther, even to a sharp recrimination, somewhat may be indulged to human frailty. Yet my resentment has not wrought so far but that I have followed Chaucer in his character of a

1. James Drake (1667–1707) published an answer to Collier's condemnation of the immorality of the stage.

holy man, and have enlarged on that subject with some pleasure, reserving to myself the right, if I shall think fit hereafter, to describe another sort of priests, such as are more easily to be found than the good Parson; such as have given the last blow to Christianity in this age by a practice so contrary to their doctrine. But this will keep cold till another time. In the meanwhile, I take up Chaucer where I left him. He must have been a man of a most wonderful comprehensive nature, because, as it has been truly observed of him, he has taken into the compass of his *Canterbury Tales* the various manners and humours (as we now call them) of the whole English nation in his age. Not a single character has escaped him. All his Pilgrims are severally distinguished from each other; and not only in their inclinations but in their very physiognomies and persons. *Baptista Porta*[1] could not have described their natures better, than by the marks which the poet gives them. The matter and manner of their tales, and of their telling, are so suited to their different educations, humours, and callings, that each of them would be improper in any other mouth. Even the grave and serious characters are distinguished by their several sorts of gravity. Their discourses are such as belong to their age, their calling, and their breeding; such as are becoming of them, and of them only. Some of his persons are vicious, and some virtuous; some are unlearned, or (as Chaucer calls them) lewd, and some are learned. Even the ribaldry of the low characters is different. The Reeve, the Miller, and the Cook are several men, and distinguished from each other as much as the mincing Lady Prioress, and the broad-speaking gap-toothed Wife of Bath. But enough of this: there is such a variety of game springing up before me that I am distracted in my choice, and know not which

1. An Italian physiognomist.

to follow. 'Tis sufficient to say according to the proverb, that here is God's plenty. We have our forefathers and great grandames all before us as they were in Chaucer's days; their general characters are still remaining in mankind, and even in England, though they are called by other names than those of monks, and friars, and canons, and lady abbesses, and nuns; for mankind is ever the same, and nothing lost out of nature, though everything is altered. May I have leave to do myself the justice (since my enemies will do me none, and are so far from granting me to be a good poet that they will not allow me so much as to be a Christian, or a moral man), may I have leave, I say, to inform my reader that I have confined my choice to such tales of Chaucer as savour nothing of immodesty. If I had desired more to please than to instruct, the Reeve, the Miller, the Shipman, the Merchant, the Sumner, and, above all, the Wife of Bath, in the Prologue to her Tale, would have procured me as many friends and readers as there are beaux and ladies of pleasure in the town. But I will no more offend against good manners. I am sensible as I ought to be of the scandal I have given by my loose writings, and make what reparation I am able by this public acknowledgement. If anything of this nature, or of profaneness, be crept into these poems, I am so far from defending it, that I disown it. *Totum hoc indictum volo.*[1] Chaucer makes another manner of apology for his broadspeaking, and Boccace makes the like; but I will follow neither of them. Our countryman, in the end of his characters, before the *Canterbury Tales*, thus excuses the ribaldry, which is very gross, in many of his novels:

> *But first, I pray you, of your courtesy,*
> *That ye ne arrete it not my villany,*

1. I would have all this unsaid.

Though that I plainly speak in this mattere
To tellen you her words, and eke her chere:
Ne though I speak her words properly,
For this ye knowen as well as I,
Who shall tellen a tale after a man
He mote rehearse as nye, as ever He can:
Everich word of it been in his charge,
All speke he, never so rudely, ne large.
Or else he mote tellen his tale untrue,
Or feine things, or find words new:
He may not spare, altho he were his brother,
He mote as well say o word as another.
Christ *spake himself full broad in holy Writ,*
And well I wote no villany is it.
Eke Plato *saith, who so can him rede,*
The words mote been cousin to the dede.

Yet if a man should have inquired of Boccace or of Chaucer what need they had of introducing such characters, where obscene words were proper in their mouths, but very undecent to be heard; I know not what answer they could have made. For that reason, such tales shall be left untold by me. You have here a specimen of Chaucer's language, which is so obsolete that his sense is scarce to be understood; and you have likewise more than one example of his unequal numbers, which were mentioned before. Yet many of his verses consist of ten syllables, and the words not much behind our present English; as for example, these two lines in the description of the Carpenter's young wife:

Wincing, she was as is a jolly Colt,
Long as a Mast, and upright as a Bolt.

I have almost done with Chaucer, when I have answered some objections relating to my present work. I find some people are offended that I have turned these tales into modern English; because they think them unworthy of my pains, and look on Chaucer as a dry, old-fashioned wit, not worth receiving. I have often heard the late Earl of Leicester[1] say that Mr Cowley himself was of that opinion, who having read him over at my Lord's request, declared he had no taste of him. I dare not advance my opinion against the judgement of so great an author; but I think it fair, however, to leave the decision to the public. Mr Cowley was too modest to set up for a dictator; and being shocked perhaps with his old style, never examined into the depth of his good sense. Chaucer, I confess, is a rough diamond, and must first be polished ere he shines. I deny not likewise that, living in our early days of poetry, he writes not always of a piece, but sometimes mingles trivial things with those of greater moment. Sometimes also, though not often, he runs riot, like Ovid, and knows not when he has said enough. But there are more great wits beside Chaucer whose fault is their excess of conceits, and those ill sorted. An author is not to write all he can, but only all he ought. Having observed this redundancy in Chaucer (as it is an easy matter for a man of ordinary parts to find a fault in one of greater), I have not tied myself to a literal translation; but have often omitted what I judged unnecessary or not of dignity enough to appear in the company of better thoughts. I have presumed farther in some places, and added somewhat of my own where I thought my author was deficient, and had not given his thoughts their true lustre for want of words in the beginning of our language. And to this I was the more emboldened, because (if I may be permitted to say it of myself) I found I had a soul congenial to his, and that I had been conversant in the same studies. Another poet in another age may take the same liberty with my writings; if at least they live long enough to

1. Philip Sidney, 3rd Earl of Leicester (1619–98), to whom Dryden dedicated *Don Sebastian*, 1690.

deserve correction. It was also necessary sometimes to re-
store the sense of Chaucer, which was lost or mangled in
the errors of the press. Let this example suffice at present in
the story of Palamon and Arcite, where the temple of Diana
is described, you find these verses, in all the editions of our
author:

> There saw I Danè *turned unto a Tree*,
> I *mean not the Goddess* Dianè,
> *But* Venus *Daughter, which that hight* Danè.

Which after a little consideration I knew was to be re-
formed into this sense, that Daphne the daughter of Peneus
was turned into a tree. I durst not make thus bold with
Ovid, lest some future Milbourne[1] should arise and say,
I varied from my author because I understood him not.

But there are other judges who think I ought not to have
translated Chaucer into English, out of a quite contrary
notion. They suppose there is a certain veneration due to
his old language; and that it is little less than profanation
and sacrilege to alter it. They are farther of opinion, that
somewhat of his good sense will suffer in this transfusion,
and much of the beauty of his thoughts will infallibly be
lost, which appear with more grace in their old habit. Of
this opinion was that excellent person, whom I mentioned,
the late Earl of Leicester, who valued Chaucer as much as
Mr Cowley despised him. My Lord dissuaded me from this
attempt (for I was thinking of it some years before his
death) and his authority prevailed so far with me as to defer
my undertaking while he lived in deference to him; yet my
reason was not convinced with what he urged against it.
If the first end of a writer be to be understood, then as his
language grows obsolete, his thoughts must grow obscure,

1. Luke Milbourne (1649–1720), a clergyman, who had published
an unsuccessful translation of Virgil in 1688, jealously criticized
Dryden's translation in a pamphlet which appeared in 1698.

multa renascuntur, quae nunc cecidere; cadentque quae nunc sunt in honore vocabula, si volet usus, quem penes arbitrium est & jus & norma loquendi.[1] When an ancient word for its sound and significancy deserves to be revived, I have that reasonable veneration for antiquity to restore it. All beyond this is superstition. Words are not like landmarks, so sacred as never to be removed. Customs are changed, and even statutes are silently repealed, when the reason ceases for which they were enacted. As for the other part of the argument, that his thoughts will lose of their original beauty by the innovation of words; in the first place, not only their beauty but their being is lost where they are no longer understood, which is the present case. I grant that something must be lost in all transfusion, that is, in all translations; but the sense will remain, which would otherwise be lost, or at least be maimed, when it is scarce intelligible, and that but to a few. How few are there who can read Chaucer so as to understand him perfectly? And if imperfectly, then with less profit and no pleasure. 'Tis not for the use of some old Saxon friends that I have taken these pains with him. Let them neglect my version, because they have no need of it. I made it for their sakes who understand sense and poetry as well as they; when that poetry and sense is put into words which they understand. I will go farther, and dare to add, that what beauties I lose in some places, I give to others which had them not originally. But in this I may be partial to myself; let the reader judge, and I submit to his decision. Yet I think I have just occasion to complain of them, who because they understand Chaucer, would deprive the greater part of their countrymen of the

---

1. Many words which have now fallen out of use will be reborn, and many now prominent will disappear, if usage (which owns the right to decide, and the law, and the canons of speech) so chooses. (Horace, *Ars Poetica* 70–2.)

same advantage, and hoard him up, as misers do their grandam gold, only to look on it themselves and hinder others from making use of it. In sum, I seriously protest that no man ever had, or can have, a greater veneration for Chaucer than myself. I have translated some part of his works only that I might perpetuate his memory, or at least refresh it, amongst my countrymen. If I have altered him anywhere for the better, I must at the same time acknowledge that I could have done nothing without him: *Facile est inventis addere*[1] is no great commendation; and I am not so vain to think I have deserved a greater. I will conclude what I have to say of him singly with this one remark: a lady of my acquaintance, who keeps a kind of correspondence with some authors of the fair sex in France, has been informed by them that Mademoiselle de Scudéry,[2] who is as old as Sibyl and inspired like her by the same god of poetry, is at this time translating Chaucer into modern French. From which I gather that he has been formerly translated into the old Provençal (for how she should come to understand old English I know not). But the matter of fact being true, it makes me think that there is something in it like fatality; that, after certain periods of time, the fame and memory of great wits should be renewed, as Chaucer is both in France and England. If this be wholly chance, 'tis extraordinary; and I dare not call it more for fear of being taxed with superstition.

Boccace comes last to be considered, who living in the same age with Chaucer, had the same genius and followed the same studies. Both writ novels, and each of them cultivated his mother tongue. But the greatest resemblance of our two modern authors being in their familiar style and

1. To add to another man's discoveries, is easy.
2. Madeleine de Scudéry (1607–1701), a voluminous author of heroic romances.

pleasing way of relating comical adventures, I may pass it over because I have translated nothing from Boccace of that nature. In the serious part of poetry, the advantage is wholly on Chaucer's side, for though the Englishman has borrowed many tales from the Italian, yet it appears that those of Boccace were not generally of his own making but taken from authors of former ages and by him only modelled; so that what there was of invention in either of them may be judged equal. But Chaucer has refined on Boccace, and has mended the stories which he has borrowed, in his way of telling; though prose allows more liberty of thought, and the expression is more easy when unconfined by numbers. Our countryman carries weight, and yet wins the race at disadvantage. I desire not the reader should take my word; and therefore I will set two of their discourses on the same subject in the same light, for every man to judge betwixt them. I translated Chaucer first, and amongst the rest, pitched on the Wife of Bath's Tale; not daring, as I have said, to adventure on her Prologue, because 'tis too licentious. There Chaucer introduces an old woman of mean parentage, whom a youthful knight of noble blood was forced to marry, and consequently loathed her. The crone being in bed with him on the wedding night, and finding his aversion, endeavours to win his affection by reason, and speaks a good word for herself (as who could blame her?) in hope to mollify the sullen bridegroom. She takes her topics from the benefits of poverty, the advantages of old age and ugliness, the vanity of youth, and the silly pride of ancestry and titles without inherent virtue, which is the true nobility. When I had closed Chaucer, I returned to Ovid and translated some more of his fables; and by this time had so far forgotten the Wife of Bath's Tale, that when I took up Boccace, unawares I fell on the same argument of preferring virtue to nobility of blood and titles, in the story of Sigismonda, which I had certainly avoided for the resemblance of the two discourses if my memory had not failed me. Let the reader weigh them both; and if he thinks me partial to Chaucer, 'tis in him to right Boccace.

I prefer in our countryman, far above all his other stories, the noble poem of Palamon and Arcite, which is of the epic kind, and perhaps not much inferior to the *Ilias* or the *Aeneis*. The story is more pleasing than either of them, the manners as perfect, the diction as poetical, the learning as deep and various, and the disposition full as artful: only it includes a greater length of time, as taking up seven years at least; but Aristotle has left undecided the duration of the action; which yet is easily reduced into the compass of a year by a narration of what preceded the return of Palamon to Athens. I had thought for the honour of our nation, and more particularly for his whose laurel, tho' unworthy, I have worn after him, that this story was of English growth and Chaucer's own. But I was undeceived by Boccace; for casually looking on the end of his seventh *Giornata*, I found Dioneo (under which name he shadows himself) and Fiametta (who represents his mistress, the natural daughter of Robert, King of Naples) of whom these words are spoken: *Dioneo e Fiametta gran pezza cantarono insieme d'Arcita, e di Palemone*. By which it appears that this story was written before the time of Boccace, but the name of its author being wholly lost, Chaucer is now become an original; and I question not but the poem has received many beauties by passing through his noble hands. Besides this tale, there is another of his own invention, after the manner of the Provençals, called *The Flower and the Leaf*; with which I was so particularly pleased, both for the invention and the moral, that I cannot hinder myself from recommending it to the reader.

As a corollary to this preface, in which I have done justice to others, I owe somewhat to myself: not that I think it worth my time to enter the lists with one *M —* ,[1] and one *B —* [2], but barely to take notice that such men there are who have written scurrilously against me without any provocation. *M —* , who is in orders, pretends amongst the rest this quarrel to me, that I have fallen foul on priesthood. If I have, I am only to ask pardon of good priests, and am afraid his part of the reparation will come to little. Let him be satisfied that he shall not be able to force himself upon me for an adversary. I contemn him too much to enter into competition with him. His own translations of Virgil have answered his criticisms on mine. If (as they say he has declared in print) he prefers the version of Ogilby[3] to mine, the world has made him the same compliment; for 'tis agreed on all hands that he writes even below Ogilby. That, you will say, is not easily to be done; but what cannot *M —* bring about? I am satisfied, however, that while he and I live together, I shall not be thought the worst poet of the age. It looks as if I had desired him underhand to write so ill against me; but upon my honest word I have not bribed him to do me this service and am wholly guiltless of his pamphlet. 'Tis true I should be glad if I could persuade him to continue his good offices and write such another critique on anything of mine; for I find by experience he has a great stroke with the reader when he condemns any of my poems to make the world have a better

1. Luke Milbourne, see p. 246, n. 1.
2. Sir Richard Blackmore (*d.* 1729), 'the City Bard, or Knight Physician' (see below); he published his epic poems, 'his *Arthurs'* (see below), *Prince Arthur* and *King Arthur*, in 1695 and 1697. Blackmore reflected unfavourably on Dryden in the first of these two poems.
3. John Ogilby's (1600–76) translation of Virgil first appeared in 1654.

opinion of them. He has taken some pains with my poetry; but nobody will be persuaded to take the same with his. If I had taken to the Church (as he affirms, but which was never in my thoughts) I should have had more sense, if not more grace, than to have turned myself out of my benefice by writing libels on my parishioners. But his account of my manners and my principles are of a piece with his cavils and his poetry: and so I have done with him for ever.

As for the City Bard, or Knight Physician, I hear his quarrel to me is that I was the author of *Absalom and Achitophel*, which he thinks is a little hard on his fanatic patrons in London.

But I will deal the more civilly with his two poems, because nothing ill is to be spoken of the dead: and therefore peace be to the *Manes* of his *Arthurs*. I will only say that it was not for this noble Knight that I drew the plan of an epic poem on King Arthur in my preface to the translation of Juvenal. The Guardian Angels of Kingdoms were machines too ponderous for him to manage; and therefore he rejected them as Dares did the whirlbats of Eryx when they were thrown before him by Entellus. Yet from that preface he plainly took his hint; for he began immediately upon the story, though he had the baseness not to acknowledge his benefactor, but instead of it to traduce me in a libel.

I shall say the less of Mr Collier, because in many things he has taxed me justly; and I have pleaded guilty to all thoughts and expressions of mine which can be truly argued of obscenity, profaneness, or immorality, and retract them. If he be my enemy, let him triumph; if he be my friend, as I have given him no personal occasion to be otherwise, he will be glad of my repentance. It becomes me not to draw my pen in the defence of a bad cause when I have so often drawn it for a good one. Yet it were not difficult to prove that in many places he has perverted my meaning by his glosses; and interpreted my words into blasphemy and bawdry of which they were not guilty. Besides that, he is too much given to horse-play in his raillery; and comes to battle like a dictator from the plough. I will not say, *The Zeal of God's House has eaten him up*; but I am sure it has devoured some part of his good manners and civility. It might also be doubted whether it were altogether zeal which prompted him to this rough manner of proceeding; perhaps it became not one of his function to rake into the rubbish of ancient and modern plays; a divine might have employed his pains to better purpose than in the nastiness of Plautus and Aristophanes, whose examples, as they excuse not me, so it might be possibly supposed that he read them not without some pleasure. They who have written commentaries on those poets, or on Horace, Juvenal, and Martial, have explained some vices, which without their interpretation had been unknown to modern times. Neither has he judged impartially betwixt the former age and us.

There is more bawdry in one play of Fletcher's, called *The Custom of the Country*, than in all ours together. Yet this has been often acted on the stage in my remembrance. Are the times so much more reformed now than they were five-and-twenty years ago? If they are, I congratulate the amendment of our morals. But I am not to prejudice the cause of my fellow-poets, though I abandon my own defence. They have some of them answered for themselves, and neither they nor I can think Mr Collier so formidable an enemy that we should shun him. He has lost ground at the latter end of the day by pursuing his point too far, like the Prince of Condé at the battle of Senneph[1]: from immoral

1. The battle was fought on 11 August 1674.

plays, to no plays, *ab abusu ad usum, non valet consequentia.*[1]
But being a party, I am not to erect myself into a judge.
As for the rest of those who have written against me, they
are such scoundrels that they deserve not the least notice
to be taken of them. *B* – and *M* – are only distinguished
from the crowd by being remembered to their infamy:

> *Demetri, teque Tigelli*
> *Discipularum inter jubeo plorare cathedras.*[2]

1. No valid inference can be made from the abuse of a thing to its
use.
2. As for you, Demetrius and Tigellius, I bid you go howl amidst
the chairs of your lady-pupils. (Horace, *Satires* 1. 10. 90–1.)

AURENG-ZEBE

A TRAGEDY

Sed, cum fregit subsellia versu,
Esurit, intactum *Paridi* nisi vendat Agaven.
J uv.[1]

PERSONS REPRESENTED

The old Emperor
Aureng-Zebe, his son
Morat, his youngest son
Arimant, governor of Agra
Dianet
Solyman
Mir Baba   Indian lords, or Omrahs,
Abas   of several factions
Asaph Chawn
Fazel Chawn
Nourmahal, the Empress
Indamora, a captive Queen
Melesinda, wife to Morat
Zayda, favourite slave to the Empress

SCENE, *Agra*, in the year 1660

PROLOGUE

Our author by experience finds it true,
'Tis much more hard to please himself than you;
And out of no feigned modesty this day
Damns his laborious trifle of a play.
Not that it's worse than what before he writ,
But he has now another taste of wit;

1. But even when an author has brought down the house with his
lines, he must go hungry if he is not prepared to sell his Agave
unspotted to his Paris (i.e. to his chief actor). (Juvenal 6. 87.)

And, to confess a truth (though out of time),
Grows weary of his long-loved mistress, rhyme.
Passion's too fierce to be in fetters bound,
And nature flies him like enchanted ground.
What verse can do, he has performed in this,
Which he presumes the most correct of his.
But spite of all his pride a secret shame
Invades his breast at Shakespeare's sacred name;
Awed when he hears his godlike Romans rage,
He, in a just despair, would quit the stage;
And to an age less polished, more unskilled,
Does with disdain the foremost honours yield.
As with the greater dead he dares not strive,
He would not match his verse with those who live.
Let him retire, betwixt two ages cast,
The first of this, and hindmost of the last.
A losing gamester, let him sneak away;
He bears no ready money from the play.
The fate which governs poets thought it fit
He should not raise his fortunes by his wit.
The clergy thrive, and the litigious bar;
Dull heroes fatten with the spoils of war;
All southern vices, heav'n be praised, are here;
But wit's a luxury you think too dear.
When you to cultivate the plant are loath,
'Tis a shrewd sign 'twas never of your growth;
And wit in northern climates will not blow,
Except, like orange trees, 'tis housed from snow.
There needs no care to put a playhouse down,
'Tis the most desert place of all the town.
We and our neighbours, to speak proudly, are
Like monarchs ruined with expensive war;
While, like wise English, unconcerned you sit,
And see us play the tragedy of wit.

AURENG-ZEBE

A TRAGEDY

ACT I

[ARIMANT, ASAPH CHAWN, FAZEL CHAWN]

ARIMANT. Heav'n seems the empire of the east to lay
    On the success of this important day;
    Their arms are to the last decision bent,
    And fortune labours with the vast event;
    She now has in her hand the greatest stake,
    Which for contending monarchs she can make.
    What e'er can urge ambitious youth to fight,
    She pompously displays before their sight;
    Laws, empire, all permitted to the sword,
    And fate could ne'er an ampler scene afford.

ASAPH CHAWN. Four several armies to the field are led,
    Which high in equal hopes four princes head.
    Indus and Ganges, our wide empire's bounds,
    Swell their dyed currents with their natives' wounds;
    Each purple river winding as he runs
    His bloody arms about his slaughtered sons.

FAZEL CHAWN. I well remember you foretold the storm,
    When first the brothers did their factions form;
    When each, by cursed cabals of women, strove
    To draw th' indulgent King to partial love.

ARIMANT. What heav'n decrees, no prudence can prevent.
    To cure their mad ambition, they were sent
    To rule a distant province each alone.
    What could a careful father more have done?
    He made provision against all, but fate;
    While, by his health, we held our peace of state.

The weight of seventy winters pressed him down,
He bent beneath the burden of a crown;
Sickness, at last, did his spent body seize,
And life almost sunk under the disease;
Mortal 'twas thought, at least by them desired,
Who, impiously, into his years inquired.
As at a signal, straight the sons prepare
For open force, and rush to sudden war;
Meeting, like winds broke loose upon the main,
To prove by arms whose fate it was to reign.

ASAPH CHAWN. Rebels and parricides!

ARIMANT. Brand not their actions with so foul a name;
Pity, at least, what we are forced to blame.
When death's cold hand has closed the father's eye,
You know the younger sons are doomed to die.
Less ills are chosen greater to avoid,
And nature's laws are by the states destroyed.
What courage tamely could to death consent,
And not, by striking first, the blow prevent?
Who falls in fight cannot himself accuse,
And he dies greatly who a crown pursues.

[*To them*, SOLYMAN AGAH]

SOLYMAN AGAH. A new express all Agra does affright:
Darah and Aureng-Zebe are joined in fight;
The press of people thickens to the court,
Th' impatient crowd devouring the report.

ARIMANT. T' each changing news they changed affections
bring,
And servilely from fate expect a king.

SOLYMAN. The ministers of state, who gave us law,
In corners with selected friends withdraw;
There, in deaf murmurs, solemnly are wise,
Whisp'ring like winds ere hurricanes arise.

The most corrupt are most obsequious grown,
And those they scorned officiously they own.

ASAPH CHAWN. In change of government
The rabble rule their great oppressors' fate:
Do sovereign justice, and revenge the state.

SOLYMAN. The little courtiers, who ne'er come to know
The depth of factions, as in mazes go,
Where int'rests meet and cross so oft that they
With too much care are wildered in their way.

ARIMANT. What of the Emperor?

SOLYMAN. Unmoved, and brave, he like himself appears,
And, meriting no ill, no danger fears;
Yet mourns his former vigour lost so far,
To make him now spectator of a war;
Repining that he must preserve his crown
By any help or courage but his own;
Wishes, each minute, he could unbeget
Those rebel-sons, who dare t' usurp his seat;
To sway his empire with unequal skill,
And mount a throne which none but he can fill.

ARIMANT. Oh! had he still that character maintained
Of valour, which in blooming youth he gained!
He promised in his east a glorious race;
Now, sunk from his meridian, sets apace.
But as the sun when he from noon declines,
And with abated heat less fiercely shines,
Seems to grow milder as he goes away,
Pleasing himself with the remains of day;
So he who in his youth for glory strove,
Would recompense his age with ease and love.

ASAPH CHAWN. The name of father hateful to him grows,
Which, for one son, produces him three foes.

FAZEL CHAWN. Darah, the eldest, bears a generous mind;
But to implacable revenge inclined.

Too openly does love and hatred show:
A bounteous master, but a deadly foe.

SOLYMAN. From Sujah's valour I should much expect,
But he's a bigot of the Persian sect;
And by a foreign int'rest seeks to reign,
Hopeless by love the sceptre to obtain.

ASAPH CHAWN. Morat's too insolent, too much a brave,
His courage to his envy is a slave.
What he attempts, if his endeavours fail
T' effect, he is resolved no other shall.

ARIMANT. But Aureng-Zebe, by no strong passion swayed,
Except his love, more temp'rate is and weighed.
This Atlas must our sinking state uphold;
In council cool, but in performance bold.
He sums their virtues in himself alone,
And adds the greatest, of a loyal son.
His father's cause upon his sword he wears,
And with his arms, we hope, his fortune bears.

SOLYMAN. Two vast rewards may well his courage move,
A parent's blessing, and a mistress' love.
If he succeed, his recompense, we hear,
Must be the captive Queen of Cassimere.

[*To them,* ABAS]

ABAS. Mischiefs on mischiefs, greater still, and more !
The neighb'ring plain with arms is covered o'er:
The vale an iron-harvest seems to yield
Of thick-sprung lances in a waving field.
The polished steel gleams terribly from far,
And every moment nearer shows the war.
The horses' neighing by the wind is blown,
And castled elephants o'erlook the town.

ARIMANT. If, as I fear, Morat these pow'rs commands,
Our empire on the brink of ruin stands.

Th' ambitious Empress with her son is joined,
And, in his brother's absence, has designed
The unprovided town to take with ease,
And then the person of the King to seize.

SOLYMAN. To all his former issue she has shown
Long hate, and laboured to advance her own.

ABAS. These troops are his.
Surat he took; and thence, preventing fame,
By quick and painful marches hither came.
Since his approach, he to his mother sent,
And two long hours in close debate were spent.

ARIMANT. I'll to my charge, the citadel, repair,
And show my duty by my timely care.

[*To them the* EMPEROR *with a letter in his hand; after him
an* AMBASSADOR, *with a train following*]

ASAPH CHAWN. But see, the Emperor! a fiery red
His brows and glowing temples does o'erspread;
Morat has some displeasing message sent.

AMBASSADOR. Do not, great Sir, misconstrue his intent;
Nor call rebellion what was prudent care,
To guard himself by necessary war.
While he believed you living, he obeyed;
His governments but as your viceroy swayed;
But when he thought you gone
T' augment the number of the blessed above,
He deemed 'em legacies of royal love;
Nor armed his brothers' portions to invade,
But to defend the present you had made.

EMPEROR. By frequent messages, and strict commands,
He knew my pleasure to discharge his bands.
Proof of my life my royal signet made;
Yet still he armed, came on, and disobeyed.

AMBASSADOR. He thought the mandate forged, your death
    concealed;
  And but delayed till truth should be revealed.
EMPEROR. News of my death from rumour he received,
  And what he wished, he easily believed;
  But long demurred, though from my hand he knew
  I lived, so loath he was to think it true.
  Since he pleads ignorance to that command,
  Now let him show his duty, and disband.
AMBASSADOR. His honour, Sir, will suffer in the cause,
  He yields his arms unjust if he withdraws;
  And begs his loyalty may be declared
  By owning those he leads to be your guard.
EMPEROR. I, in myself, have all the guard I need;
  Bid the presumptuous boy draw off with speed.
  If his audacious troops one hour remain,
  My cannon from the fort shall scour the plain.
AMBASSADOR. Since you deny him entrance, he demands
  His wife, whom cruelly you hold in bands;
  Her, if unjustly you from him detain,
  He justly will by force of arms regain.
EMPEROR. O'er him and his a right from heav'n I
    have;
  Subject and son, he's doubly born my slave.
  But whatsoe'er his own demerits are,
  Tell him, I shall not make on women, war.
  And yet I'll do her innocence the grace,
  To keep her here, as in the safer place.
  But thou, who dar'st this bold defiance bring,
  May'st feel the rage of an offended King.
  Hence from my sight, without the least reply:
  One word, nay, one look more, and thou shalt die.

[*Exit* AMBASSADOR]

[*Re-enter* ARIMANT]

ARIMANT. May heav'n, great monarch, still augment your
    bliss
  With length of days, and every day like this.
  For, from the banks of Gemna news is brought,
  Your army has a bloody battle fought.
  Darah from loyal Aureng-Zebe is fled,
  And forty thousand of his men lie dead.
  To Sujah next your conquering army drew;
  Him they surprised, and easily o'erthrew.

EMPEROR. 'Tis well.

ARIMANT. But well! what more could at your wish be
    done,
  Than two such conquests gained by such a son?
  Your pardon, mighty Sir;
  You seem not high enough your joys to rate;
  You stand indebted a vast sum to fate,
  And should large thanks for the great blessing pay.

EMPEROR. My fortune owes me greater every day;
  And should my joy more high for this appear,
  It would have argued me before of fear.
  How is heav'n kind, where I have nothing won,
  And fortune only pays me with my own?

ARIMANT. Great Aureng-Zebe did duteous care express;
  And durst not push too far his good success.
  But lest Morat the city should attack,
  Commanded his victorious army back;
  Which, left to march as swiftly as they may,
  Himself comes first and will be here this day,
  Before a close-formed siege shut up his way.

EMPEROR. Prevent his purpose! hence, hence with all thy
    speed.
  Stop him; his entrance to the town forbid.

ARIMANT. How, Sir? your loyal, your victorious son?

EMPEROR. Him would I, more than all the rebels, shun.

ARIMANT. Whom with your pow'r and fortune, Sir, you
    trust,
  Now to suspect is vain, as 'tis unjust.
  He comes not with a train to move your fear,
  But trusts himself, to be a pris'ner here.
  You knew him brave, you know him faithful now;
  He aims at fame, but fame from serving you.
  'Tis said, ambition in his breast does rage;
  Who would not be the hero of an age?
  All grant him prudent; prudence interest weighs,
  And interest bids him seek your love and praise.
  I know you grateful; when he marched from hence,
  You bade him hope an ample recompense;
  He conquered in that hope; and from your hands,
  His love, the precious pledge he left, demands.

EMPEROR. No more! you search too deep my wounded
    mind;
  And show me what I fear, and would not find.
  My son has all the debts of duty paid;
  Our Prophet sends him to my present aid.
  Such virtue to distrust were base and low;
  I'm not ungrateful – or I was not so!
  Inquire no farther, stop his coming on;
  I will not, cannot, dare not see my son.

ARIMANT. 'Tis now too late his entrance to prevent;
  Nor must I to your ruin give consent.
  At once your people's heart and son's you lose;
  And give him all, when you just things refuse.

EMPEROR. Thou lov'st me sure; thy faith has oft been tried,
  In ten pitched fields not shrinking from my side,
  Yet giv'st me no advice to bring me ease.

ARIMANT. Can you be cured, and tell not your disease?
  I asked you, Sir?

EMPEROR.   Thou shouldst have asked again:
There hangs a secret shame on guilty men.
Thou shouldst have pulled the secret from my breast,
Torn out the bearded steel to give me rest.
At least, thou shouldst have guessed –
Yet thou art honest, thou couldst ne'er have guessed.
Hast thou been never base? did love ne'er bend
Thy frailer virtue to betray thy friend?
Flatter me, make thy court, and say, it did:
Kings in a crowd would have their vices hid.
We would be kept in count'nance, saved from shame;
And owned by others who commit the same.
Nay, now I have confessed. –
Thou seest me naked, and without disguise;
I look on Aureng-Zebe with rival's eyes.
He has abroad my enemies o'ercome,
And I have sought to ruin him at home.

ARIMANT. This free confession shows you long did
      strive;
And virtue, though oppressed, is still alive.
But what success did your injustice find?

EMPEROR. What it deserved, and not what I designed.
Unmoved she stood, and deaf to all my prayers,
As seas and winds to sinking mariners.
But seas grow calm, and winds are reconciled;
Her tyrant beauty never grows more mild.
Pray'rs, promises, and threats were all in vain.

ARIMANT. Then cure yourself by generous disdain.

EMPEROR. Virtue, disdain, despair, I oft have tried,
And foiled, have with new arms my foe defied.
This made me with so little joy to hear
The victory, when I the victor fear.

ARIMANT. Something you swiftly must resolve to do,
Lest Aureng-Zebe your secret love should know.

Morat without does for your ruin wait;
And would you lose the buckler of your state?
A jealous Empress lies within your arms,
Too haughty to endure neglected charms.
Your son is duteous, but (as man) he's frail;
And just revenge o'er virtue may prevail.

EMPEROR. Go then to Indamora, say from me,
Two lives depend upon her secrecy.
Bid her conceal my passion from my son.
Though Aureng-Zebe return a conqueror,
Both he and she are still within my pow'r.
Say, I'm a father, but a lover too;
Much to my son, more to myself I owe.
When she receives him, to her words give law;
And even the kindness of her glances awe.
See, he appears!

[*After a short whisper*, ARIMANT *departs*]

[*Enter* AURENG-ZEBE, DIANET, *and attendants.—*
AURENG-ZEBE *kneels to his father, and kisses his hand*]

AURENG-ZEBE. My vows have been successful as my
sword;
My pray'rs are heard, you have your health restored.
Once more 'tis given me to behold your face;
The best of kings and fathers to embrace.
Pardon my tears; 'tis joy which bids 'em flow,
A joy which never was sincere till now.
That which my conquest gave I could not prize;
Or 'twas imperfect till I saw your eyes.

EMPEROR. Turn the discourse: I have a reason why
I would not have you speak so tenderly.
Knew you what shame your kind expressions bring,
You would in pity spare a wretched King.

AURENG-ZEBE. A King! you rob me, Sir, of half my due!
  You have a dearer name, a father too.
EMPEROR. I had that name.
AURENG-ZEBE.   What have I said or done,
  That I no longer must be called your son?
  'Tis in that name, heav'n knows, I glory more,
  Than that of prince, or that of conqueror.
EMPEROR. Then you upbraid me; I am pleased to see
  You're not so perfect, but can fail, like me.
  I have no god to deal with.
AURENG-ZEBE.   Now I find
  Some sly court-devil has seduced your mind;
  Filled it with black suspicions not your own,
  And all my actions through false optics shown.
  I ne'er did crowns ambitiously regard;
  Honour I sought, the generous mind's reward.
  Long may you live! while you the sceptre sway
  I shall be still most happy to obey.
EMPEROR. Oh, Aureng-Zebe! thy virtues shine too bright,
  They flash too fierce; I, like the bird of night,
  Shut my dull eyes and sicken at the sight.
  Thou hast deserved more love than I can show;
  But 'tis thy fate to give, and mine to owe.
  Thou seest me much distempered in my mind;
  Pulled back, and then pushed forward to be kind.
  Virtue, and – fain I would my silence break,
  But have not yet the confidence to speak.
  Leave me, and to thy needful rest repair.
AURENG-ZEBE. Rest is not suiting with a lover's care.
  I have not yet my Indamora seen.   [*Is going*]
EMPEROR. Somewhat I had forgot; come back again:
  So weary of a father's company!
AURENG-ZEBE. Sir, you were pleased yourself to license
  me.

EMPEROR. You made me no relation of the fight.
    Besides, a rebel's army is in sight.
    Advise me first; yet go –
    He goes to Indamora; I should take   *[Aside]*
    A kind of envious joy to keep him back.
    Yet to detain him makes my love appear;
    I hate his presence, and his absence fear.   *[Exit]*
AURENG-ZEBE. To some new clime, or to thy native
    sky,
    Oh, friendless and forsaken virtue fly!
    Thy Indian air is deadly to thee grown;
    Deceit and cankered malice rule thy throne.
    Why did my arms in battle prosp'rous prove,
    To gain the barren praise of filial love?
    The best of kings by women is misled,
    Charmed by the witchcraft of a second bed.
    Against myself I victories have won,
    And by my fatal absence am undone.

[To him INDAMORA, *with* ARIMANT *]*

But here she comes!
In the calm harbour of whose gentle breast
My tempest-beaten soul may safely rest.
Oh, my heart's joy! whate'er my sorrows be,
They cease and vanish in beholding thee!
Care shuns thy walks; as at the cheerful light,
The groaning ghosts and birds obscene take flight.
By this one view, all my past pains are paid;
And all I have to come more easy made.
INDAMORA. Such sullen planets at my birth did shine,
    They threaten every fortune mixed with mine.
    Fly the pursuit of my disastrous love,
    And from unhappy neighbourhood remove.

AURENG-ZEBE. Bid the laborious hind,
 Whose hardened hands did long in tillage toil,
 Neglect the promised harvest of the soil,
 Should I, who cultivated love with blood,
 Refuse possession of approaching good?

INDAMORA. Love is an airy good, opinion makes;
 Which he, who only thinks he has, partakes.
 Seen by a strong imagination's beam,
 That tricks and dresses up the gaudy dream.
 Presented so, with rapture 'tis enjoyed;
 Raised by high fancy, and by low destroyed.

AURENG-ZEBE. If love be vision, mine has all the fire
 Which, in first dreams, young prophets does inspire.
 I dream, in you, our promised paradise;
 An age's tumult of continued bliss.
 But you have still your happiness in doubt;
 Or else 'tis past, and you have dreamt it out.

INDAMORA. Perhaps not so.

AURENG-ZEBE.   Can Indamora prove
 So altered? Is it but, perhaps you love?
 Then farewell all! I thought in you to find
 A balm to cure my much distempered mind.
 I came to grieve a father's heart estranged;
 But little thought to find a mistress changed.
 Nature herself is changed to punish me;
 Virtue turned vice, and faith inconstancy.

INDAMORA. You heard me not inconstancy confess!
 'Twas but a friend's advice to love me less.
 Who knows what adverse fortune may befall?
 Arm well your mind; hope little, and fear all.
 Hope with a goodly prospect feeds your eye;
 Shows from a rising ground possession nigh;
 Shortens the distance, or o'erlooks it quite;
 So easy 'tis to travel with the sight.

AURENG-ZEBE. Then to despair you would my love betray
    By taking hope, its last kind friend, away.
    You hold the glass, but turn the perspective;
    And farther off the lessened object drive.
    You bid me fear: in that your change I know;
    You would prepare me for the coming blow.
    But, to prevent you, take my last adieu;
    I'll sadly tell myself you are untrue,
    Rather than stay to hear it told by you.   *[Going]*
INDAMORA. Stay, Aureng-Zebe, I must not let you go.
    And yet believe yourself your own worst foe,
    Think I am true, and seek no more to know.
    Let in my breast the fatal secret lie,
    'Tis a sad riddle, which, if known, we die.
                             [Seeming to pause]
AURENG-ZEBE. Fair hypocrite, you seek to cheat in vain;
    Your silence argues you ask time to feign.
    Once more, farewell; the snare in sight is laid,
    'Tis my own fault if I am now betrayed. *[Going again]*
INDAMORA. Yet once more stay; you shall believe me
    true,
    Though in one fate I wrap myself and you.
    Your absence –
ARIMANT.   Hold; you know the hard command
    I must obey; you only can withstand
    Your own mishap. I beg you on my knee,
    Be not unhappy by your own decree.
AURENG-ZEBE. Speak, Madam, by (if that be yet an
    oath)
    Your love, I'm pleased we should be ruined both.
    Both is a sound of joy:
    In death's dark bow'rs our bridals we will keep,
    And his cold hand
    Shall draw the curtain when we go to sleep.

INDAMORA. Know then, that man whom both of us did
    trust,
  Has been to you unkind, to me unjust.
  The guardian of my faith so false did prove,
  As to solicit me with lawless love.
  Prayed, promised, threatened, all that man could do,
  Base as he's great; and need I tell you who?

AURENG-ZEBE. Yes! for I'll not believe my father meant.
  Speak quickly, and my impious thoughts prevent.

INDAMORA. You've said; I wish I could some other name!

ARIMANT. My duty must excuse me, Sir, from blame.
  A guard there!

              [Enter Guards]

AURENG-ZEBE.   Slave, for me?

ARIMANT.   My orders are
  To seize this Princess, whom the laws of war
  Long since made prisoner.

AURENG-ZEBE. Villain!

ARIMANT.   Sir, I know
  Your birth, nor durst another call me so.

AURENG-ZEBE. I have redeemed her; and as mine she's
  free.

ARIMANT. You may have right to give her liberty;
  But with your father, Sir, that right dispute,
  For his commands to me were absolute;
  If she disclosed his love, to use the right
  Of war and to secure her from your sight.

AURENG-ZEBE. I'll rescue her, or die.   *[Draws]*
  And you, my friends, though few, are yet too brave
  To see your Gen'ral's mistress made a slave.

               [All draw]

INDAMORA. Hold, my dear love! if so much pow'r there
    lies,
  As once you owned, in Indamora's eyes,

Lose not the honour you have early won;
But stand the blameless pattern of a son.
My love your claim inviolate secures;
'Tis writ in fate, I can be only yours.
My suff'rings for you make your heart my due;
Be worthy me, as I am worthy you.

AURENG-ZEBE [*putting up his sword*]. I've thought, and
    blessed be you who gave me time;
My virtue was surprised into a crime.
Strong virtue, like strong nature, struggles still;
Exerts itself, and then throws off the ill.
I to a son's and lover's praise aspire;
And must fulfil the parts which both require.
How dear the cure of jealousy has cost!
With too much care and tenderness you're lost.
So the fond youth from hell redeemed his prize,
Till looking back she vanished from his eyes!

[*Exeunt severally*]

ACT II

[*Betwixt the Acts, a warlike tune is played, shooting off guns,
and shouts of soldiers are heard as in an assault*]

[AURENG-ZEBE, ARIMANT, ASAPH CHAWN,
FAZEL CHAWN, SOLYMAN]

AURENG-ZEBE. What man could do was by Morat per-
    formed;
The fortress thrice himself in person stormed.
Your valour bravely did th' assault sustain;
And filled the moats and ditches with the slain.
Till, mad with rage, into the breach he fired;
Slew friends and foes, and in the smoke retired

ARIMANT. To us you give what praises are not due;
  Morat was thrice repulsed, but thrice by you.
  High, over all, was your great conduct shown;
  You sought our safety, but forgot your own.

ASAPH CHAWN. Their standard, planted on the battle-
    ment,
  Despair and death among the soldiers sent.
  You, the bold Omrah tumbled from the wall;
  And shouts of victory pursued his fall.

FAZEL CHAWN. To you, alone, we owe this prosp'rous
    day;
  Our wives and children rescued from the prey.
  Know your own int'rest, Sir, where'er you lead,
  We jointly vow to own no other head.

SOLYMAN. Your wrongs are known. Impose but your
    commands;
  This hour shall bring you twenty thousand hands.

AURENG-ZEBE. Let them who truly would appear my
    friends,
  Employ their swords, like mine, for noble ends.
  No more: remember you have bravely done;
  Shall treason end what loyalty begun?
  I own no wrongs; some grievance I confess,
  But kings, like gods, at their own time redress.
  Yet, some becoming boldness I may use;
  I've well deserved, nor will he now refuse.   [*Aside*]
  I'll strike my fortunes with him at a heat;
  And give him not the leisure to forget.

    [*Exit, attended by the* OMRAHS]

ARIMANT. Oh! Indamora, hide these fatal eyes;
  Too deep they wound whom they too soon surprise.
  My virtue, prudence, honour, interest, all
  Before this universal monarch fall.

Beauty, like ice, our footing does betray;
Who can tread sure on the smooth slippery way?
Pleased with the passage, we slide swiftly on;
And see the dangers which we cannot shun.

[*To him,* INDAMORA]

INDAMORA. I hope my liberty may reach thus far?
These terrace walks within my limits are.
I came to seek you, and to let you know,
How much I to your generous pity owe.
The King, when he designed you for my guard,
Resolved he would not make my bondage hard;
If otherwise, you have deceived his end,
And whom he meant a guardian made a friend.
ARIMANT. A guardian's title I must own with shame;
But should be prouder of another name.
INDAMORA. And therefore 'twas I changed that name before;
I called you friend, and could you wish for more?
ARIMANT. I dare not ask for what you would not grant;
But wishes, Madam, are extravagant.
They are not bounded with things possible;
I may wish more than I presume to tell.
Desire's the vast extent of human mind,
It mounts above, and leaves poor hope behind.
I could wish –
INDAMORA. What?
ARIMANT. Why did you speak? you've dashed my fancy quite;
Ev'n in th' approaching minute of delight.
I must take breath –
Ere I the rapture of my wish renew,
And tell you then, it terminates in you.

INDAMORA. Have you considered what th'event would be?
  Or know you, Arimant, yourself, or me?
  Were I no Queen, did you my beauty weigh,
  My youth in bloom, your age in its decay?
ARIMANT. I my own judge, condemned myself before;
  For pity aggravate my crime no more.
  So weak I am, I with a frown am slain;
  You need have used but half so much disdain.
INDAMORA. I am not cruel yet to that degree;
  Have better thoughts both of yourself and me.
  Beauty a monarch is,
  Which kingly power magnificently proves,
  By crowds of slaves, and peopled empire loves.
  And such a slave as you, what Queen would lose?
  Above the rest, I Arimant would choose;
  For counsel, valour, truth, and kindness too,
  All I could wish in man, I find in you.
ARIMANT. What lover could to greater joy be raised!
  I am, methinks, a god, by you thus praised.
INDAMORA. To what may not desert like yours pretend?
  You have all qualities – that fit a friend.
ARIMANT. So mariners mistake the promised coast,
  And with full sails on the blind rocks are lost.
  Think you my aged veins so faintly beat,
  They rise no higher than to friendship's heat?
  So weak your charms, that, like a winter's night,
  Twinkling with stars, they freeze me while they light?
INDAMORA. Mistake me not, good Arimant, I know
  My beauty's power, and what my charms can do.
  You your own talent have not learned so well;
  But practise one, where you can ne'er excel.
  You can at most
  To an indiff'rent lover's praise pretend;
  But you would spoil an admirable friend.

ARIMANT. Never was amity so highly prized;
 Nor ever any love so much despised.
 Ev'n to myself ridiculous I grow,
 And would be angry, if I knew but how.
INDAMORA. Do not. Your anger, like your love, is vain;
 Whene'er I please, you must be pleased again.
 Knowing what pow'r I have your will to bend,
 I'll use it; for I need just such a friend.
 You must perform, not what you think is fit;
 But, to whatever I propose, submit.
ARIMANT. Madam, you have a strange ascendant gained;
 You use me like a courser, spurred and reined;
 If I fly out, my fierceness you command,
 Then sooth and gently stroke me with your hand.
 Impose, but use your pow'r of taxing well;
 When subjects cannot pay they soon rebel.

   [*Enter the* EMPEROR, *unseen by them*]

INDAMORA. My rebel's punishment would easy prove;
 You know you're in my pow'r by making love.
ARIMANT. Would I, without dispute, your will obey,
 And could you, in return, my life betray?
EMPEROR. What danger, Arimant, is this you fear?
 Or what love-secret which I must not hear?
 These altered looks some inward motion show.
 His cheeks are pale, and yours with blushes glow.
          [*To her*]
INDAMORA. 'Tis what, with justice, may my anger move;
 He has been bold, and talked to me of love.
ARIMANT. I am betrayed, and shall be doomed to die!
          [*Aside*]
EMPEROR. Did he, my slave, presume to look so high?
 That crawling insect, who from mud began,
 Warmed by my beams and kindled into man?

Durst he, who does but for my pleasure live,
Entrench on love, my great prerogative?
Print his base image on his sovereign's coin?
'Tis treason if he stamp his love with mine.

ARIMANT. 'Tis true, I have been bold; but if it be
    A crime —

INDAMORA.   He means, 'tis only so to me.
You, Sir, should praise what I must disapprove;
He insolently talked to me of love;
But, Sir, 'twas yours, he made it in your name.
You, if you please, may all he said disclaim.

EMPEROR. I must disclaim whate'er he can express:
His grovelling sense will show my passion less.
But stay, if what he said my message be,
What fear, what danger could arrive from me?
He said, he feared you would his life betray.

INDAMORA. Should he presume again, perhaps I may.
Though in your hands he hazard not his life,
Remember, Sir, your fury of a wife;
Who, not content to be revenged on you,
The agents of your passion will pursue.

EMPEROR. If I but hear her named, I'm sick that day;
The sound is mortal, and frights life away.
Forgive me, Arimant, my jealous thought;
Distrust in lovers is the tend'rest fault.
Leave me, and tell thyself in my excuse,
Love, and a crown, no rivalship can bear;
And precious things are still possessed with fear.

[*Exit* ARIMANT *bowing*]

This, Madam, my excuse to you may plead;
Love should forgive the faults which love has made.

INDAMORA. From me what pardon can you hope to have,
Robbed of my love, and treated as a slave?

EMPEROR. Force is the last relief which lovers find;
And 'tis the best excuse of womankind.

INDAMORA. Force never yet a generous heart did gain;
We yield on parley, but are stormed in vain.
Constraint, in all things, makes the pleasure less;
Sweet is the love which comes with willingness.

EMPEROR. No; 'tis resistance that inflames desire;
Sharpens the darts of love, and blows his fire.
Love is disarmed that meets with too much ease;
He languishes, and does not care to please.
And therefore 'tis your golden fruit you guard
With so much care, to make possession hard.

INDAMORA. Was't not enough you took my crown away,
But cruelly you must my love betray?
I was well pleased to have transferred my right,
And better changed your claim of lawless might
By taking him, whom you esteemed above
Your other sons, and taught me first to love.

EMPEROR. My son by my command his course must steer;
I bade him love, I bid him now forbear.
If you have any kindness for him still,
Advise him not to shock a father's will.

INDAMORA. Must I advise?
Then let me see him, and I'll try t' obey.

EMPEROR. I had forgot, and dare not trust your way.
But send him word.
He has not here an army to command:
Remember he and you are in my hand.

INDAMORA. Yes, in a father's hand, whom he has served,
And, with the hazard of his life, preserved!
But piety to you, unhappy Prince,
Becomes a crime, and duty an offence;
Against yourself, you with your foes combine,
And seem your own destruction to design.

EMPEROR. You may be pleased your politics to spare;
  I'm old enough, and can myself take care.
INDAMORA. Advice from me was, I confess, too bold;
  You're old enough; it may be, Sir, too old!
EMPEROR. You please yourself with your contempt of
    age;
  But love, neglected, will convert to rage.
  If on your head my fury does not turn,
  Thank that fond dotage which so much you scorn.
  But in another's person you may prove
  There's warmth for vengeance left, though not for love.

[*Re-enter* ARIMANT]

ARIMANT. The Empress has the ante-chambers past,
  And this way moves with a disordered haste;
  Her brows the stormy marks of anger bear.
EMPEROR. Madam, retire; she must not find you here.

[*Exit* INDAMORA *with* ARIMANT]

[*Enter* NOURMAHAL *hastily*]

NOURMAHAL. What have I done, that Nourmahal must
    prove
  The scorn and triumph of a rival's love?
  My eyes are still the same, each glance, each grace,
  Keep their first lustre, and maintain their place;
  Not second yet to any other face.
EMPEROR. What rage transports you? are you well awake?
  Such dreams distracted minds in fevers make.
NOURMAHAL. Those fevers you have giv'n, those dreams
    have bred,
  By broken faith and an abandoned bed.
  Such visions hourly pass before my sight,
  Which from my eyes their balmy slumbers fright
  In the severest silence of the night.

Visions, which in this citadel are seen;
Bright, glorious visions of a rival queen.

EMPEROR. Have patience, my first flames can ne'er decay;
These are but dreams, and soon will pass away.
Thou know'st, my heart, my empire, all is thine:
In thy own heav'n of love serenely shine:
Fair as the face of nature did appear
When flowers first peeped and trees did blossoms bear,
And winter had not yet deformed th' inverted year.
Calm as the breath which fans our eastern groves,
And bright as when thy eyes first lighted up our loves.
Let our eternal peace be sealed by this,
With the first ardour of a nuptial kiss. [*Offers to kiss her*]

NOURMAHAL. Me would you have, me your faint kisses
prove,
The dregs and droppings of enervate love?
Must I your cold long-labouring age sustain,
And be to empty joys provoked in vain?
Receive you sighing after other charms,
And take an absent husband in my arms?

EMPEROR. Even these reproaches I can bear from you;
You doubted of my love, believe it true.
Nothing but love this patience could produce;
And I allow your rage that kind excuse.

NOURMAHAL. Call it not patience, 'tis your guilt stands
mute;
You have a cause too foul to bear dispute.
You wrong me first, and urge my rage to rise,
Then I must pass for mad; you, meek and wise,
Good man, plead merit by your soft replies.
Vain privilege poor women have of tongue!
Men can stand silent and resolve on wrong.

EMPEROR. What can I more? my friendship you refuse,
And even my mildness, as my crime, accuse.

NOURMAHAL. Your sullen silence cheats not me, false
    man;
  I know you think the bloodiest things you can.
  Could you accuse me, you would raise your voice;
  Watch for my crimes, and in my guilt rejoice.
  But my known virtue is from scandal free,
  And leaves no shadow for your calumny.
EMPEROR. Such virtue is the plague of human life;
  A virtuous woman, but a cursed wife.
  In vain of pompous chastity you're proud;
  Virtue's adultery of the tongue when loud;
  I, with less pain, a prostitute could bear,
  Than the shrill sound of virtue, virtue hear.
  In unchaste wives –
  There's yet a kind of recompensing ease.
  Vice keeps 'em humble, gives 'em care to please;
  But against clamorous virtue, what defence?
  It stops our mouths, and gives your noise pretence.
NOURMAHAL. Since virtue does your indignation raise,
  'Tis pity but you had that wife you praise.
  Your own wild appetites are prone to range,
  And then you tax our humours with your change.
EMPEROR. What can be sweeter than our native home!
  Thither for ease, and soft repose, we come.
  Home is the sacred refuge of our life;
  Secured from all approaches, but a wife.
  If thence we fly, the cause admits no doubt;
  None but an inmate foe could force us out.
  Clamours, our privacies uneasy make;
  Birds leave their nests disturbed, and beasts their haunts
    forsake.
NOURMAHAL. Honour's my crime that has your loathing
    bred;
  You take no pleasure in a virtuous bed.

EMPEROR. What pleasure can there be in that estate,
    Which your unquietness has made me hate?
    I shrink far off –
    Dissembling sleep, but wakeful with the fright.
    The day takes off the pleasure of the night.

NOURMAHAL. My thoughts no other joys but pow'r
    pursue;
    Or, if they did, they must be lost in you.
    And yet the fault's not mine –
    Though youth and beauty cannot warmth command,
    The sun in vain shines on the barren sand.

EMPEROR. 'Tis true, of marriage-bands I'm weary
    grown.
    Love scorns all ties, but those that are his own.
    Chains that are dragged must needs uneasy prove;
    For there's a god-like liberty in love.

NOURMAHAL. What's love to you?
    The bloom of beauty other years demands,
    Nor will be gathered by such withered hands;
    You importune it with a false desire,
    Which sparkles out and makes no solid fire.
    This impudence of age, whence can it spring?
    All you expect, and yet you nothing bring.
    Eager to ask, when you are past a grant;
    Nice in providing what you cannot want.
    Have conscience; give not her you love this pain;
    Solicit not yourself, and her, in vain.
    All other debts may compensation find;
    But love is strict, and will be paid in kind.

EMPEROR. Sure, of all ills, domestic are the worst;
    When most secure of blessings, we are cursed.
    When we lay next us what we hold most dear,
    Like Hercules, envenomed shirts we wear,
    And cleaving mischiefs.

NOURMAHAL. What you merit, have;
And share, at least, the miseries you gave.
Your days I will alarm, I'll haunt your nights;
And, worse than age, disable your delights.
May your sick fame still languish till it die;
All offices of pow'r neglected lie,
And you grow cheap in every subject's eye.
Then, as the greatest curse that I can give,
Unpitied be deposed, and after live. [*Going off*]

EMPEROR. Stay! and now learn
How criminal soe'er we husbands are
'Tis not for wives to push our crimes too far.
Had you still mistress of your temper been,
I had been modest and not owned my sin.
Your fury hardens me; and whate'er wrong
You suffer, you have cancelled by your tongue.
A guard there! seize her! she shall know this
hour,
What is a husband's and a monarch's pow'r.
[*Guard seizes her*]

[*Enter* AURENG-ZEBE]

NOURMAHAL. I see for whom your charter you maintain;
I must be fettered and my son be slain,
That Zelyma's ambitious race may reign.
Not so you promised, when my beauty drew
All Asia's vows; when Persia left for you,
The realm of Candahar for dow'r I brought,
That long contended prize for which you fought.

AURENG-ZEBE. The name of step-mother, your practised
art,
By which you have estranged my father's heart,
All you have done against me, or design,
Shows your aversion, but begets not mine.

Long may my father India's empire guide;
And may no breach your nuptial vows divide.

EMPEROR. Since love obliges not, I from this hour
Assume the right of man's despotic pow'r.
Man is by nature formed your sex's head;
And is himself the canon of his bed.
In bands of iron fettered you shall be;
An easier yoke than what you put on me.

AURENG-ZEBE. Though much I fear my int'rest is not
      great,   [*Kneeling*]
Let me your royal clemency entreat.
Secrets of marriage still are sacred held;
Their sweet and bitter by the wise concealed.
Errors of wives reflect on husbands still;
And when divulged proclaim you've chosen ill;
And the mysterious pow'r of bed and throne
Should always be maintained, but rarely shown.

EMPEROR. To so perverse a sex all grace is vain.
It gives 'em courage to offend again,
For with feigned tears they penitence pretend;
Again are pardoned, and again offend.
Fathom our pity when they seem to grieve,
Only to try how far we can forgive.
Till launching out into a sea of strife,
They scorn all pardon and appear all wife.
But be it as you please; for your loved sake,
This last and fruitless trial I will make.
In all requests, your right of merit use,
And know, there is but one I can refuse.

[*He signs to the guards, and they remove from the Empress*]

NOURMAHAL. You've done enough, for you designed my
      chains;
The grace is vanished, but th' affront remains.

Nor is't a grace, or for his merit done;
You durst no farther for you feared my son.
This you have gained by the rough course you prove;
I'm past repentance, and you past my love.   [*Exit*]

EMPEROR. A spirit so untamed the world ne'er bore.

AURENG-ZEBE. And yet worse usage had incensed her
        more.
But since by no obligement she is tied,
You must betimes for your defence provide.
I cannot idle in your danger stand,
But beg once more I may your arms command.
Two battles your auspicious cause has won;
My sword can perfect what it has begun,
And from your walls dislodge that haughty son.

EMPEROR. My son, your valour has, this day, been
        such,
None can enough admire, or praise too much.
But now, with reason, your success I doubt;
Her faction's strong within, his arms without.

AURENG-ZEBE. I left the city in a panic fright;
Lions they are in council, lambs in fight.
But my own troops, by Mirzah led, are near;
I, by to-morrow's dawn, expect 'em here.
To favour 'em, I'll sally out ere day,
And through our slaughtered foes enlarge their way.

EMPEROR. Age has not yet
So shrunk my sinews, or so chilled my veins,
But conscious virtue in my breast remains.
But had I now
That strength, with which my boiling youth was fraught,
When in the vale of Balasor I fought,
And from Bengal their captive monarch brought;
When elephant 'gainst elephant did rear
His trunk, and castles justled in the air;

My sword thy way to victory had shown,
And owed the conquest to itself alone.

AURENG-ZEBE. Those fair ideas to my aid I'll call,
And emulate my great original.
Or, if they fail, I will invoke in arms,
The pow'r of love, and Indamora's charms.

EMPEROR. I doubt the happy influence of your star;
T' invoke a captive's name bodes ill in war.

AURENG-ZEBE. Sir, give me leave to say, whatever now
The omen prove, it boded well to you.
Your royal promise, when I went to fight,
Obliged me to resign a victor's right.
Her liberty I fought for, and I won;
And claim it as your general, and your son.

EMPEROR. My ears still ring with noise, I'm vexed to
death;
Tongue-killed, and have not yet recovered breath.
Nor will I be prescribed my time by you;
First end the war, and then your claim renew.
While to your conduct I my fortune trust,
To keep this pledge of duty is but just.

AURENG-ZEBE. Some hidden cause your jealousy does
move,
Or you could ne'er suspect my loyal love.

EMPEROR. What love soever by an heir is shown,
He waits but time to step into the throne.
You're neither justified, nor yet accused;
Meanwhile, the pris'ner with respect is used.

AURENG-ZEBE. I know the kindness of her guardian such,
I need not fear too little, but too much.
But how, Sir, how have you from virtue swerved?
Or what so ill return have I deserved?
You doubt not me, nor have I spent my blood,
To have my faith no better understood.

Your soul's above the baseness of distrust;
Nothing but love could make you so unjust.
EMPEROR. You know your rival then; and know 'tis fit,
The son's should to the father's claim submit.
AURENG-ZEBE. Sons may have right, which they can
    never quit.
Yourself first made that title which I claim;
First bid me love, and authorized my flame.
EMPEROR. The value of my gift I did not know;
If I could give, I can resume it too.
AURENG-ZEBE. Recall your gift, for I your power confess;
But first, take back my life, a gift that's less.
Long life would now but a long burden prove;
You're grown unkind, and I have lost your love.
My grief lets unbecoming speeches fall;
I should have died, and not complained at all.
EMPEROR. Witness ye pow'rs,
How much I suffered, and how long I strove
Against th' assaults of this imperious love!
I represented to myself the shame
Of perjured faith, and violated fame;
Your great deserts, how ill they were repaid;
All arguments, in vain, I urged and weighed.
For mighty love, who prudence does despise,
For reason, showed me Indamora's eyes.
What would you more, my crime I sadly view,
Acknowledge, am ashamed, and yet pursue.
AURENG-ZEBE. Since you can love, and yet your error see,
The same resistless pow'r may plead for me.
With no less ardour I my claim pursue;
I love, and cannot yield her ev'n to you.
EMPEROR. Your elder brothers, though o'ercome, have
    right;
The youngest yet in arms prepared to fight;

But, yielding her, I firmly have decreed,
That you alone to Empire shall succeed.

AURENG-ZEBE. To after ages let me stand a shame,
When I exchange for crowns my love or fame.
You might have found a mercenary son,
To profit of the battles he had won.
Had I been such, what hindered me to take
The crown? nor had th' exchange been yours to make.
While you are living, I no right pretend;
Wear it, and let it where you please descend.
But from my love, 'tis sacrilege to part;
There, there's my throne in Indamora's heart.

EMPEROR. 'Tis in her heart alone that you must reign;
You'll find her person difficult to gain.
Give willingly what I can take by force;
And know, obedience is your safest course.

AURENG-ZEBE. I'm taught by honour's precepts to obey:
Fear to obedience is a slavish way.
If aught my want of duty could beget,
You take the most prevailing means, to threat.
Pardon your blood that boils within my veins;
It rises high, and menacing disdains.
Even death's become to me no dreadful name:
I've often met him, and have made him tame;
In fighting fields, where our acquaintance grew,
I saw him, and contemned him first for you.

EMPEROR. Of formal duty make no more thy boast;
Thou disobey'st where it concerns me most.
Fool, with both hands thus to push back a crown,
And headlong cast thyself from empire down.
Though Nourmahal I hate, her son shall reign;
Inglorious thou, by thy own fault remain.
Thy younger brother I'll admit this hour;
So mine shall be thy mistress, his thy pow'r.   [*Exit*]

AURENG-ZEBE. How vain is virtue which directs our ways
    Through certain danger to uncertain praise!
    Barren and airy name! thee fortune flies;
    With thy lean train, the pious and the wise.
    Heav'n takes thee at thy word, without regard,
    And lets thee poorly be thy own reward.
    The world is made for the bold impious man,
    Who stops at nothing, seizes all he can.
    Justice to merit does weak aid afford;
    She trusts her balance, and neglects her sword.
    Virtue is nice to take what's not her own,
    And, while she long consults, the prize is gone.

[*To him,* DIANET]

DIANET. Forgive the bearer of unhappy news.
    Your altered father openly pursues
    Your ruin; and, to compass his intent,
    For violent Morat in haste has sent.
    The gates he ordered all to be unbarred,
    And from the market-place to draw the guard.
AURENG-ZEBE. How look the people in this turn of state?
DIANET. They mourn your ruin as their proper fate.
    Cursing the Empress; for they think it done
    By her procurement to advance her son.
    Him too, though awed, they scarcely can forbear;
    His pride they hate, his violence they fear.
    All bent to rise, would you appear their chief,
    Till your own troops come up to your relief.
AURENG-ZEBE. Ill treated, and forsaken, as I am,
    I'll not betray the glory of my name.
    'Tis not for me, who have preserved a state,
    To buy an empire at so base a rate.
DIANET. The points of honour poets may produce;
    Trappings of life, for ornament not use.

K   289

Honour, which only does the name advance,
Is the mere raving madness of romance.
Pleased with a word, you may sit tamely down,
And see your younger brother force the crown.

AURENG-ZEBE. I know my fortune in extremes does lie;
The sons of Indostan must reign, or die;
That desperate hazard courage does create,
As he plays frankly who has least estate;
And that the world the coward will despise,
When life's a blank, who pulls not for a prize.

DIANET. Of all your knowledge, this vain fruit you have,
To walk with eyes broad open to your grave.

AURENG-ZEBE. From what I've said, conclude, without
    reply,
I neither would usurp, nor tamely die.
Th' attempt to fly would guilt betray, or fear;
Besides, 'twere vain; the fort's our prison here.
Somewhat I have resolved –
Morat, perhaps, has honour in his breast;
And, in extremes, bold counsels are the best.
Like emp'ric remedies, they last are tried,
And by th' event condemned, or justified.
Presence of mind and courage in distress,
Are more than armies to procure success.

[*Exit*]

ACT III

[ARIMANT, *with a letter in his hand.* INDAMORA]

ARIMANT. And I the messenger to him from you?
Your empire you to tyranny pursue;
You lay commands, both cruel and unjust,
To serve my rival, and betray my trust.

INDAMORA. You first betrayed your trust in loving me,
    And should not I my own advantage see?
    Serving my love, you may my friendship gain,
    You know the rest of your pretences vain.
    You must, my Arimant, you must be kind:
    'Tis in your nature, and your noble mind.
ARIMANT. I'll to the King, and straight my trust resign.
INDAMORA. His trust you may, but you shall never
    mine.
    Heav'n made you love me for no other end,
    But to become my confidant and friend:
    As such, I keep no secret from your sight,
    And therefore make you judge how ill I write.
    Read it, and tell me freely then your mind;
    If 'tis indited as I meant it, kind.
ARIMANT *reading*: I ask not heav'n my freedom to restore,
    But only for your sake – I'll read no more:
    And yet I must –
    [*Reading*] Less for my own, than for your sorrow, sad –
    Another line, like this, would make me mad –
    [*As reading*] Heav'n! she goes on – yet more – and yet
    more kind!
    Each sentence is a dagger to my mind.
    [*Reading*] See me this night –
    Thank fortune, who did such a friend provide,
    For faithful Arimant shall be your guide.
    Not only to be made an instrument,
    But pre-engaged without my own consent!
INDAMORA. Unknown t' engage you still augments my
    score,
    And gives you scope of meriting the more.
ARIMANT. The best of men
    Some int'rest in their actions must confess;
    None merit but in hope they may possess.

    The fatal paper rather let me tear,
    Than, like Bellerophon, my own sentence bear.
INDAMORA. You may; but 'twill not be your best advice;
    'Twill only give me pains of writing twice.
    You know you must obey me, soon or late;
    Why should you vainly struggle with your fate?
ARIMANT. I thank thee, heav'n, thou hast been
        wondrous kind!
    Why am I thus to slavery designed,
    And yet am cheated with a free-born mind?
    Or make thy orders with my reason suit,
    Or let me live by sense a glorious brute – [*She frowns*]
    You frown, and I obey with speed, before
    That dreadful sentence comes, *See me no more*;
    See me no more! that sound, methinks, I hear
    Like the last trumpet thund'ring in my ear.

[*Enter* SOLYMAN]

SOLYMAN. The Princess Melesinda, bathed in tears,
    And tossed alternately with hopes and fears,
    If your affairs such leisure can afford,
    Would learn from you the fortunes of her lord.
ARIMANT. Tell her, that I some certainty may bring;
    I go this minute to attend the King.
INDAMORA. This lonely turtle I desire to see;
    Grief, though not cured, is eased by company.
ARIMANT *to* SOLYMAN. Say, if she please, she hither
        may repair,
    And breathe the freshness of the open air.
                    [*Exit* SOLYMAN]
INDAMORA. Poor Princess! how I pity her estate,
    Wrapped in the ruins of her husband's fate!
    She mourned Morat should in rebellion rise;
    Yet he offends, and she's the sacrifice.

ARIMANT. Not knowing his design, at Court she stayed;
    Till, by command, close pris'ner she was made.
    Since when,
    Her chains with Roman constancy she bore;
    But that, perhaps, an Indian wife's is more.
INDAMORA. Go, bring her comfort; leave me here alone.
ARIMANT. My love must still be in obedience shown.
                                [*Exit* ARIMANT]

        [*Enter* MELESINDA, *led by* SOLYMAN,
            who retires afterwards]

INDAMORA. When graceful sorrow in her pomp appears,
    Sure she is dressed in Melesinda's tears.
    Your head reclined (as hiding grief from view)
    Droops like a rose surcharged with morning dew.
MELESINDA. Can flowers but droop in absence of the sun,
    Which waked their sweets? and mine, alas! is gone.
    But you the noblest charity express;
    For they who shine in Courts still shun distress.
INDAMORA. Distressed myself, like you, confined I live;
    And therefore can compassion take, and give.
    We're both love's captives, but with fate so cross,
    One must be happy by the other's loss.
    Morat, or Aureng-Zebe must fall this day.
MELESINDA. Too truly Tamerlain's successors they,
    Each thinks a world too little for his sway.
    Could you and I the same pretences bring,
    Mankind should with more ease receive a king:
    I would to you the narrow world resign,
    And want no empire while Morat was mine.
INDAMORA. Wished freedom I presage you soon will find;
    If heav'n be just, and be to virtue kind.
MELESINDA. Quite otherwise my mind foretells my fate;
    Short is my life, and that unfortunate.

                    293

Yet should I not complain, would heav'n afford
Some little time ere death to see my lord.

INDAMORA. These thoughts are but your melancholy's
food;
Raised from a lonely life and dark abode.
But whatsoe'er our jarring fortunes prove,
Though our lords hate, methinks we two may love.

MELESINDA. Such be our loves as may not yield to fate;
I bring a heart more true than fortunate.

[*Giving their hands*]

[*To them* ARIMANT]

ARIMANT. I come with haste surprising news to bring.
In two hours' time, since last I saw the King,
Th' affairs of Court have wholly changed their face.
Unhappy Aureng-Zebe is in disgrace;
And your Morat (proclaimed the successor)
Is called to awe the city with his power.
Those trumpets his triumphant entry tell.
And now the shouts waft near the citadel.

INDAMORA. See, Madam, see th' event by me fore-
shown;
I envy not your chance, but grieve my own.

MELESINDA. A change so unexpected must surprise;
And more, because I am unused to joys.

INDAMORA. May all your wishes ever prosp'rous be;
But I'm too much concerned th' event to see.
My eyes too tender are –
To view my lord become the public scorn.
I came to comfort, and I go to mourn.

[*Taking her leave*]

MELESINDA. Stay, I'll not see my lord,
Before I give your sorrow some relief,
And pay the charity you lent my grief.

Here he shall see me first with you confined;
And if your virtue fail to move his mind,
I'll use my int'rest that he may be kind.
Fear not, I never moved him yet in vain.
INDAMORA. So fair a pleader any cause may gain.
MELESINDA. I have no taste, methinks, of coming joy;
For black presages all my hopes destroy.
Die, something whispers, Melesinda, die;
Fulfil, fulfil, thy mournful destiny.
Mine is a gleam of bliss, too hot to last,
Watery it shines, and will be soon o'ercast.

[INDAMORA *and* MELESINDA *re-enter, as into the chamber*]

ARIMANT. Fortune seems weary grown of Aureng-Zebe,
While to her new-made favourite, Morat,
Her lavish hand is wastefully profuse;
With fame and flowing honours tided in,
Borne on a swelling current smooth beneath him.
The King and haughty Empress, to our wonder,
If not atoned, yet seemingly at peace,
As fate for him that miracle reserved.

[*Enter in triumph,* EMPEROR, MORAT, *and train*]

EMPEROR. I have confessed I love.
As I interpret fairly your design,
So look not with severer eyes on mine.
Your fate has called you to th' imperial seat;
In duty be, as you in arms are, great.
For Aureng-Zebe a hated name is grown,
And love less bears a rival than the throne.
MORAT. To me, the cries of fighting fields are charms,
Keen be my sabre, and of proof my arms,

I ask no other blessing of my stars;
No prize but fame, nor mistress but the wars.
I scarce am pleased I tamely mount the throne.
Would Aureng-Zebe had all their souls in one,
With all my elder brothers I would fight,
And so from partial nature force my right.
EMPEROR. Had we but lasting youth, and time to spare,
Some might be thrown away on fame and war;
But youth, the perishing good, runs on too fast,
And unenjoyed will spend itself to waste;
Few knew the use of life before 'tis past.
Had I once more thy vigour to command,
I would not let it die upon my hand;
No hour of pleasure should pass empty by;
Youth should watch joys, and shoot 'em as they fly.
MORAT. Methinks all pleasure is in greatness found.
Kings, like heav'n's eye, should spread their beams
      around,
Pleased to be seen while glory's race they run;
Rest is not for the chariot of the sun.
Subjects are stiff-necked animals, they soon
Feel slackened reins and pitch their rider down.
EMPEROR. To thee that drudgery of pow'r I give.
Cares be thy lot; reign thou, and let me live.
The fort I'll keep for my security,
Bus'ness and public state resign to thee.
MORAT. Luxurious kings are to their people lost;
They live, like drones, upon the public cost.
My arms, from pole to pole, the world shall shake;
And, with myself, keep all mankind awake.
EMPEROR. Believe me, son, and needless trouble spare;
'Tis a base world, and is not worth our care.
The vulgar, a scarce animated clod,
Ne'er pleased with aught above 'em, prince or god.

Were I a god, the drunken globe should roll;
The little emmets with the human soul
Care for themselves, while at my ease I sat,
And second causes did the work of fate.
Or, if I would take care, that care should be
For wit that scorned the world, and lived like me.

[*To them*, NOURMAHAL, ZAYDA, *and attendants*]

NOURMAHAL. My dear Morat,   [*Embracing her son*]
   This day propitious to us all has been;
   You're now a monarch's heir, and I a Queen.
   Your faithful father now may quit the state,
   And find the ease he sought, indulged by fate.
   Cares shall not keep him on the throne awake,
   Nor break the golden slumbers he would take.
EMPEROR. In vain I struggled to the goal of life,
   While rebel-sons and an imperious wife
   Still dragged me backward into noise and strife.
MORAT. Be that remembrance lost; and be't my pride
   To be your pledge of peace on either side.

[*To them*, AURENG-ZEBE]

AURENG-ZEBE. With all th' assurance innocence can
      bring,
   Fearless without, because secure within,
   Armed with my courage, unconcerned I see
   This pomp; a shame to you, a pride to me.
   Shame is but where with wickedness 'tis joined,
   And, while no baseness in this breast I find,
   I have not lost the birthright of my mind.
EMPEROR. Children (the blind effect of love and chance,
   Formed by their sportive parents' ignorance)

Bear from their birth th' impressions of a slave;
Whom heav'n for play-games first, and then for service
   gave.
One then may be displaced, and one may reign;
And want of merit, render birthright vain.

MORAT. Comes he t' upbraid us with his innocence?
Seize him, and take the preaching Brahmin hence.

AURENG-ZEBE. Stay, Sir! I, from my years, no merit
   plead;   [*To his father*]
All my designs and acts to duty lead.
Your life and glory are my only end;
And for that prize I with Morat contend.

MORAT. Not him alone; I all mankind defy.
Who dares adventure more for both than I?

AURENG-ZEBE. I know you brave, and take you at your word;
That present service which you vaunt, afford.
Our two rebellious brothers are not dead;
Though vanquished, yet again they gather head.
I dare you, as your rival in renown,
March out your army from th' imperial town;
Choose whom you please, the other leave to me;
And set our father absolutely free.
This, if you do, to end all future strife,
I am content to lead a private life;
Disband my army to secure the state,
Nor aim at more, but leave the rest to fate.

MORAT. I'll do't. Draw out my army on the plain;
War is to me a pastime, peace a pain.

EMPEROR *to* MORAT. Think better first.
   [*To* AURENG-ZEBE] You see yourself enclosed beyond
   escape,
And therefore, Proteus-like, you change your shape.
Of promise prodigal, while pow'r you want,
And preaching in the self-denying cant.

MORAT. Plot better; for these arts too obvious are,
    Of gaining time, the masterpiece of war.
    Is Aureng-Zebe so known?
AURENG-ZEBE.   If acts like mine,
    So far from int'rest, profit, or design,
    Can show my heart, by those I would be known;
    I wish you could as well defend your own.
    My absent army for my father fought;
    Yours, in these walls, is to enslave him brought.
    If I come singly, you an armed guest,
    The world with ease may judge whose cause is
        best.
MORAT. My father saw you ill designs pursue;
    And my admission showed his fear of you.
AURENG-ZEBE. Himself best knows why he his love
        withdraws;
    I owe him more than to declare the cause.
    But still I press our duty may be shown
    By arms.
MORAT.   I'll vanquish all his foes alone.
AURENG-ZEBE. You speak as if you could the fates com-
        mand,
    And had no need of any other hand.
    But, since my honour you so far suspect,
    'Tis just I should on your designs reflect.
    To prove yourself a loyal son, declare
    You'll lay down arms when you conclude the war.
MORAT. No present answer your demand requires;
    The war once done, I'll do what heav'n inspires.
    And while the sword this monarchy secures,
    'Tis managed by an abler arm than yours.
EMPEROR. Morat's design a doubtful meaning bears;
                            [Apart]

  In Aureng-Zebe true loyalty appears.

He, for my safety, does his own despise;
Still, with his wrongs, I find his duty rise.
I feel my virtue struggling in my soul,
But stronger passion does its pow'r control.
Yet be advised your ruin to prevent.

[*To* AURENG-ZEBE *apart*]

You might be safe, if you would give consent.

AURENG-ZEBE. So to your welfare I of use may be,
My life or death are equal both to me.

EMPEROR. The people's hearts are yours, the fort yet
    mine;
Be wise, and Indamora's love resign.
I am observed: remember that I give
This my last proof of kindness, die, or live.

AURENG-ZEBE. Life, with my Indamora, I would choose;
But, losing her, the end of living lose.
I had considered all I ought before;
And fear of death can make me change no more.
The people's love so little I esteem,
Condemned by you, I would not live by them.
May he who must your favour now possess,
Much better serve you, and not love you less.

EMPEROR. I've heard you; and, to finish the debate,

[*Aloud*]

Commit that rebel pris'ner to the state.

MORAT. The deadly draught he shall begin this day;
And languish with insensible decay.

AURENG-ZEBE. I hate the ling'ring summons to attend,
Death all at once would be the nobler end.
Fate is unkind! methinks a general
Should warm and at the head of armies fall.
And my ambition did that hope pursue;
That so I might have died in fight for you.

[*To his father*]

300

MORAT. Would I had been disposer of thy stars;
 Thou shouldst have had thy wish, and died in wars.
 'Tis I, not thou, have reason to repine,
 That thou shouldst fall by any hand, but mine.
AURENG-ZEBE. When thou wert formed, heav'n did a
   man begin;
 But the brute soul, by chance, was shuffled in.
 In woods and wilds thy monarchy maintain,
 Where valiant beasts, by force and rapine, reign;
 In life's next scene, if transmigration be,
 Some bear or lion is reserved for thee.
MORAT. Take heed thou com'st not in that Lion's way!
 I prophesy thou wilt thy soul convey
 Into a lamb, and be again my prey.
 Hence with that dreaming priest.
NOURMAHAL.   Let me prepare
 The pois'nous draught; his death shall be my care.
 Near my apartment let him pris'ner be,
 That I his hourly ebbs of life may see.
AURENG-ZEBE. My life I would not ransom with a
   pray'r;
 'Tis vile, since 'tis not worth my father's care.
 I go not, Sir, indebted to my grave;
 You paid yourself, and took the life you gave.[*Exit*]
EMPEROR. Oh, that I had more sense of virtue left,[*Aside*]
 Or were of that, which yet remains, bereft.
 I've just enough to know how I offend,
 And, to my shame, have not enough to mend.
 Lead to the mosque –
MORAT. Love's pleasures why should dull devotion stay?
 Heav'n to my Melesinda's but the way.
    [*Exeunt* EMPEROR, MORAT, *and train*]
ZAYDA. Sure Aureng-Zebe has somewhat of divine,
 Whose virtue through so dark a cloud can shine.

Fortune has from Morat this day removed
The greatest rival, and the best beloved.

NOURMAHAL. He is not yet removed.

ZAYDA.   He lives, 'tis true;
But soon must die, and, what I mourn, by you.

NOURMAHAL. My Zayda, may thy words prophetic be;

[*Embracing her eagerly*]

I take the omen, let him die by me.
He stifled in my arms shall lose his breath,
And life itself shall envious be of death.

ZAYDA. Bless me, you pow'rs above!

NOURMAHAL.   Why dost thou start?
Is love so strange? or have not I a heart?
Could Aureng-Zebe so lovely seem to thee,
And I want eyes that noble worth to see?
Thy little soul was but to wonder moved;
My sense of it was higher, and I loved.
That man, that god-like man, so brave, so great!
But these are thy small praises I repeat.
I'm carried by a tide of love away;
He's somewhat more than I myself can say.

ZAYDA. Though all th' ideas you can form be true,
He must not, cannot be possessed by you.
If contradicting int'rests could be mixt,
Nature herself has cast a bar betwixt;
And, ere you reach to this incestuous love,
You must divine and human rights remove.

NOURMAHAL. Count this among the wonders love has
done;
I had forgot he was my husband's son!

ZAYDA. Nay, more; you have forgot who is your
own;
For whom your care so long designed the throne.
Morat must fall if Aureng-Zebe should rise.

NOURMAHAL. 'Tis true; but who was e'er in love and wise?
Why was that fatal knot of marriage tied,
Which did, by making us too near, divide?
Divides me from my sex! for heav'n, I find,
Excludes but me alone of woman-kind.
I stand with guilt confounded, lost with shame,
And yet made wretched only by a name.
If names have such command on human life,
Love sure's a name that's more divine than wife.
That sovereign power all guilt from action takes,
At least the stains are beautiful it makes.
ZAYDA. Th' encroaching ill you early should oppose;
Flattered 'tis worse, and by indulgence grows.
NOURMAHAL. Alas! and what have I not said or done?
I fought it to the last; and love has won.
A bloody conquest; which destruction brought,
And ruined all the country where he fought.
Whether this passion from above was sent,
The fate of him heav'n favours to prevent;
Or as the curse of fortune in excess,
That, stretching, would beyond its reach possess,
And, with a taste which plenty does deprave,
Loathes lawful good, and lawless ill does crave?
ZAYDA. But yet consider –
NOURMAHAL.   No, 'tis loss of time.
Think how to farther, not divert my crime.
My artful engines instantly I'll move;
And choose the soft and gentlest hour of love.
The under-provost of the fort is mine.
But see, Morat! I'll whisper my design.

[*Enter* MORAT *with* ARIMANT, *as talking. Attendants*]

ARIMANT. And for that cause was not in public seen;
But stays in prison with the captive Queen.

MORAT. Let my attendants wait, I'll be alone;
 Where least of state, there most of love is shown.
NOURMAHAL. My son, your bus'ness is not hard to guess;
                                                 [*To* MORAT]
 Long absence makes you eager to possess.
 I will not importune you by my stay;
 She merits all the love which you can pay.
                                     [*Exit with* ZAYDA]

[*Re-enter* ARIMANT, *with* MELESINDA; *then exit.*

 MORAT *runs to* MELESINDA, *and embraces her*]

MORAT. Should I not chide you, that you chose to stay
 In gloomy shades, and lost a glorious day?
 Lost the first fruits of joy you should possess
 In my return, and made my triumph less?
MELESINDA. Should I not chide, that you could stay and see
 Those joys, preferring public pomp to me?
 Through my dark cell your shouts of triumph rung;
 I heard with pleasure, but I thought 'em long.
MORAT. The public will in triumphs rudely share,
 And kings the rudeness of their joys must bear;
 But I made haste to set my captive free,
 And thought that work was only worthy me.
 The fame of ancient matrons you pursue,
 And stand a blameless pattern to the new.
 I have not words to praise such acts as these;
 But take my heart, and mould it as you please.
MELESINDA. A trial of your kindness I must make,
 Though not for mine so much as virtue's sake.
 The Queen of Cassimeer —
MORAT.   No more, my love;
 That only suit I beg you not to move.

That she's in bonds for Aureng-Zebe I know,
And should, by my consent, continue so.
The good old man, I fear, will pity show.
My father dotes, and let him still dote on;
He buys his mistress dearly with his throne.

MELESINDA. See her; and then be cruel if you can.

MORAT. 'Tis not with me as with a private man.
Such may be swayed by honour, or by love;
But monarchs, only by their int'rest move.

MELESINDA. Heav'n does a tribute for your pow'r
demand;
He leaves th' oppressed and poor upon your hand.
And those, who stewards of his pity prove,
He blesses in return with public love.
In his distress, some miracle is shown;
If exiled, heav'n restores him to his throne.
He needs no guard while any subject's near,
Nor, like his tyrant neighbours, lives in fear;
No plots th' alarm to his retirements give;
'Tis all mankind's concern that he should live.

MORAT. You promised friendship in your low estate,
And should forget it in your better fate;
Such maxims are more plausible than true;
But somewhat must be given to love and you.
I'll view this captive Queen; to let her see,
Pray'rs and complaints are lost on such as me.

MELESINDA. I'll bear the news. Heav'n knows how much
I'm pleased,
That, by my care, th' afflicted may be eased.

[*As she is going off, enter* INDAMORA]

INDAMORA. I'll spare your pains, and venture out
alone,
Since you, fair Princess, my protection own.

305

But you, brave Prince, a harder task must find;
        [*To* MORAT *kneeling, who takes her up*]
In saving me, you would but half be kind.
A humble suppliant at your feet I lie;
You have condemned my better part to die.
Without my Aureng-Zebe I cannot live;
Revoke his doom, or else my sentence give.

MELESINDA. If Melesinda in your love have part,
  Which, to suspect, would break my tender heart;
  If love, like mine, may for a lover plead,
  By the chaste pleasures of our nuptial bed,
  By all the int'rest my past suff'rings make,
  And all I yet would suffer for your sake;
  By you yourself, the last and dearest tie –

MORAT. You move in vain; for Aureng-Zebe must die.

INDAMORA. Could that decree from any brother come?
  Nature herself is sentenced in your doom.
  Piety is no more, she sees her place
  Usurped by monsters and a savage race.
  From her soft eastern climes you drive her forth,
  To the cold mansions of the utmost north.
  How can our Prophet suffer you to reign,
  When he looks down and sees your brother slain?
  Avenging furies will your life pursue;
  Think there's a heav'n, Morat, though not for you.

MELESINDA. Her words imprint a terror on my mind.
  What if this death, which is for him designed,
  Had been your doom (far be that augury!),
  And you, not Aureng-Zebe, condemned to die?
  Weigh well the various turns of human fate,
  And seek, by mercy, to secure your state.

INDAMORA. Had heav'n the crown for Aureng-Zebe designed,
  Pity, for you, had pierced his generous mind.

Pity does with a noble nature suit;
A brother's life had suffered no dispute.
All things have right in life, our Prophet's care
Commands the beings ev'n of brutes to spare.
Though int'rest his restraint has justified,
Can life, and to a brother, be denied?

MORAT. All reasons for his safety urged, are weak;
And yet, methinks, 'tis heav'n to hear you speak.

MELESINDA. 'Tis part of your own being to invade –

MORAT. Nay, if she fail to move, would you persuade?
                              [*Turning to* INDAMORA]
My brother does a glorious fate pursue.
I envy him, that he must fall for you.
He had been base had he released his right;
For such an empire none but kings should fight.
If with a father he disputes this prize,
My wonder ceases when I see these eyes.

MELESINDA. And can you then deny those eyes you praise?
Can beauty wonder, and not pity raise?

MORAT. Your intercession now is needless grown:
Retire, and let me speak with her alone.
[MELESINDA *retires, weeping, to the side of the theatre*]
Queen, that you may not fruitless tears employ,
                              [*Taking* INDAMORA's *hand*]
I bring you news to fill your heart with joy.
Your lover king of all the east shall reign;
For Aureng-Zebe to-morrow shall be slain.

INDAMORA. The hopes you raised, you've blasted with a
          breath!   [*Starting back*]
With triumphs you began, but end with death.
Did you not say, my lover should be king?

MORAT. I, in Morat, the best of lovers bring!
For one forsaken both of earth and heav'n,
Your kinder stars a nobler choice have given.

My father, while I please, a king appears;
His pow'r is more declining than his years;
An emperor and lover, but in show;
But you, in me, have youth and fortune too.
As heav'n did to your eyes and form divine,
Submit the fate of all th' Imperial line;
So was it ordered by its wise decree,
That you should find 'em all comprised in me.

INDAMORA. If, Sir, I seem not discomposed with rage,
Feed not your fancy with a false presage.
Farther to press your courtship is but vain;
A cold refusal carries more disdain.
Unsettled virtue stormy may appear;
Honour, like mine, serenely is severe.
To scorn your person, and reject your crown,
Disorder not my face into a frown. [*Turns from him*]

MORAT. Your fortune you should rev'rently have used;'
Such offers are not twice to be refused.
I go to Aureng-Zebe, and am in haste;
For your commands, they're like to be the last.

INDAMORA. Tell him,
With my own death I would his life redeem;
But, less than honour, both our lives esteem.

MORAT. Have you no more?

INDAMORA.   What shall I do or say? [*Aside*]
He must not in this fury go away.
Tell him, I did in vain his brother move,
And yet he falsely said, he was in love.
Falsely; for had he truly loved, at least,
He would have giv'n one day to my request.

MORAT. A little yielding may my love advance:
She darted from her eyes a sidelong glance,
Just as she spoke; and, like her words, it flew;
Seemed not to beg what yet she bid me do.

A brother, madam, cannot give a day;   [*To her*]
A servant, and who hopes to merit, may.
MELESINDA. If, Sir –   [*coming to him*]
MORAT. No more – set speeches, and a formal tale,
    With none but statesmen and grave fools prevail.
    Dry up your tears, and practise every grace,
    That fits the pageant of your royal place.   [*Exit*]
MELESINDA. Madam, the strange reverse of fate you see;
                         [*To* INDAMORA]
    I pitied you, now you may pity me.   [*Exit after him*]
INDAMORA. Poor Princess! thy hard fate I could bemoan,
    Had I not nearer sorrows of my own.
    Beauty is seldom fortunate, when great;
    A vast estate, but overcharged with debt.
    Like those whom want to baseness does betray;
    I'm forced to flatter him I cannot pay.
    Oh, would he be content to seize the throne!
    I beg the life of Aureng-Zebe alone.
    Whom heav'n would bless, from pomp it will remove,
    And make their wealth in privacy and love.

                 [*Exit*]

ACT IV

[AURENG-ZEBE *solus*]

Distrust and darkness of a future state,
Make poor mankind so fearful of their fate.
Death, in itself, is nothing; but we fear
To be we know not what, we know not where.
                 [*Soft music*]
This is the ceremony of my fate;
A parting treat, and I'm to die in state.

They lodge me as I were the Persian King;
And with luxurious pomp my death they bring.

[*To him* NOURMAHAL]

NOURMAHAL. I thought, before you drew your latest
    breath,
To smooth your passage and to soften death;
For I would have you, when you upward move,
Speak kindly of me to our friends above;
Nor name me there th' occasion of your fate,
Or what my interest does impute to hate.

AURENG-ZEBE. I ask not for what end your pomp's
    designed;
Whether t' insult or to compose my mind.
I marked it not,
But, knowing death would soon th' assault begin,
Stood firm collected in my strength within;
To guard that breach did all my forces guide,
And left unmanned the quiet senses' side.

NOURMAHAL. Because Morat from me his being took,
All I can say will much suspected look.
'Tis little to confess your fate I grieve;
Yet more than you would easily believe.

AURENG-ZEBE. Since my inevitable death you know,
You safely unavailing pity show;
'Tis popular to mourn a dying foe.

NOURMAHAL. You made my liberty your late request;
Is no return due from a grateful breast?
I grow impatient, till I find some way
Great offices, with greater, to repay.

AURENG-ZEBE. When I consider life, 'tis all a cheat;
Yet, fooled with hope, men favour the deceit;
Trust on, and think to-morrow will repay:
To-morrow's falser than the former day;

Lies worse; and while it says, we shall be blessed
With some new joys, cuts off what we possessed.
Strange couzenage! none would live past years
    again,
Yet all hope pleasure in what yet remain;
And, from the dregs of life, think to receive
What the first sprightly running could not give.
I'm tired with waiting for this chymic gold,
Which fools us young, and beggars us when old.

NOURMAHAL. 'Tis not for nothing that we life pursue;
It pays our hopes with something still that's new.
Each day's a mistress, unenjoyed before;
Like travellers, we're pleased with seeing more.
Did you but know what joys your way attend,
You would not hurry to your journey's end.

AURENG-ZEBE. I need not haste the end of life to meet;
The precipice is just beneath my feet.

NOURMAHAL. Think not my sense of virtue is so small;
I'll rather leap down first, and break your fall.
My Aureng-Zebe, (may I not call you so?)
                                        [*Taking him by the hand*]
Behold me now no longer for your foe;
I am not, cannot be your enemy.
Look, is there any malice in my eye?
Pray sit –   [*Both sit*]
That distance shows too much respect, or fear;
You'll find no danger in approaching near.

AURENG-ZEBE. Forgive th' amazement of my doubtful
    state;
This kindness from the mother of Morat!
Or is't some angel, pitying what I bore,
Who takes that shape to make my wonder more?

NOURMAHAL. Think me your better genius in disguise;
Or anything that more may charm your eyes.

311

Your guardian angel never could excel
In care, nor could he love his charge so well.

AURENG-ZEBE. Whence can proceed so wonderful a
change?

NOURMAHAL. Can kindness to desert, like yours, be
strange?
Kindness by secret sympathy is tied;
For noble souls in nature are allied.
I saw with what a brow you braved your fate;
Yet with what mildness bore your father's hate.
My virtue, like a string wound up by art,
To the same sound, when yours was touched, took
part,
At distance shook and trembled at my heart.

AURENG-ZEBE. I'll not complain my father is unkind,
Since so much pity from a foe I find.
Just heav'n reward this act.

NOURMAHAL. 'Tis well the debt no payment does demand,
You turn me over to another hand.
But happy, happy she,
And with the blessed above to be compared,
Whom you yourself would, with yourself, reward;
The greatest, nay, the fairest of her kind,
Would envy her that bliss which you designed.

AURENG-ZEBE. Great princes thus, when favourites they
raise,
To justify their grace, their creatures praise.

NOURMAHAL. As love the noblest passion we account,
So to the highest object it should mount.
It shows you brave when mean desires you shun.
An eagle only can behold the sun;
And so must you; if yet, presage divine
There be in dreams, or was't a vision mine?

AURENG-ZEBE. Of me?

NOURMAHAL. And who could else employ my
    thought?
I dreamed your love was by love's goddess sought;
Officious cupids, hov'ring o'er your head,
Held myrtle wreaths; beneath your feet were spread
What sweets soe'er Sabean springs disclose,
Our Indian jasmine, or the Syrian rose.
The wanton ministers around you strove
For service, and inspired their mother's love;
Close by your side, and languishing, she lies,
With blushing cheeks, short breath, and wishing
    eyes;
Upon your breast supinely lay her head,
While, on your face, her famished sight she fed.
Then, with a sigh, into these words she broke,
(And gathered humid kisses as she spoke.)
Dull, and ungrateful! must I offer love?
Desired of gods, and envied ev'n by Jove;
And dost thou ignorance or fear pretend?
Mean soul! and dar'st not gloriously offend?
Then, pressing thus his hand –
AURENG-ZEBE.   I'll hear no more. [*Rising up*]
'Twas impious to have understood before;
And I, till now, endeavoured to mistake
Th' incestuous meaning which too plain you make.
NOURMAHAL. And why this niceness to that pleasure
    shown,
Where nature sums up all her joys in one;
Gives all she can, and labouring still to give,
Makes it so great, we can but taste and live.
So fills the senses, that the soul seems fled,
And thought itself does, for the time, lie dead;
Till, like a string screwed up with eager haste,
It breaks, and is too exquisite to last?

AURENG-ZEBE. Heav'ns! can you this, without just ven-
geance, hear?
When will you thunder, if it now be clear?
Yet her alone let not your thunder seize;
I, too, deserve to die, because I please.
NOURMAHAL. Custom our native royalty does awe;
Promiscuous love is nature's general law.
For whosoever the first lovers were,
Brother and sister made the second pair,
And doubled, by their love, their piety.
AURENG-ZEBE. Hence, hence, and to some barbarous
climate fly,
Which only brutes in human form does yield,
And man grows wild in nature's common field.
Who eat their parents, piety pretend;
Yet there no sons their sacred bed ascend.
To veil great sins, a greater crime you choose;
And, in your incest, your adult'ry lose.
NOURMAHAL. In vain this haughty fury you have shown.
How I adore a soul so like my own!
You must be mine, that you may learn to live;
Know joys which only she who loves can give.
Nor think that action you upbraid, so ill:
I am not changed; I love my husband still,
But love him as he was, when youthful grace
And the first down began to shade his face.
That image does my virgin-flames renew,
And all your father shines more bright in you.
AURENG-ZEBE. In me a horror of myself you raise;
Cursed by your love, and blasted by your praise.
You find new ways to prosecute my fate;
And your least-guilty passion was your hate.
NOURMAHAL. I beg my death, if you can love deny.
                                    [*Offering him a dagger*]

AURENG-ZEBE. I'll grant you nothing; no, not ev'n to die.
NOURMAHAL. Know then, you are not half so kind as I.
                    [*Stamps with her foot*]

[*Enter mutes, some with swords drawn, one with a cup*]
You've chosen, and may now repent too late.
Behold th' effect of what you wished, my hate.
                    [*Taking the cup to present him*]
This cup, a cure for both our ills has brought;
You need not fear a philtre in the draught.
AURENG-ZEBE. All must be poison which can come from
    thee;   [*Receiving it from her*]
But this the least. T' immortal liberty,
This first I pour – like dying Socrates;
                    [*Spilling a little of it*]
Grim though he be, death pleases when he frees.

[*As he is going to drink, enter* MORAT *attended*]
MORAT. Make not such haste, you must my leisure stay:
Your fate's deferred, you shall not die to-day.
                    [*Taking the cup from him*]
NOURMAHAL. What foolish pity has possessed your mind,
To alter what your prudence once designed?
MORAT. What if I please to lengthen out his date
A day, and take a pride to cozen fate?
NOURMAHAL. 'Twill not be safe to let him live an hour.
MORAT. I'll do't, to show my arbitrary pow'r.
NOURMAHAL. Fortune may take him from your hands
    again,
And you repent th' occasion lost in vain.
MORAT. I smile at what your female fear foresees;
I'm in fate's place and dictate her decrees.
Let Arimant be called.   [*Exit one of the attendants*]

AURENG-ZEBE. Give me the poison, and I'll end your
      strife;
I hate to keep a poor precarious life.
Would I my safety on base terms receive,
Know, Sir, I could have lived without your leave.
But those I could accuse, I can forgive;
By my disdainful silence, let 'em live.

NOURMAHAL. What am I, that you dare to bind my
      hand?   [*To* MORAT]
So low, I've not a murder at command!
Can you not one poor life to her afford,
Her who gave up whole nations to your sword?
And from th' abundance of whose soul and heat,
Th' o'erflowing served to make your mind so great.

MORAT. What did that greatness in a woman's mind?
Ill lodged, and weak to act what it designed.
Pleasure's your portion, and your slothful ease;
When man's at leisure, study how to please.
Soften his angry hours with servile care,
And when he calls, the ready feast prepare.
From wars, and from affairs of state abstain;
Women emasculate a monarch's reign;
And murmuring crowds, who see 'em shine with
      gold,
That pomp as their own ravished spoils behold.

NOURMAHAL. Rage chokes my words; 'tis womanly to
      weep.   [*Aside*]
In my swoll'n breast my close revenge I'll keep;
I'll watch his tender'st part, and there strike deep.
                            [*Exit*]

AURENG-ZEBE. Your strange proceeding does my wonder
      move;
Yet seems not to express a brother's love.
Say to what cause my rescued life I owe.

MORAT. If what you ask would please, you should not know;
 But since that knowledge, more than death, will grieve,
 Know, Indamora gained you this reprieve.
AURENG-ZEBE. And whence had she the pow'r to work
  your change?
MORAT. The pow'r of beauty is not new or strange.
 Should she command me more, I could obey;
 But her reqûest was bounded with a day.
 Take that; and, if you'll spare my farther crime,
 Be kind, and grieve to death against your time.

   [*Enter* ARIMANT]

Remove this pris'ner to some safer place.
He has, for Indamora's sake, found grace;
And from my mother's rage must guarded be,
Till you receive a new command from me.
ARIMANT. This love, and fortune, persecute me still,
 And make me slave to every rival's will. [*Aside*]
AURENG-ZEBE. How I disdain a life, which I must buy
 With your contempt, and her inconstancy!
 For a few hours my whole content I pay;
 You shall not force on me another day.
      [*Exit with* ARIMANT]

   [*Enter* MELESINDA]

MELESINDA. I have been seeking you this hour's long
  space,
 And feared to find you in another place;
 But, since you're here, my jealousy grows less;
 You will be kind to my unworthiness.
 What shall I say? I love to that degree,
 Each glance another way is robbed from me.
 Absence and prisons I could bear again;
 But sink and die beneath your least disdain.

MORAT. Why do you give your mind this needless care,
And, for yourself, and me, new pains prepare?
I ne'er approved this passion in excess;
If you would show your love, distrust me less.
I hate to be pursued from place to place;
Meet, at each turn, a stale domestic face.
Th' approach of jealousy love cannot bear,
He's wild and soon on wing if watchful eyes come near.

MELESINDA. From your loved presence how can I depart?
My eyes pursue the object of my heart.

MORAT. You talk as if it were our bridal night.
Fondness is still th' effect of new delight,
And marriage but the pleasure of a day;
The metal's base the gilding worn away.

MELESINDA. I fear I'm guilty of some great offence,
And that has bred this cold indifference.

MORAT. The greatest in the world to flesh and blood;
You fondly love much longer than you should.

MELESINDA. If that be all which makes your discontent,
Of such a crime I never can repent.

MORAT. Would you force love upon me, which I shun?
And bring coarse fare when appetite is gone?

MELESINDA. Why did I not in prison die before
My fatal freedom made me suffer more?
I had been pleased to think I died for you,
And doubly pleased, because you then were true;
Then I had hope, but now, alas, have none.

MORAT. You say you love me; let that love be shown.
'Tis in your power to make my happiness.

MELESINDA. Speak quickly; to command me is to bless.

MORAT. To Indamora you my suit must move;
You'll sure speak kindly of the man you love.

MELESINDA. Oh! rather let me perish by your hand,
Than break my heart by this unkind command;

Think 'tis the only one I could deny,
And that 'tis harder to refuse than die.
Try, if you please, my rival's heart to win;
I'll bear the pain, but not promote the sin.
You own whate'er perfections man can boast,
And if she view you with my eyes, she's lost.

MORAT. Here I renounce all love, all nuptial ties;
Henceforward live a stranger to my eyes.
When I appear, see you avoid the place,
And haunt me not with that unlucky face.

MELESINDA. Hard as it is, I this command obey,
And haste, while I have life, to go away.
In pity stay some hours, till I am dead,
That blameless you may court my rival's bed.
My hated face I'll not presume to show;
Yet I may watch your steps where'er you go.
Unseen, I'll gaze; and with my latest breath
Bless, while I die, the author of my death. [*Weeping*]

[*Enter* EMPEROR]

EMPEROR. When your triumphant fortune high appears,
What cause can draw these unbecoming tears?
Let cheerfulness on happy fortune wait,
And give not thus the counter-time to fate.

MELESINDA. Fortune long frowned, and has but lately
    smiled;
I doubt a foe so newly reconciled.
You saw but sorrow in its waning form,
A working sea remaining from a storm;
When the now weary waves roll o'er the deep,
And faintly murmur ere they fall asleep.

EMPEROR. Your inward griefs you smother in your
    mind;
But fame's loud voice proclaims your lord unkind.

MORAT. Let fame be busy where she has to do;
    Tell of fought fields, and every pompous show.
    Those tales are fit to fill the people's ears;
    Monarchs, unquestioned, move in higher spheres.
MELESINDA. Believe not rumour, but yourself; and see
    The kindness 'twixt my plighted lord and me.
                         [*Kissing* MORAT]
    This is our state; thus happily we live;
    These are the quarrels which we take and give.
    [*Aside to* MORAT] I had no other way to force a kiss.
    Forgive my last farewell to you, and bliss.   [*Exit*]
EMPEROR. Your haughty carriage shows too much of
    scorn,
    And love, like hers, deserves not that return.
MORAT. You'll please to leave me judge of what I do,
    And not examine by the outward show.
    Your usage of my mother might be good;
    I judged it not.
EMPEROR.   Nor was it fit you should.
MORAT. Then in as equal balance weigh my deeds.
EMPEROR. My right and my authority exceeds.
    Suppose (what I'll not grant) injustice done;
    Is judging me the duty of a son?
MORAT. Not of a son, but of an emperor.
    You cancelled duty when you gave me pow'r.
    If your own actions on your will you ground,
    Mine shall hereafter know no other bound.
    What meant you when you called me to a throne?
    Was it to please me with a name alone?
EMPEROR. 'Twas that I thought your gratitude would
    know
    What to my partial kindness you did owe;
    That what your birth did to your claim deny,
    Your merit of obedience might supply.

MORAT. To your own thoughts such hopes you might
  propose;
 But I took empire not on terms like those.
 Of business you complained; now take your ease;
 Enjoy whate'er decrepit age can please.
 Eat, sleep, and tell long tales of what you were
 In flow'r of youth, if anyone will hear.
EMPEROR. Pow'r like new wine does your weak brain
  surprise,
 And its mad fumes in hot discourses rise;
 But time these giddy vapours will remove;
 Meanwhile I'll taste the sober joys of love.
MORAT. You cannot love, nor pleasures take, or
  give;
 But life begin when 'tis too late to live.
 On a tired courser you pursue delight,
 Let slip your morning and set out at night.
 If you have lived, take thankfully the past;
 Make, as you can, the sweet remembrance last.
 If you have not enjoyed what youth could give,
 But life sunk through you like a leaky sieve,
 Accuse yourself you lived not while you might;
 But in the captive Queen resign your right.
 I've now resolved to fill your useless place;
 I'll take that post to cover your disgrace,
 And love her for the honour of my race.
EMPEROR. Thou dost but try how far I can forbear,
 Nor art that monster which thou wouldst appear.
 But do not wantonly my passion move;
 I pardon nothing that relates to love.
 My fury does, like jealous forts, pursue
 With death ev'n strangers who but come to view.
MORAT. I did not only view, but will invade.
 Could you shed venom from your reverend shade,

Like trees beneath whose arms 'tis death to sleep;
Did rolling thunder your fenced fortress keep,
Thence would I snatch my Semele like Jove,
And midst the dreadful rack enjoy my love.

EMPEROR. Have I for this, ungrateful as thou art,
When right, when nature, struggled in my heart;
When heav'n called on me for thy brother's claim,
Broke all, and sullied my unspotted fame?
Wert thou to empire, by my baseness brought,
And wouldst thou ravish what so dear I bought?
Dear! for my conscience and its peace I gave;
Why was my reason made my passion's slave?
I see heav'n's justice; thus the pow'rs divine
Pay crimes with crimes and punish mine by thine.

MORAT. Crimes let them pay, and punish as they please;
What pow'r makes mine, by pow'r I mean to seize.
Since 'tis to that they their own greatness owe
Above, why should they question mine below? [*Exit*]

EMPEROR. Prudence, thou vainly in our youth art sought,
And with age purchased art too dearly bought.
We're past the use of wit for which we toil;
Late fruit, and planted in too cold a soil.
My stock of fame is lavished and decayed;
No profit of the vast profusion made.
Too late my folly I repent; I know
My Aureng-Zebe would ne'er have used me so.
But by his ruin I prepared my own;
And, like a naked tree, my shelter gone,
To winds and winter-storms must stand exposed alone.

[*Exit*]

[AURENG-ZEBE, ARIMANT]

ARIMANT. Give me not thanks, which I will ne'er deserve;
But know, 'tis for a noble price I serve.

322

By Indamora's will you're hither brought;
All my reward in her command I sought.
The rest your letter tells you. – See, like light
She comes; and I must vanish, like the night.   [*Exit*]

[*Enter* INDAMORA]

INDAMORA. 'Tis now that I begin to live again.
Heav'ns, I forgive you all my fear and pain;
Since I behold my Aureng-Zebe appear,
I could not buy him at a price too dear.
His name alone afforded me relief,
Repeated as a charm to cure my grief.
I that loved name did, as some god, invoke,
And printed kisses on it while I spoke.

AURENG-ZEBE. Short ease, but long, long pains from you
    I find;
Health to my eyes, but poison to my mind.
Why are you made so excellently fair?
So much above what other beauties are,
That ev'n in cursing you new form my breath,
And make me bless those eyes which give me death?

INDAMORA. What reason for your curses can you find?
My eyes your conquest, not your death, designed.
If they offend, 'tis that they are too kind.

AURENG-ZEBE. The ruins they have wrought you will not
    see;
Too kind they are, indeed, but not to me.

INDAMORA. Think you base interest souls like mine can sway?
Or that for greatness I can love betray?
No, Aureng-Zebe, you merit all my heart,
And I'm too noble but to give a part.
Your father, and an Empire! am I known
No more? Or have so weak a judgement shown,
In choosing you, to change you for a throne?

AURENG-ZEBE. How with a truth you would a falsehood
    blind!
  'Tis not my father's love you have designed;
  Your choice is fixed where youth and pow'r are joined.
INDAMORA. Where youth and power are joined! has he
    a name?
AURENG-ZEBE. You would be told; you glory in your
    shame.
  There's music in the sound; and, to provoke
  Your pleasure more, by me it must be spoke.
  Then, then it ravishes, when your pleased ear
  The sound does from a wretched rival hear.
  Morat's the name your heart leaps up to meet,
  While Aureng-Zebe lies dying at your feet.
INDAMORA. Who told you this?
AURENG-ZEBE.   Are you so lost to shame?
  Morat, Morat, Morat! You love the name
  So well you ev'ry question ends in that;
  You force me still to answer you, Morat.
  Morat, who best could tell what you revealed;
  Morat, too proud to keep his joy concealed.
INDAMORA. Howe'er unjust your jealousy appear,
  It shows the loss, of what you love, you fear;
  And does my pity, not my anger move:
  I'll fond it, as the froward child of love.
  To show the truth of my unaltered breast,
  Know, that your life was given at my request;
  At least reprieved. When heav'n denied you aid,
  She brought it; she, whose falsehood you upbraid.
AURENG-ZEBE. And 'tis by that you would your falsehood
    hide;
  Had you not asked how happy had I died!
  Accurst reprieve! not to prolong my breath,
  It brought a ling'ring and more painful death.

I have not lived since first I heard the news;
The gift the guilty giver does accuse.
You knew the price, and the request did move
That you might pay the ransom with your love.

INDAMORA. Your accusation must, I see, take place;
And I am guilty, infamous, and base!

AURENG-ZEBE. If you are false, those epithets are small;
You're then the things, the abstract of 'em all.
And you are false; you promised him your love.
No other price a heart so hard could move.
Do not I know him? could his brutal mind
Be wrought upon? could he be just or kind?
Insultingly he made your love his boast;
Gave me my life, and told me what it cost.
Speak; answer. I would fain yet think you true.
Lie; and I'll not believe myself but you.
Tell me you love; I'll pardon the deceit,
And, to be fooled, myself assist the cheat.

INDAMORA. No; 'tis too late. I have no more to say.
If you'll believe I have been false, you may.

AURENG-ZEBE. I would not, but your crimes too plain
    appear;
Nay, even that I should think you true, you fear.
Did I not tell you, I would be deceived?

INDAMORA. I'm not concerned to have my truth believed.
You would be cozened! would assist the cheat!
But I'm too plain to join in the deceit;
I'm pleased you think me false –
And whatsoe'er my letter did pretend,
I made this meeting for no other end.

AURENG-ZEBE. Kill me not quite with this indifference;
When you are guiltless, boast not an offence.
I know you better than yourself you know;
Your heart was true, but did some frailty show.

You promised him your love that I might live;
But promised what you never meant to give.
Speak, was't not so? confess; I can forgive.

INDAMORA. Forgive what dull excuses you prepare!
As if your thoughts of me were worth my care.

AURENG-ZEBE. Ah trait'ress! Ah ingrate! Ah faithless
mind!
Ah sex, invented first to damn mankind!
Nature took care to dress you up for sin;
Adorned, without; unfinished left, within.
Hence, by no judgement you your loves direct;
Talk much, ne'er think, and still the wrong affect.
So much self-love in your composures mixed,
That love to others still remains unfixed.
Greatness, and noise, and show, are your delight;
Yet wise men love you, in their own despite:
And, finding in their native wit no ease,
Are forced to put your folly on to please.

INDAMORA. Now you shall know what cause you have to
rage;
But to increase your fury, not assuage.
I found the way your brother's heart to move,
Yet promised not the least return of love.
His pride and brutal fierceness I abhor;
But scorn your mean suspicions of me more.
I owed my honour and my fame this care;
Know what your folly lost you, and despair.
                                    [Turning from him]

AURENG-ZEBE. Too cruelly your innocence you tell;
Show heav'n, and damn me to the pit of hell.
Now I believe you; 'tis not yet too late;
You may forgive, and put a stop to fate;
Save me, just sinking, and no more to rise. [She frowns]
How can you look with such relentless eyes?

Or let your mind by penitence be moved,
Or I'm resolved to think you never loved.
You are not cleared unless you mercy speak;
I'll think you took th' occasion thus to break.

INDAMORA. Small jealousies, 'tis true, inflame desire;
Too great, not fan, but quite blow out the fire.
Yet I did love you, till such pains I bore
That I dare trust myself and you no more.
Let me not love you, but here end my pain;
Distrust may make me wretched once again.
Now, with full sails, into the port I move,
And safely can unlade my breast of love;
Quiet and calm. Why should I then go back,
To tempt the second hazard of a wrack?

AURENG-ZEBE. Behold these dying eyes, see their sub-
        missive awe;
These tears, which fear of death could never draw;
Heard you that sigh? from my heaved heart it past,
And said, if you forgive not 'tis my last.
Love mounts, and rolls about my stormy mind,
Like fire that's borne by a tempestuous wind.
Oh, I could stifle you with eager haste!
Devour your kisses with my hungry taste!
Rush on you! eat you! wander o'er each part,
Raving with pleasure, snatch you to my heart!
Then hold you off, and gaze! then, with new rage,
Invade you till my conscious limbs presage
Torrents of joy, which all their banks o'erflow!
So lost, so blest, as I but then could know!

INDAMORA. Be no more jealous. [*Giving him her hand*]
AURENG-ZEBE.   Give me cause no more:
The danger's greater after than before.
If I relapse, to cure my jealousy,
Let me (for that's the easiest parting) die.

INDAMORA. My life!

AURENG-ZEBE.   My soul!

INDAMORA.   My all that heav'n can give!
    Death's life with you; without you, death to live.

[*To them* ARIMANT *hastily*]

ARIMANT. Oh, we are lost, beyond all human aid!
    The citadel is to Morat betrayed.
    The traitor, and the treason, known too late;
    The false Abas delivered up the gate.
    Ev'n while I speak, we're compassed round with fate.
    The valiant cannot fight, or coward fly;
    But both in undistinguished crowds must die.

AURENG-ZEBE. Then my prophetic fears are come to pass:
    Morat was always bloody, now, he's base;
    And has so far in usurpation gone,
    He will by paricide secure the throne.

[*To them the* EMPEROR]

EMPEROR. Am I forsaken and betrayed by all?
    Not one brave man dare, with a monarch, fall?
    Then, welcome death, to cover my disgrace;
    I would not live to reign o'er such a race.
    My Aureng-Zebe!   [*Seeing* AURENG-ZEBE]
    But thou no more art mine; my cruelty
    Has quite destroyed the right I had in thee.
    I have been base.
    Base ev'n to him from whom I did receive
    All that a son could to a parent give;
    Behold me punished in the self-same kind,
    Th' ungrateful does a more ungrateful find.

AURENG-ZEBE. Accuse yourself no more; you could not be
    Ungrateful; could commit no crime to me.

I only mourn my yet uncancelled score;
You put me past the pow'r of paying more.
That, that's my grief, that I can only grieve,
And bring but pity where I would relieve;
For had I yet ten thousand lives to pay,
The mighty sum should go no other way.

EMPEROR. Can you forgive me? 'tis not fit you should.
Why will you be so excellently good?
'Twill stick too black a brand upon my name;
The sword is needless; I shall die with shame.
What had my age to do with love's delight,
Shut out from all enjoyments but the sight?

ARIMANT. Sir, you forget the danger's imminent;
This minute is not for excuses lent.

EMPEROR. Disturb me not —
How can my latest hour be better spent?
To reconcile myself to him is more
Than to regain all I possessed before.
Empire and life are now not worth a pray'r;
His love alone deserves my dying care.

AURENG-ZEBE. Fighting for you, my death will glorious
be.

INDAMORA. Seek to preserve yourself, and live for me.

ARIMANT. Lose then no farther time.
Heav'n has inspired me with a sudden thought,
Whence your unhoped for safety may be wrought,
Though with the hazard of my blood 'tis bought.
But since my life can ne'er be fortunate,
'Tis so much sorrow well redeemed from fate.
You, Madam, must retire;
Your beauty is its own security;
And leave the conduct of the rest to me.
Glory will crown my life if I succeed;
If not, she may afford to love me dead.   [*Aside*]

AURENG-ZEBE. My father's kind, and, Madam, you
    forgive;
Were heav'n so pleased, I now could wish to live.
And, I shall live.
With glory and with love at once I burn;
I feel th' inspiring heat and absent god return.

[Exeunt]

ACT V

[INDAMORA alone]

THE night seems doubled with the fear she brings,
And, o'er the citadel, new spreads her wings.
The morning, as mistaken, turns about,
And all her early fires again go out.
Shouts, cries, and groans, first pierce my ears, and then
A flash of lightning draws the guilty scene,
And shows me arms, and wounds, and dying men.
Ah, should my Aureng-Zebe be fighting there,
And envious winds distinguished to my ear
His dying groans, and his last accents bear!

[To her MORAT, attended]

MORAT. The bloody bus'ness of the night is done,
And, in the citadel, an empire won.
Our swords so wholly did the fates employ,
That they, at length, grew weary to destroy;
Refused the work we brought, and, out of breath,
Made sorrow and despair attend for death.
But what of all my conquest can I boast?
My haughty pride before your eyes is lost;
And victory but gains me to present
That homage, which our eastern world has sent.

INDAMORA. Your victory, alas, begets my fears;
　　Can you not then triumph without my tears?
　　Resolve me (for you know my destiny
　　In Aureng-Zebe's); say, do I live, or die?
MORAT. Urged by my love, by hope of empire fired,
　　'Tis true I have performed what both required;
　　What fate decreed; for when great souls are giv'n,
　　They bear the marks of sov'reignty from heav'n.
　　My elder brothers my forerunners came;
　　Rough-draughts of nature, ill designed, and lame;
　　Blown off like blossoms never made to bear;
　　Till I came finished; her last-laboured care.
INDAMORA. This prologue leads to your succeeding
　　　　sin;
　　Blood ended what ambition did begin.
MORAT. 'Twas rumoured, but by whom I cannot tell,
　　My father 'scaped from out the citadel;
　　My brother too may live.
INDAMORA. 　　　　　　　He may?
MORAT. 　　　　　　　　　　He must!
　　I killed him not; and a less fate's unjust.
　　Heav'n owes it me that I may fill his room;
　　A phoenix-lover, rising from his tomb.
　　In whom you'll lose your sorrows for the dead;
　　More warm, more fierce, and fitter for your bed.
INDAMORA. Should I from Aureng-Zebe my heart divide,
　　To love a monster and a paricide?
　　These names your swelling titles cannot hide.
　　Severe decrees may keep our tongues in awe,
　　But to our thoughts what edict can give law?
　　Ev'n you yourself, to your own breast, shall tell
　　Your crimes; and your own conscience be your hell.
MORAT. What bus'ness has my conscience with a crown?
　　She sinks in pleasures, and in bowls will drown.

If mirth should fail, I'll busy her with cares;
Silence her clamorous voice with louder wars.
Trumpets and drums shall fright her from the throne,
As sounding cymbals aid the lab'ring moon.

INDAMORA. Repelled by these, more eager she will
    grow;
Spring back more strongly than a Scythian bow.
Amidst your train this unseen judge will wait,
Examine how you came by all your state;
Upbraid your impious pomp; and, in your ear,
Will hallow, rebel, tyrant, murderer.
Your ill-got pow'r wan looks and care shall bring;
Known but by discontent to be a king.
Of crowds afraid, yet anxious when alone;
You'll sit and brood your sorrows on a throne.

MORAT. Birthright's a vulgar road to kingly sway;
'Tis ev'ry dull-got elder brother's way.
Dropped from above, he lights into a throne;
Grows of a piece with that he sits upon,
Heav'n's choice, a low, inglorious rightful drone.
But who by force a sceptre does obtain,
Shows he can govern that which he could gain.
Right comes of course, whate'er he was before;
Murder and usurpation are no more.

INDAMORA. By your own laws you such dominion make,
As ev'ry stronger pow'r has right to take;
And paricide will so deform your name,
That dispossessing you will give a claim.
Who next usurps will a just prince appear;
So much your ruin will his reign endear.

MORAT. I without guilt would mount the royal seat;
But yet 'tis necessary to be great.

INDAMORA. All greatness is in virtue understood;
'Tis only necessary to be good.

Tell me, what is't at which great spirits aim,
What most yourself desire?
MORAT.   Renown and fame,
And pow'r, as uncontrolled as is my will.
INDAMORA. How you confound desires of good and ill!
For true renown is still with virtue joined,
But lust of pow'r lets loose th' unbridled mind.
Yours is a soul irregularly great,
Which wanting temper yet abounds with heat;
So strong, yet so unequal pulses beat.
A sun which does through vapours dimly shine;
What pity 'tis you are not all divine!
New moulded, thorough lightened, and a breast
So pure to bear the last severest test;
Fit to command an empire you should gain
By virtue, and without a blush to reign.
MORAT. You show me somewhat I ne'er learnt before;
But 'tis the distant prospect of a shore,
Doubtful in mists; which, like enchanted ground,
Flies from my sight before 'tis fully found.
INDAMORA. Dare to be great without a guilty crown;
View it, and lay the bright temptation down.
'Tis base to seize on all because you may;
That's empire, that which I can give away.
There's joy when to wild will you laws prescribe,
When you bid fortune carry back her bribe;
A joy, which none but greatest minds can taste;
A fame which will to endless ages last.
MORAT. Renown and fame in vain I courted long,
And still pursued 'em, though directed wrong.
In hazard and in toils I heard they lay;
Sailed farther than the coast, but missed my way.
Now you have giv'n me virtue for my guide;
And, with true honour, ballasted my pride.

Unjust dominion I no more pursue;
I quit all other claims but those to you.

INDAMORA. Oh, be not just to halves! pay all you owe.
Think, there's a debt to Melesinda too.
To leave no blemish on your after life;
Reward the virtue of a suff'ring wife.

MORAT. To love once past, I cannot backward move;
Call yesterday again, and I may love.
'Twas not for nothing I the crown resigned;
I still must own a mercenary mind.
I in this venture double gains pursue,
And laid out all my stock to purchase you.

[*To them* ASAPH CHAWN]

Now, what success? does Aureng-Zebe yet live?

ASAPH CHAWN. Fortune has giv'n you all that she can
give
Your brother –

MORAT.   Hold; thou show'st an impious joy,
And think'st I still take pleasure to destroy;
Know, I am changed, and would not have him slain.

ASAPH CHAWN. 'Tis past; and you desire his life in
vain.
He prodigal of soul rushed on the stroke
Of lifted weapons, and did wounds provoke.
In scorn of night, he would not be concealed;
His soldiers, where he fought, his name revealed.
In thickest crowds still Aureng-Zebe did sound;
The vaulted roofs did Aureng-Zebe rebound,
Till late, and in his fall, the name was drowned.

INDAMORA. Wither that hand which brought him to his
fate,
And blasted be the tongue which did relate.

ASAPH CHAWN. His body –

MORAT.　　　　Cease to enhance her misery;
　　Pity the Queen, and show respect to me.
　　'Tis ev'ry painter's art to hide from sight
　　And cast in shades what seen would not delight.
　　Your grief in me such sympathy has bred,　　　[*To her*]
　　I mourn; and wish I could recall the dead.
　　Love softens me; and blows up fires, which pass
　　Through my tough heart, and melt the stubborn mass.
INDAMORA. Break, heart; or choke, with sobs, my hated
　　　　breath;
　　Do thy own work! admit no foreign death.
　　Alas! why do I make this useless moan?
　　I'm dead already, for my soul is gone.

[*To them*, MIR BABA]

MIR BABA. What tongue the terror of this night can tell,
　　Within, without, and round the citadel!
　　A new-formed faction does your pow'r oppose;
　　The fight's confused, and all who meet are foes.
　　A second clamour, from the town, we hear;
　　And the far noise so loud, it drowns the near.
　　Abas, who seemed our friend, is either fled,
　　Or, what we fear, our enemies does head.
　　Your frighted soldiers scarce their ground maintain.
MORAT. I thank their fury; we shall fight again.
　　They rouse my rage; I'm eager to subdue;
　　'Tis fatal to withhold my eyes from you.
　　　　　　　　　[*Exit with the two* OMRAHS]

[*Enter* MELESINDA]

MELESINDA. Can misery no place of safety know?
　　The noise pursues me wheresoe'er I go,
　　As fate sought only me, and where I fled,
　　Aimed all its darts at my devoted head.

And let it; I am now past care of life;
The last of women: an abandoned wife.

INDAMORA. Whether design or chance has brought you here,
I stand obliged to fortune, or to fear;
Weak women should in danger herd like deer.
But say, from whence this new combustion springs?
Are there yet more Morats? more fighting kings?

MELESINDA. Him from his mother's love your eyes divide,
And now her arms the cruel strife decide.

INDAMORA. What strange misfortunes my vexed life attend?
Death will be kind, and all my sorrows end.
If Nourmahal prevail, I know my fate.

MELESINDA. I pity, as my own, your hard estate;
But what can my weak charity afford?
I have no longer int'rest in my lord.
Nor in his mother, he! she owns her hate
Aloud, and would herself usurp the state.

INDAMORA. I'm stupefied with sorrow, past relief
Of tears; parched up and withered with my grief.

MELESINDA. Dry mourning will decays more deadly bring,
As a north wind burns a too forward spring.
Give sorrow vent, and let the sluices go.

INDAMORA. My tears are all congealed, and will not flow,

MELESINDA. Have comfort; yield not to the blows of fate.

INDAMORA. Comfort, like cordials after death, comes late.
Name not so vain a word; my hopes are fled.
Think your Morat were kind, and think him dead.

MELESINDA. I can no more –
Can no more arguments for comfort find.
Your boding words have quite o'erwhelmed my mind.

[*Clattering of weapons within*]

INDAMORA. The noise increases, as the billows roar.
  When rolling from afar they threat the shore.
  She comes; and feeble nature now I find
  Shrinks back in danger, and forsakes my mind.
  I wish to die, yet dare not death endure;
  Detest the med'cine, yet desire the cure.
  I would have death, but mild and at command;
  I dare not trust him in another's hand.
  In Nourmahal's he would not mine appear,
  But armed with terror and disguised with fear.
MELESINDA. Beyond this place you can have no retreat;
  Stay here, and I the danger will repeat.
  I fear not death because my life I hate;
  And envious death will shun th' unfortunate.
INDAMORA. You must not venture.
MELESINDA.   Let me; I may do
  Myself a kindness in obliging you.
  In your loved name I'll seek my angry lord,
  And beg your safety from his conqu'ring sword;
  So his protection all your fears will ease,
  And I shall see him once, and not displease.   [Exit]
INDAMORA. O wretched Queen! what pow'r thy life can
      save?
  A stranger, and unfriended, and a slave!

[Enter NOURMAHAL, ZAYDA, and ABAS, with soldiers]

  Alas, she's here!

  [INDAMORA withdraws to the inner part of the scene]

NOURMAHAL. Heartless they fought, and quitted soon
      their ground,
  While ours with easy victory were crowned.
  To you, Abas, my life and empire too,
  And, what's yet dearer, my revenge, I owe.

ABAS. The vain Morat, by his own rashness wrought,
    Too soon discovered his ambitious thought;
    Believed me his because I spoke him fair,
    And pitched his head into the ready snare.
    Hence 'twas I did his troops at first admit,
    But such whose numbers could no fears beget;
    By them th' Emperor's party first I slew,
    Then turned my arms the victors to subdue.

NOURMAHAL. Now let the headstrong boy my will control!
    Virtue's no slave of man; no sex confines the soul.
    I, for myself, th' imperial seat will gain,
    And he shall wait my leisure for his reign.
    But Aureng-Zebe is nowhere to be found.
    And now perhaps in death's cold arms he lies;
    I fought and conquered, yet have lost the prize.

ZAYDA. The chance of war determined well the strife
    That racked you, 'twixt the lover and the wife;
    He's dead, whose love had sullied all your reign,
    And made you empress of the world in vain.

NOURMAHAL. No; I my pow'r and pleasure would divide;
    The drudge had quenched my flames, and then had died.
    I rage to think without that bliss I live;
    That I could wish what fortune would not give.
    But what love cannot, vengeance must supply;
    She, who bereaved me of his heart, shall die.

ZAYDA. I'll search; far distant hence she cannot be.

                            [Goes in]

NOURMAHAL. This wondrous masterpiece I fain would see;
    This fatal Helen, who can wars inspire,
    Make kings her slaves, and set the world on fire.
    My husband locked his jewel from my view;
    Or durst not set the false one by the true.

[*Re-enter* ZAYDA, *leading* INDAMORA]

ZAYDA. Your frighted captive, ere she dies, receive;
  Her soul's just going else, without your leave.

NOURMAHAL. A fairer creature did my eyes ne'er
    see!
  Sure she was formed by heav'n in spite to me!
  Some angel copied, while I slept, each grace,
  And moulded ev'ry feature from my face.
  Such majesty does from her forehead rise,
  Her cheeks such blushes cast, such rays her eyes,
  Nor I, nor envy, can a blemish find;
  The palace is, without, too well designed:
  Conduct me in, for I will view thy mind.   [*To her*]
  Speak, if thou hast a soul, that I may see
  If heav'n can make throughout another me.

INDAMORA. My tears and miseries must plead my
    cause;   [*Kneeling*]
  My words, the terror of your presence awes.
  Mortals, in sight of angels, mute become;
  The nobler nature strikes th' inferior dumb.

NOURMAHAL. The palm is, by the foe's confession, mine;
  But I disdain what basely you resign.
  Heav'n did, by me, the outward model build;
  Its inward work, the soul, with rubbish filled.
  Yet, oh! th' imperfect piece moves more delight;
  'Tis gilded o'er with youth to catch the sight.
  The gods have poorly robbed my virgin bloom,
  And what I am, by what I was, o'ercome.
  Trait'ress, restore my beauty and my charms,
  Nor steal my conquest with my proper arms.

INDAMORA. What have I done, thus to inflame your
    hate?
  I am not guilty, but unfortunate.

NOURMAHAL. Not guilty, when thy looks my pow'r
    betray,
    Seduce mankind, my subject, from my sway,
    Take all my hearts, and all my eyes away?
    My husband first; but that I could forgive:
    He only moved and talked, but did not live.
    My Aureng-Zebe, for I dare own the name,
    The glorious sin, and the more glorious flame;
    Him, from my beauty, have thy eyes misled,
    And starved the joys of my expected bed.
INDAMORA. His love, so sought, he's happy that he's
    dead.
    Oh, had I courage but to meet my fate;
    That short dark passage to a future state;
    That melancholy riddle of a breath.
NOURMAHAL. That something, or that nothing, after
    death: [*Giving a dagger*]
    Take this, and teach thyself.
INDAMORA. Alas!
NOURMAHAL.   Why dost thou shake?
    Dishonour not the vengeance I designed;
    A Queen, and own a base plebeian mind!
    Let it drink deep in thy most vital part;
    Strike home, and do me reason in thy heart.
INDAMORA. I dare not.
NOURMAHAL.   Do't, while I stand by and see,
    At my full gust, without the drudgery.
    I love a foe who dares my stroke prevent,
    Who gives me the full scene of my content,
    Shows me the flying soul's convulsive strife,
    And all the anguish of departing life.
    Disdain my mercy, and my rage defy;
    Curse me with thy last breath, and make me see
    A spirit worthy to have rivalled me.

INDAMORA. Oh, I desire to die; but dare not yet.
Give me some respite, I'll discharge the debt.
Without my Aureng-Zebe I would not live.

NOURMAHAL. Thine, traitress! thine! that word has
winged thy fate,
And put me past the tedious forms of hate.
I'll kill thee with such eagerness and haste,
As fiends, let loose, would lay all nature waste.

[INDAMORA *runs back; as* NOURMAHAL *is running to
her. Clashing of swords is heard within*]

SOLDIER. Yield, you're o'erpow'red; resistance is in
vain.   [*Within*]

MORAT. Then death's my choice; submission I disdain.
[*Within*]

NOURMAHAL. Retire, you slaves! Ah whither does he
run   [*At the door*]
On pointed swords? Disarm, but save my son.

[*Enter* MORAT *staggering, and upheld by soldiers*]

MORAT. She lives! and I shall see her once again!
I have not thrown away my life in vain.

[*Catches hold of* INDAMORA'S *gown, and falls by her;
she sits*]

I can no more; yet, ev'n in death, I find
My fainting body biased by my mind.
I fall toward you; still my contending soul
Points to your breast, and trembles to its pole.

[*To them* MELESINDA, *hastily, casting herself on the
other side of* MORAT]

MELESINDA. Ah woe, woe, woe! the worst of woes I find!
Live still; oh, live; live ev'n to be unkind.
With half-shut eyes he seeks the doubtful day;
But, ah! he bends his sight another way.

He faints! and in that sigh his soul is gone;
Yet heaven's unmoved, yet heav'n looks careless on.

NOURMAHAL. Where are those pow'rs which monarchs
should defend?
Or do they vain authority pretend
O'er human fates, and their weak empire show,
Which cannot guard their images below?
If, as their image, he was not divine,
They ought to have respected him as mine.
I'll waken them with my revenge; and she,
Their Indamora, shall my victim be,
And helpless heav'n shall mourn in vain, like me.

[*As she is going to stab* INDAMORA, MORAT *raises
himself, and holds her hand*]

MORAT. Ah, what are we
Who dare maintain with heav'n this wretched strife,
Puffed with the pride of heav'n's own gift, frail life?
That blast which my ambitious spirit swelled,
See, by how a weak a tenure it was held!
I only stay to save the innocent;
Oh, envy not my soul its last content.

INDAMORA. No, let me die; I'm doubly summoned
now;
First, by my Aureng-Zebe; and, since, by you.
My soul grows hardy, and can death endure;
Your convoy makes the dang'rous way secure.

MELESINDA. Let me, at least, a funeral marriage crave;
Nor grudge my cold embraces in the grave.
I have too just a title in the strife;
By me, unhappy me, he lost his life.
I called him hither; 'twas my fatal breath;
And I the screech-owl that proclaimed his death.

[*Shout within*]

ABAS. What new alarms are these? I'll haste and see.

           [*Exit*]

NOURMAHAL. Look up, and live; an empire shall be
 thine.

MORAT. That I contemned, ev'n when I thought it mine.
 Oh, I must yield to my hard destinies,

        [*To* INDAMORA]

 And must for ever cease to see your eyes.

MELESINDA. Ah turn your sight to me, my dearest lord!
 Can you not one, one parting look afford?
 Ev'n so unkind in death? but 'tis in vain;
 I lose my breath, and to the winds complain.
 Yet 'tis as much in vain your cruel scorn;
 Still I can love without this last return.
 Nor fate, nor you, can my vowed faith control;
 Dying, I'll follow your disdainful soul;
 A ghost, I'll haunt your ghost, and, where you go,
 With mournful murmurs fill the plains below.

MORAT. Be happy, Melesinda, cease to grieve,
 And for a more deserving husband live.
 Can you forgive me?

MELESINDA.   Can I! Oh, my heart!
 Have I heard one kind word before I part?
 I can, I can forgive; is that a task
 To love like mine? Are you so good to ask?
 One kiss – Oh, 'tis too great a blessing this;

        [*Kisses him*]

 I would not live to violate the bliss.

   [*Re-enter* ABAS]

ABAS. Some envious devil has ruined us yet more!
 The fort's revolted to the emperor;
 The gates are opened, the portcullis drawn,
 And deluges of armies from the town

Come pouring in. I heard the mighty flaw
When first it broke; the crowding ensigns saw
Which choked the passage; and (what least I feared)
The waving arms of Aureng-Zebe appeared,
Displayed with your Morat's.
In either's flag the golden serpents bear,
Erected crests alike, like volumes rear,
And mingle friendly hissings in the air.
Their troops are joined, and our destruction nigh.
NOURMAHAL. 'Tis vain to fight, and I disdain to fly.
I'll mock the triumphs which our foes intend,
And, spite of fortune, make a glorious end.
In pois'nous draughts my liberty I'll find,
And from the nauseous world set free my mind. [*Exit*]

[*At the other end of the stage enter* AURENG-ZEBE,
DIANET, *and attendants.* AURENG-ZEBE *turns back,
and speaks, entering*]

AURENG-ZEBE. The lives of all who cease from combat
    spare;
My brother's be your most peculiar care;
Our impious use no longer shall obtain,
Brothers no more by brothers shall be slain.

            [*Seeing* INDAMORA *and* MORAT]

Ha! do I dream? is this my hoped success?
I grow a statue, stiff and motionless.
Look, Dianet; for I dare not trust these eyes;
They dance in mists, and dazzle with surprise.
DIANET. Sir, 'tis Morat; dying he seems, or dead;
And Indamora's hand –
AURENG-ZEBE.   Supports his head!   [*Sighing*]
Thou shalt not break yet heart, nor shall she know
My inward torments by my outward show;

To let her see my weakness were too base;
Dissembled quiet sit upon my face;
My sorrow to my eyes no passage find,
But let it inward sink and drown my mind.
Falsehood shall want its triumph. I begin
To stagger, but I'll prop myself within.
The specious tow'r no ruin shall disclose,
Till down, at once, the mighty fabric goes.

MORAT. In sign that I die yours, reward my love,

                                     [*To* INDAMORA]

And seal my passport to the blessed above.

                                   [*Kissing her hand*]

INDAMORA. Oh, stay, or take me with you when you
    go;
There's nothing now worth living for below.

MORAT. I leave you not; for my expanded mind
Grows up to heav'n while it to you is joined;
Not quitting, but enlarged! A blazing fire,
Fed from the brand.   [*Dies*]

MELESINDA. Ah me! he's gone! I die!   [*Swoons*]

INDAMORA.   Oh, dismal day!
Fate, thou hast ravished my last hope away.
Oh, heav'n! my Aureng-Zebe –
                What strange surprise!

    [*She turns and sees* AURENG-ZEBE *standing by
                   her, and starts*]

Or does my willing mind delude my eyes,
And shows the figure always present there?
Or liv'st thou? am I blessed, and see thee
    here?

AURENG-ZEBE. My brother's body see conveyed with
    care,   [*Turning from her to his attendants*]
Where we may royal sepulture prepare.

With speed to Melesinda bring relief;
Recall her spirits and moderate her grief. –
                    [*Half turning to* INDAMORA]
I go, to take for ever from your view
Both the loved object and the hated too.
        [*Going away after the bodies, which are carried off*]
INDAMORA. Hear me; yet think not that I beg your stay.
                    [*Laying hold of him*]
I will be heard, and after take your way.
Go; but your late repentance shall be vain:
                    [*He struggles still. She lets him go*]
I'll never, never see your face again.   [*Turning away*]
AURENG-ZEBE. Madam, I know whatever you can say;
    You might be pleased not to command my stay.
    All things are yet disordered in the fort;
    I must crave leave your audience may be short.
INDAMORA. You need not fear I shall detain you long;
    Yet you may tell me your pretended wrong.
AURENG-ZEBE. Is that the bus'ness? then my stay is vain.
INDAMORA. How are you injured?
AURENG-ZEBE.   When did I complain?
INDAMORA. Leave off your forced respect –
    And show your rage in its most furious form;
    I'm armed with innocence to brave the storm.
    You heard, perhaps, your brother's last desire,
    And after saw him in my arms expire;
    Saw me, with tears, so great a loss bemoan;
    Heard me complaining my last hopes were gone.
AURENG-ZEBE. Oh, stay, and take me with you when you go,
    There's nothing new worth living for below.
    Unhappy sex! whose beauty is your snare;
    Exposed to trials; made too frail to bear.
    I grow a fool, and show my rage again.
    'Tis Nature's fault; and why should I complain?

INDAMORA. Will you yet hear me?

AURENG-ZEBE. Yes, till you relate
What pow'rful motives did your change create.
You thought me dead, and prudently did weigh
Tears were but vain, and brought but youth's decay.
Then, in Morat, your hopes a crown designed;
And all the woman worked within your mind.
I rave again, and to my rage return,
To be again subjected to your scorn.

INDAMORA. I wait till this long storm be over-blown.

AURENG-ZEBE. I'm conscious of my folly; I have done.
I cannot rail; but silently I'll grieve.
How did I trust! and how did you deceive!
Oh, Arimant, would I had died for thee!
I dearly buy thy generosity.

INDAMORA. Alas, is he then dead?

AURENG-ZEBE. Unknown to me,
He took my arms; and while I forced my way
Through troops of foes, which did our passage stay,
My buckler o'er my aged father cast,
Still fighting, still defending as I past,
The noble Arimant usurped my name;
Fought, and took from me, while he gave me fame.
To Aureng-Zebe, he made his soldiers cry,
And seeing not, where he heard danger nigh,
Shot, like a star, through the benighted sky.
A short but mighty aid; at length he fell.
My own adventures 'twere lost time to tell;
Or how my army, entering in the night,
Surprised our foes; the dark disordered fight;
How my appearance, and my father shown,
Made peace; and all the rightful monarch own.
I've summed it briefly, since it did relate
Th' unwelcome safety of the man you hate.

INDAMORA. As briefly will I clear my innocence.
　　Your altered brother died in my defence.
　　Those tears you saw, that tenderness I showed,
　　Were just effects of grief and gratitude.
　　He died my convert.
AURENG-ZEBE. 　　　　　　But your lover too!
　　I heard his words, and did your actions view;
　　You seemed to mourn another lover dead;
　　My sighs you gave him, and my tears you shed.
　　But worst of all,
　　Your gratitude for his defence was shown;
　　It proved you valued life when I was gone.
INDAMORA. Not that I valued life but feared to die;
　　Think that my weakness, not inconstancy.
AURENG-ZEBE. Fear showed you doubted of your own
　　　　intent;
　　And she who doubts becomes less innocent.
　　Tell me not you could fear;
　　Fear's a large promiser, who subject live
　　To that base passion know not what they give.
　　No circumstance of grief you did deny;
　　And what could she give more who durst not die?
INDAMORA. My love, my faith.
AURENG-ZEBE. 　　　　　Both so adult'rate grown,
　　When mixed with fear, they never could be known.
　　I wish no ill might her I love befall;
　　But she ne'er loved who durst not venture all.
　　Her life and fame should my concernment be;
　　But she should only be afraid for me.
INDAMORA. My heart was yours; but, oh! you left it
　　　　here.
　　Abandoned to those tyrants, hope and fear.
　　If they forced from me one kind look or word,
　　Could you not that, not that small part afford?

AURENG-ZEBE. If you had loved, you nothing yours
    could call;
  Giving the least of mine, you gave him all.
  True love's a miser; so tenacious grown,
  He weighs to the least grain of what's his own.
  More delicate than honour's nicest sense;
  Neither to give nor take the least offence.
  With, or without you, I can have no rest.
  What shall I do? you're lodged within my breast;
  Your image never will be thence displaced,
  But there it lies, stabbed, mangled, and defaced.

INDAMORA. Yet, to restore the quiet of your
    heart,
  There's one way left.

AURENG-ZEBE.   Oh, name it.

INDAMORA.   'Tis to part.
  Since perfect bliss with me you cannot prove,
  I scorn to bless by halves the man I love.

AURENG-ZEBE. Now you distract me more; shall then
    the day,
  Which views my triumph see our loves decay?
  Must I new bars to my own joy create?
  Refuse, myself, what I had forced from fate?
  What though I am not loved?
  Reason's nice taste does our delights destroy;
  Brutes are more blessed, who grossly feed on joy.

INDAMORA. Such endless jealousies, your love
    pursue,
  I can no more be fully blessed than you.
  I therefore go, to free us both from pain;
  I prized your person, but your crown disdain.
  Nay, ev'n my own –
  I give it you; for since I cannot call
  Your heart my subject, I'll not reign at all.   [*Exit*]

AURENG-ZEBE. Go: though thou leav'st me tortured on
    the rack,
'Twixt shame and pride, I cannot call thee back.
She's guiltless, and I should submit; but oh!
When she exacts it, can I stoop so low?
Yes; for she's guiltless – but she's haughty too.
Great souls long struggle ere they own a crime.
She's gone; and leaves me no repenting time.
I'll call her now; sure, if she loves, she'll stay;
Linger at least, or not go far away.

              [*Looks to the door, and returns*]

Forever lost, and I repent too late.
My foolish pride would set my whole estate,
Till, at one throw, I lost all back to fate.

   [*To him the Emperor, drawing in* INDAMORA.
        Attendants]

EMPEROR. It must not be that he, by whom we live,
Should no advantage of his gift receive.
Should he be wholly wretched? he alone
In this blessed day, a day so much his own?

                 [*To* INDAMORA]

I have not quitted yet a victor's right;
I'll make you happy in your own despite.
I love you still; and if I struggle hard
To give, it shows the worth of the reward.
INDAMORA. Suppose he has o'ercome? must I find place
Among his conquered foes and sue for grace?
Be pardoned and confess I loved not well?
What though none live my innocence to tell?
I know it; truth may own a gen'rous pride;
I clear myself, and care for none beside.
AURENG-ZEBE. Oh, Indamora, you would break my heart!
Could you resolve, on any terms, to part?

I thought your love eternal! was it tied
So loosely that a quarrel could divide?
I grant that my suspicions were unjust;
But would you leave me for a small distrust?
Forgive those foolish words –   [*Kneeling to her*]
They were the froth my raging folly moved
When it boiled up. I knew not then I loved;
Yet then loved most.

INDAMORA *to* AURENG-ZEBE. You would but half be
    blest!   [*Giving her hand, smiling*]

AURENG-ZEBE.   Oh, do but try
My eager love; I'll give myself the lie.
The very hope is a full happiness;
Yet scantly measures what I shall possess.
Fancy itself ev'n in enjoyment, is
But a dumb judge, and cannot tell its bliss.

EMPEROR. Her eyes a secret yielding do confess,
And promise to partake your happiness.
May all the joys I did myself pursue
Be raised by her, and multiplied on you!

[*A procession of priests, slaves following, and last*
MELESINDA *in white*]

INDAMORA. Alas! what means this pomp?

AURENG-ZEBE. 'Tis the procession of a funeral vow,
Which cruel laws to Indian wives allow,
When fatally their virtue they approve;
Cheerful in flames, and martyrs of their love.

INDAMORA. Oh, my foreboding heart! th' event I fear;
And see! sad Melesinda does appear.

MELESINDA. You wrong my love; what grief do I betray?
This is the triumph of my nuptial day.
My better nuptials; which, in spite of fate,
For ever join me to my dear Morat.

Now I am pleased; my jealousies are o'er;
He's mine, and I can lose him now no more.
EMPEROR. Let no false show of fame your reason blind.
INDAMORA. You have no right to die; he was not kind.
MELESINDA. Had he been kind, I could no love have
    shown;
Each vulgar virtue would as much have done.
My love was such, it needed no return;
But could, though he supplied no fuel, burn.
Rich in itself, like elemental fire,
Whose pureness does no aliment require.
In vain you would bereave me of my lord;
For I will die. Die is too base a word;
I'll seek his breast, and kindling by his side,
Adorned with flames, I'll mount a glorious bride. [*Exit*]

[*Enter* NOURMAHAL *distracted, with* ZAYDA]

ZAYDA. She's lost, she's lost! but why do I complain
    For her, who generously did life disdain!
Poisoned, she raves —
Th' envenomed body does the soul attack;
Th' envenomed soul works its own poison back.
NOURMAHAL. I burn, I more than burn; I am all fire;
See how my mouth and nostrils flame expire.
I'll not come near myself —
Now I'm a burning lake, it rolls and flows;
I'll rush, and pour it all upon my foes.
Pull, pull that reverend piece of timber near;
Throw't on — 'tis dry — 'twill burn —
Ha, ha! how my old husband crackles there!
Keep him down, keep him down, turn him about;
I know him; he'll but whizz, and straight go out.
Fan me, you winds; what, not one breath of air?
I burn 'em all, and yet have flames to spare.

Quench me; pour on whole rivers. 'Tis in vain!
Morat stands there to drive 'em back again;
With those huge bellows in his hands, he blows
New fire into my head; my brain-pan glows.
See, see! there's Aureng-Zebe too takes his part;
But he blows all his fire into my heart.

AURENG-ZEBE. Alas, what fury's this?

NOURMAHAL.   That's he, that's he!
          [*Staring upon him, and catching at him*]
I know the dear man's voice;
And this my rival, this the cursed she.
They kiss; into each other's arms they run.
Close, close, close! must I see, and must have none?
Thou art not hers; give me that eager kiss.
Ungrateful! have I lost Morat for this?
Will you? – before my face? – poor helpless I
See all, and have my hell before I die!

                              [*Sinks down*]

EMPEROR. With thy last breath thou hast thy crimes
          confessed;
Farewell, and take, what thou ne'er gav'st me, rest.
But you, my son, receive it better here.
          [*Giving him* INDAMORA'S *hand*]
The just rewards of love and honour wear.
Receive the mistress you so long have served;
Receive the crown your loyalty preserved.
Take you the reins, while I from cares remove,
And sleep within the chariot which I drove.

EPILOGUE

A pretty task! and so I told the fool,
Who needs would undertake to please by rule.
He thought that if his characters were good,
The scenes entire, and freed from noise and blood;
The action great, yet circumscribed by time,
The words not forced, but sliding into rhyme,
The passions raised and calmed by just degrees,
As tides are swelled, and then retire to seas;
He thought, in hitting these, his bus'ness done,
Though he, perhaps, has failed in ev'ry one.
But, after all, a poet must confess
His art's like physic, but a happy guess.
Your pleasure on your fancy must depend;
The lady's pleased, just as she likes her friend.
No song! no dance! no show! he fears you'll say,
You love all naked beauties, but a play.
He much mistakes your methods to delight,
And, like the French, abhors our target-fight;
But those damned dogs can never be i' th' right.
True English hate your monsieur's paltry arts;
For you are all silk-weavers,[1] *in your hearts.*
Bold Britons at a brave bear-garden fray
Are roused, and, clatt'ring sticks, cry, play, play, play.
Meantime, your filthy foreigner will stare,
And mutter to himself, Ha, gens barbare!
And, gad, 'tis well he mutters; well for him;
Our butchers else would tear him limb from limb.
'Tis true, the time may come, your sons may be
Infected with this French civility;
But this in after-ages will be done:

1. The London silk-weavers were always threatened with unemployment by the import of French silks.

Our poet writes a hundred years too soon.
This age comes on too slow, or he too fast;
And early springs are subject to a blast!
Who would excel, when few can make a test
Betwixt indiff'rent writing and the best?
For favours cheap and common who would strive,
Which, like abandoned prostitutes, you give?
Yet scattered here and there I some behold,
Who can discern the tinsel from the gold;
To these he writes, and if by them allowed,
'Tis their prerogative to rule the crowd.
For he more fears (like a presuming man)
Their votes who cannot judge, than theirs who can.

INDEX OF FIRST LINES

356

*A selection of
books of various kinds
published in Penguins
is described on the
remaining pages*

THE PENGUIN POETS

Matthew Arnold – edited by Kenneth Allott

A Book of English Poetry – edited by G. B. Harrison

Border Ballads – edited by William Beattie

Robert Browning – edited by W. E. Williams

Robert Burns – edited by H. W. Meikle and W. Beattie

Lord Byron – edited by A. S. B. Glover

The Centuries' Poetry – edited by D. Kilham Roberts

   1. *Chaucer to Shakespeare*   3. *Pope to Keats*
   2. *Donne to Dryden*   4. *Hood to Hardy*
          5. *Hopkins to Sitwell* *

John Dryden – edited by Douglas Grant

Robert Frost – selected by himself †

Gerard Manley Hopkins – edited by W. H. Gardner

John Keats – edited by J. E. Morpurgo

D. H. Lawrence – selected by W. E. Williams

C. Day Lewis – selected by himself *

John Milton – selected by L. D. Lerner

The Penguin Book of Comic and Curious Verse *
   – edited by J. M. Cohen

The Penguin Book of Contemporary Verse *
   – edited by Kenneth Allott

The Penguin Book of Modern American Verse *
   – edited by Geoffrey Moore

Alexander Pope – edited by Douglas Grant

Edith Sitwell – selected by herself *

Tennyson – edited by W. E. Williams

Wordsworth – edited by W. E. Williams

*Not for sale in the U.S.A.

†Not for sale in the U.S.A. or Canada

A Guide to English Literature

1. THE AGE OF CHAUCER

2. THE AGE OF SHAKESPEARE

This series, of which the first two volumes are now ready, is not a *Bradshaw* or a *Whitaker's Almanack* of information; nor has it been designed on the lines of the standard histories of literature. It is intended for those many thousands of general readers who accept with genuine respect what is known as our 'literary heritage', but who might none the less hesitate to describe intimately the work of such writers as Pope, George Eliot, Langland, Marvell, Yeats, Tourneur, Hopkins, Crabbe, or D. H. Lawrence, or to fit them into any larger pattern of growth and development.

The first volume (A 290) covers the period from Chaucer to Spenser. It includes two general surveys of the literature of the period, one on the poetry and the other on prose; an account of the social context of literature at the time; a specially edited anthology of medieval texts that are otherwise virtually inaccessible to the general reader, texts such as the complete version of the great alliterative poem *Sir Gawayne and the Grene Knight*.

The second volume (A 291) covers the period of Shakespeare's own lifetime. It contains a long general survey of the English literary renaissance, and also an account of the social context of literature in the period.

Reviewing the first volume, the Birmingham Post *said, 'It is an imaginative publishing venture. There is an abundance of enthusiasm, much intelligence, and no pedantry.'*

THE PENGUIN SHAKESPEARE

Edited by Dr G. B. Harrison

ANTONY AND CLEOPATRA

AS YOU LIKE IT

CORIOLANUS

HAMLET

HENRY IV, PART I

HENRY IV, PART II

JULIUS CAESAR

KING LEAR

LOVE'S LABOUR'S LOST

MACBETH

MEASURE FOR MEASURE

THE MERCHANT OF VENICE

A MIDSUMMER NIGHT'S DREAM

MUCH ADO ABOUT NOTHING

OTHELLO

RICHARD II

RICHARD III

ROMEO AND JULIET

THE SONNETS

THE TAMING OF THE SHREW

THE TEMPEST

TROYLUS AND CRESSIDA

TWELFTH NIGHT

THE WINTER'S TALE

Not for sale in the U.S.A.

THE PELICAN
HISTORY OF THE WORLD

It is often urged that world history is best written without the limitations of frontiers, that, for example, a history of the development of Western Europe has more historical validity than 'nationalist' histories of France, Germany, the Low Countries, and Britain. Nevertheless it is national character, national development, and national power which incite the curiosity of most of us, and it is these things which seem to be behind most of the international problems with which we are faced to-day. Therefore, in preparing the plan of THE PELICAN HISTORY OF THE WORLD the editor, J. E. Morpurgo, has decided that the old and familiar emphasis upon national history has meant sufficient to justify its continuance in this series.

Each volume is written by a specialist, and the emphasis given to such matters as trade, religion, politics, foreign relations, intellectual and social life, varies and must vary between volume and volume, but the interplay of nationalisms is as much part of national history as internal events, and it is hoped that THE PELICAN HISTORY OF THE WORLD will be both a series of national histories and, in the true sense, a history of the modern world.

FIRST VOLUME NOW READY

A HISTORY OF MODERN CHINA by *Kenneth Scott Latourette* (A 302)

IN PREPARATION

HISTORY OF THE UNITED STATES; VOL. 1: COLONIES TO NATION; VOL. 2: NATION TO WORLD POWER by *J. E. Morpurgo and Russel B. Nye, Professor at Michigan State College*

HISTORY OF MODERN FRANCE by *J. A. Cobban, Professor of French History, University College, London*

HISTORY OF SPAIN AND PORTUGAL by *W. C. Atkinson, Stevenson Professor of Spanish, Glasgow University*

THE PELICAN
HISTORY OF ENGLAND

While each volume is complete in itself, the whole series, edited by J. E. Morpurgo, has been planned to provide an intelligent and consecutive guide to the development of English society in all its aspects. The eight volumes are:

1. ROMAN BRITAIN *by Professor Ian Richmond,* King's College, Newcastle upon Tyne

2. THE BEGINNINGS OF ENGLISH SOCIETY (from the Anglo-Saxon Invasion) *by Dorothy Whitelock,* Fellow of St Hilda's College, Oxford

3. ENGLISH SOCIETY IN THE EARLY MIDDLE AGES *by Doris Mary Stenton,* Lecturer at Reading University

4. ENGLAND IN THE LATE MIDDLE AGES *by A. R. Myers,* Lecturer at Liverpool University

5. TUDOR ENGLAND *by S. T. Bindoff,* Professor of History at Queen Mary College, London

6. ENGLAND IN THE SEVENTEENTH CENTURY *by Maurice Ashley, M.A.*

7. ENGLAND IN THE EIGHTEENTH CENTURY *by J. H. Plumb,* Fellow of Christ's College, Cambridge

8. ENGLAND IN THE NINETEENTH CENTURY *by David Thomson,* Fellow of Sidney Sussex College, Cambridge

'As a portent in the broadening of popular culture the influence of this wonderful series has yet to receive full recognition and precise assessment. No venture could be more enterprising or show more confidence in the public's willingness to purchase thoughtful books...' The Listener

ALDOUS HUXLEY

*

The name of Aldous Huxley, which became known in the twenties, rapidly developed into a password for his generation. At cocktail parties, which were becoming fashionable in the same period, it was bandied about as if the mere mention of it were enough to show that one was brilliant, witty, and cynically up to date. What was behind the *éclat* of Huxley's success? To start with, as Cyril Connolly has written, 'witty, serious, observant, well-read, sensitive, intelligent, there can have been few young writers as gifted as Huxley.' Born in 1894, he belongs to a family of great talent: he is the grandson of the famous Thomas Henry Huxley, the son of Leonard Huxley, the editor of *The Cornhill Magazine*, and the brother of Dr Julian Huxley. He was educated at Eton and Balliol, and before devoting himself entirely to writing worked as a journalist and dramatic critic.

He first attracted attention with a volume of stories published in 1920, following this up with his provoking and amusing novel, *Crome Yellow* (1921), and in 1922 with some more stories in the same vein, *Mortal Coils*, which contains *The Gioconda Smile* (later made into a successful play). His next novel, *Antic Hay* (1923), a brilliant satire, gave such an accurate picture of the aimless life of various intellectuals after the First World War that Huxley was accused of approving of their outlook. *Those Barren Leaves* (1925), his next novel, also describes an incongruous group of people in this period of social unrest. But the accusations of his less perceptive critics were completely off the mark, for in spite of Huxley's brilliant sense of light comedy, he has always been fundamentally serious. Too good an artist to become a preacher, he has never disguised his disillusionment, which in one form or another has been the basis of his satire.

In 1928, *Point Counter Point*, the outstanding novel which was the culmination of this early period, appeared. It was followed in 1932 by *Brave New World*, which has become not only one of his best-known books but also one of the three or four best-known books of the thirties, satirizing as it does the Utopia resulting from the popular idea of 'progress'. Four years later he produced a further *tour de force*, *Eyeless in Gaza* (1936), in which while experimenting with the chronological sequence, Huxley showed himself for the first time to be a mystic – a role with which he has been preoccupied since he went to live in California in 1937. As a result he has become more and more concerned in his books with contrasting reality and illusion. *After Many a Summer*, which appeared in 1939, is a fantastic parable treating of the ultimate topics of philosophy, and at the same time a nightmarish tale, as brilliant and amusing as anything Huxley has written.

As well as novelist, Aldous Huxley is a writer in many different genres. He has written poems, biographies, travel books, essays, plays, a book about curing bad eyesight, books of a political nature, and most recently an essay on perception, based on his conclusions about the effect of the drug mescalin. In fact he is one of the most versatile writers of his age. *Music at Night* (1931), a selection of essays ranging over a wide variety of subjects, and *Beyond the Mexique Bay* (1934), a traveller's journal of an excursion to Guatemala and Mexico, have been chosen to represent Huxley's non-fiction in this Penguin selection of his books.

The Ten Volumes are:

CROME YELLOW	THOSE BARREN LEAVES
MORTAL COILS	POINT COUNTER POINT
ANTIC HAY	AFTER MANY A SUMMER
BRAVE NEW WORLD	EYELESS IN GAZA
MUSIC AT NIGHT	BEYOND THE MEXIQUE BAY

Three Great English Novels

JOSEPH ANDREWS

HENRY FIELDING

One of the most entertaining novels of the eighteenth century, about which Hazlitt said: '. . . I should be at a loss where to find in any authentic documents of the same period so satisfactory an account of the general state of society, and of moral, political, and religious feelings in the reign of George II as we meet with in the Adventures of Joseph Andrews and his friend Mr Abraham Adams.' (1013)

SYBIL

BENJAMIN DISRAELI

First published in 1845, *Sybil, or The Two Nations* is one of Disraeli's most famous novels. The 'two nations' are the rich and the poor, and the conditions of the working classes in the hungry forties are described with sympathy, and an understanding of the discontent which led up to the Chartist riots. (1012)

GREAT EXPECTATIONS

CHARLES DICKENS

This Dickens favourite first appeared in serial form in 1860–1. Philip Pirip, known as 'Pip', a village boy brought up by his sister, the termagant wife of the blacksmith, is befriended by Miss Havisham, a woman of strange eccentricity caused by being deserted on her wedding day. It is at her house that Pip meets Estella, a beautiful girl who has been taught by the revengeful Miss Havisham to use her beauty to torture men. (1041)